Green Thoughts, Green Shades

Green Thoughts, Green Shades

ESSAYS BY CONTEMPORARY POETS
ON THE EARLY MODERN LYRIC

Edited by Jonathan F. S. Post

UNIVERSITY OF CALIFORNIA PRESS

BERKELEY   LOS ANGELES   LONDON

University of California Press
Berkeley and Los Angeles, California

University of California Press, Ltd.
London, England

A slightly different version of chapter 9 appeared in Alice
Fulton, *Feeling as a Foreign Language: The Good Strange-
ness of Poetry* (St. Paul, Minn.: Graywolf Press, 1999),
85–124.

James Merrill's poem "Tomorrows" appears in chapter 2
by kind permission of Random House, Inc., publisher of
James Merrill, *Collected Poems*, ed. by J. D. McClatchy
and Stephen Yenser (New York: Alfred A. Knopf, 2001).

Elizabeth Bishop's poems "A Miracle for Breakfast" and
"Sestina" appear in chapter 2, from Elizabeth Bishop, *The
Complete Poems: 1927–1979*. Copyright © 1979, 1983 by
Alice Helen Methfessel. Reprinted by permission of Far-
rar, Straus and Giroux, LLC.

Library of Congress Cataloging-in-Publication Data
Green thoughts, green shades : essays by contemporary
poets on the early modern lyric / Jonathan F. S. Post, edi-
tor.
    p. cm.
  Includes bibliographical references and index.
  ISBN 0-520-21455-2 (alk. paper).—ISBN 0-520-22752-2
(pbk. : alk. paper)
    1. English poetry—Early modern, 1500–1700—History
and criticism. I. Post, Jonathan F. S., 1947–

PR533 .G74 2002
821'.040903—dc21   2001048051

Manufactured in Canada

12   11   10   09   08   07   06   05   04   03   02

10   9   8   7   6   5   4   3   2   1

The paper used in this publication is both acid-free and
totally chlorine-free (TCF). It meets the minimum
requirements of ANSI/NISO Z39.48–1992 (R 1997)
(Permanence of Paper). ∞

FOR SUSAN, JESSICA, AND FRED

Joys oft are there

GEORGE HERBERT
"THE FAMILY"

Meanwhile the mind, from pleasure less,
Withdraws into its happiness:
The mind, that ocean where each kind
Does straight its own resemblance find,
Yet it creates, transcending these,
Far other worlds, and other seas,
Annihilating all that's made
To a green thought in a green shade.

ANDREW MARVELL
"THE GARDEN"

CONTENTS

ACKNOWLEDGMENTS

WERE IT NOT FOR THE HELP OF SEVERAL PEOPLE, *Green Thoughts, Green Shades* would never have been more than an idea. So let me thank them at the outset: Calvin Bedient and Stephen Yenser, my colleagues at UCLA; and Linda Norton, literary acquisitions editor at the University of California Press. That it had a chance at life is owing to the nourishing hospitality of Doris and Darryl Curran, who feted, fed, and occasionally housed a number of the contributors: for thirty years these two made poetry part of the Los Angeles climate until the end of the millennium, when, to the great sadness of all, Doris died, leaving me, and others, with many unpaid debts. That *Green Thoughts* finally grew into a book, of course, is a matter of the goodwill and huge talent of the contributors themselves.

I continue to learn much about poetry from my UCLA students, most recently those who have taken my smorgasbord of a seminar, "How to Read a Poem," which has frequently included poems both discussed and written by the contributors. Two of my early teachers, Harvard Knowles and David Sofield, showed me their ways with verse some years ago; it is high time I thanked them in public—the latter, as luck would have it, too, for continuing a lifelong conversation about poetry in the form of a wonderfully useful reader's report he provided the press. I want to express my appreciation as well to the press's second reader for an astute response to the manuscript. It is a pleasure to acknowledge both Anne Myers and

Curt Whitaker, my graduate research assistants, for their superb help in preparing the manuscript for publication; my colleague Michael Colacurcio and former student Diana Engelman for some quick answers when I needed them; and the Council on Research of the Academic Senate of the Los Angeles Division of the University of California for continuing to support my research. As manuscript editor, Joe Abbott was resourceful, as well as restrained, in his suggestions for improvement. Rachel Berchten moved this book through the production phase with great expedition. My deepest thanks to them both. Special thanks also to Peter Reill, the director of the Clark Library and the UCLA Center for Seventeenth- and Eighteenth-Century Studies, and to the staffs of each for their many kindnesses over the years.

All the essays were written specifically for this collection.

Green Thoughts, Green Shades

Green Thoughts, Green Shades

JONATHAN F. S. POST

> The poet's instinct is to shun or shed more knowledge
> than he can swing or sing.
>
> ROBERT FROST
> *New Poets of England and America*

GREEN THOUGHTS, GREEN SHADES IS a book of original essays about lyric poetry written in English during the sixteenth and seventeenth centuries. What differentiates it from other recent collections concerned with the early modern period—to adopt momentarily the period nomenclature currently in use among historicist scholars—is the simple fact that all the essays printed here are written by practicing poets, by people who spend much of their lives thinking in verse and about verse. All the contributors are or have been distinguished teachers of poetry, often in workshop settings, sometimes in lecture halls at their schools and around the country; and almost all have written important criticism, some over the course of four decades, although only a few have concentrated their interpretive energies in print on poetry of the early modern period. Underlying the invitation issued to contemporary poets to write about lyrics of the sixteenth and seventeenth centuries was, therefore, the potential novelty of the encounter itself. What might some of today's poets find of special interest in their forebears and worth retrieving for fellow readers of poetry? And of equal interest, what do their emphases tell us about their own poetry and, more broadly, about how the past continues to form the present?

To be more specific still: given that theoretical and political considerations have dominated the last two decades of "literary" criticism (even necessitating the frequent use of quotation marks and sometimes a strict division of labor within English departments), I began to wonder, both as an interested reader of lyric poetry of the early modern period and as one who envies at times the direct encounter with verse characteristic of contemporary writers and writing, what a series of readings of early lyrics and their authors might look like if these readings were performed by poets who have themselves lived through, indeed participated in, the culture of change that has affected "literary" studies. What, for example, might a reading of George Herbert look like by the author of *From the Devotions* (1998), bearing an epigraph from Donne's "Hymn to God, My God in My Sickness"? Or of Anne Bradstreet by the author of *Outside History* (1990) and *Object Lessons* (1995)? Or of the earl of Rochester by the author of *My Sad Captains* (1961) and, more recently, *The Man with Night Sweats* (1992)? How would a poet and critic of the American sublime regard Donne? Or a self-identified logophile follow the curve of a copia-happy English Renaissance? Where might be the new angles and emphases? What new "figures" might emerge, in person or in form, especially if one invited the author of *Dance Script with Electric Ballerina* (1982) to think about Margaret Cavendish, the duchess of Newcastle; or was lucky enough to have the poet of "The Book of Yolek" and the author of *Promised Lands* (1990) concentrating, respectively, on unfolding those seminal Renaissance forms, the sestina and the sonnet?

By way of Andrew Marvell's "The Garden," the title of the book seeks to call attention to the concinnity of these encounters. For the most part poets chose—or were chosen by—their poets or their subjects; or with the slightest of editorial nudging, they were pointed in one of several possible directions. (How could one resist, again, asking the poet of *Vain Empires* [1998] to take on Milton, or the author of the horticultural sequence "Vertumnal" to muse over Andrew Marvell, or a "daughter of Ben" from Stanford to measure Jonson anew?) But if some attention to chronology as well as to major poets governed the pairings, it would be misleading to suggest that the only motive for the collection was to find an appropriate green shade for each green thought. "The Garden," too, begins and ends in the world of time, notwithstanding disclaiming against ambition; so it might be said that the return to poetry represented here is also not without mundane considerations, not the least of which is the belief that the time is ripe to offer readers of the early modern lyric an alternative to the dominant discourse of political criticism. (As with Marvell, the essays by Eavan Boland and Alice Fulton forcibly remind us that a "retreat" to the muse's garden is not the same thing as an escape from the world.) And the point is better made collectively—in essaying numbers, from the Atlantic seaboard to the Pacific shore, as it happens—rather than with the "odd" essay, although I hasten to add that it is precisely what is "curious" about poetry that *Green Thoughts* seeks to entertain and retain.

An age or so ago, but not so long ago as the Renaissance, when Sidney produced England's first *Apology for Poetry*, this defensive claim would hardly have seemed necessary. This is especially true for the English poetry of the seventeenth century, which owed much of the elevated status it acquired earlier in the twentieth century to T. S. Eliot's influential comments. Indeed, C. S. Lewis was driven once to wonder whether "we (mere critics) have any right to talk" at all.[1] But Eliot's long and complicated connections to the seventeenth century—to say nothing about the rise of critical "talk"—is more a matter now for historical inquiry itself than a calling for others to follow; and although Eliot's presence is occasionally felt in this collection, especially in a stated preference for intellectually complex verse—I have in mind the vigorous thinking, often about body and soul, found in Donne, Marvell, and Rochester, for instance—or in a recalculated use of an Eliotic phrase (like "dissociated sensibility"), the collection as a whole is decidedly post-Eliotic: departing from Eliot's preferred line of poets and downplaying or ignoring a number of Eliot's more cherished views, especially those involving his epochal valuations of the amalgamating power of wit.

Post-Eliotic "marvelry," as Stephen Yenser might say: no doubt the fascination with "reading," mine included, is a legacy of New Criticism. But neither is the collection unequivocally postmodern. Authorship remains, and sometimes reigns: in the figure of Donne's "sovereignty" (Bedient), Cavendish's "unordinary passions" (Fulton), Milton's "modernity" (Logan), Rochester's rakishness (McHugh, Gunn), Jonson's "loathèd word" (Gregerson). If so diverse a group of essays can be said to have a common purpose, it is to stake a claim for reading *poetically*, in all that that tricky word implies. It is to prize (and to "prise") the curious, explore the unusual, hunker down with the unordinary—sometimes with *OED* in hand. It is to analyze verbal particulars, even to make value judgments about specific lines, but also to find metaphors—key words, as it were—and analogues in other poets and poems for explaining the place of the particular in the larger structures of thought as these affect the practice of reading. In an important sense, as the essays in *Green Thoughts* individually testify, responses to poetry almost always begin with the immediate, the personal; and good criticism might be characterized in part, at least, as the intelligent hunt for the appropriate metaphor for generalizing about this experience.

Yet it must be said, too, that reading poetically can only mean something different for each author. As a glance at the contents of the collection will perhaps indicate, the language of critical perception is inseparable from the angle of inquiry. Idiomatic difference is a strong feature of the volume. For Anthony Hecht it means beginning (with humor) but hardly ending with the challenge presented by the six terminal words used in a sestina—twice the challenge in Sidney's double sestina, "Ye Gote-heard gods"—and the *terrible* monotony they can provoke (the adjective is necessary); then to elaborate on the mysteries of the form and the feats to which it is put not only in Sidney but in the hands of present-day masters like Elizabeth Bishop and James Merrill. With its potential for the ludic as well as the melancholic—Hecht has provided striking examples of each in his own poetry—the sestina, for all its byzantine elaborations, has come to seem, once again, strangely modern: the mental landscape of Sidney's double sestina still reverberating in poems that, in turn, create superb commentaries on their origins.

In tracing out a tradition, Hecht's essay points toward how poets and their poems constantly recuperate the past. Sidney's sestina cannot be fully appreciated without a knowledge of what preceded it, but it also becomes newly intelligible because of the offspring it has enabled. (I say this as a teacher of students who, amazed by the spider-like artistry required of the form, find their way back to Sidney.) Peter Sacks also takes a long view of the Renaissance, but what catches his eye, aided by a directing glance from John Ashbery, is the peculiar, almost talismanic association of the sonnet form with the subject of the face or "fayned visage." The latter phrase is from Wyatt's "The longe love, that in my thought doeth harbar," the sonnet that forms the centerpiece of Sacks's study. And here we do enter into postmodern terrain involving the role of representation in the never-finished project of constructing subjectivity that we regard as one salient feature of the Renaissance. The clunk in that last sentence has, at least, the virtue of indicating the divide separating a recycled cultural cliché from the more genuinely speculative processes whereby, thinking through examples ranging from the thirteenth-century sonneteer Niccolo Degli Abbizi to Ashbery himself, Sacks arrives at "the inner lineaments of the tradition" and points to a new way to conceive of that most identifiably original of Renaissance poetic forms.

Looking further ahead in the collection for a moment (and along in time), one might gauge the perspicuity of Sacks's thinking as well as discover an adroitly explicit "defense" of form in William Logan's "Milton in the Modern: The Invention of Personality," which begins by proposing that "Milton's sonnets represent one of the first moments—perhaps *the* first moment—when a poet writing in English took his or her form for granted." Although Logan is wary of granting "intrinsic" character to particular forms, he's equally suspicious of the counterclaim "that form has no character *whatsoever* and in *no* way responds to certain types of inspiration"; and his vigorous inquiry into Milton's huge place in literature hinges on the sonnets, which might be said to reveal gradually more and more of the author's face, or personality, as the youthful imitator of Petrarch matures into the deeply etched figure of the blind poet of "When I consider" and the other late sonnets. A strength of Logan's essay, sometimes missing from both general and specialized studies of Milton, is the extended attention paid to Milton's Civil War sonnets and their "heterodoxy of style": "These three sonnets are among the most thrilling in the rise of colloquial idiom in English verse." Although I have placed his essay in the collection with other single-author studies, Logan's remark here provides a transition to Heather McHugh, for there is practically nothing not heterodoxical, or paradoxical, with "Naked Numbers: A Curve from Wyatt to Rochester."

McHugh's twist on the never-quite-dead formalist debate: "A poem's content no less than its form can be a cover: *what* it means may reveal less than *how* it is seen *through*." And if you're Heather McHugh, there's little you don't see. Or say. I can think of few essays—and certainly none published in the scholarly literature of the period—so committed to laying bare what is both moving and outrageous (and often very funny) about some of the period's lyrics. Her "curve," in short, is not chronologically conceived any more than it stops with Rochester. It is in the eye of the beholder; and what the eye focuses on now, as it often did then, is the materiality of the poem's "numbers": the "wild civility" with word turning that, along with turning on a reader like McHugh, can also, in the name of talent, make a poem like Wyatt's "The piller pearisht" stick long in the ear.

"Naked Numbers" could have been placed at the beginning or the end of *Green Thoughts,* as either signal call or fiery coda, but because it "covers" a number of poets, I've elected to group it with the longer views provided by Sacks and Hecht. Readers, of course, are free to pick and choose among the essays as they wish—to continue with a leisurely garden metaphor. But the sharp contrast between McHugh's essay and Linda Gregerson's "Ben Jonson and the Loathèd Word" is much to the point, for it is precisely what is apparently repellent in Jonson that initially provokes Gregerson's analysis. What critical rewards—to say nothing of pleasures—can be found in stripping away what is almost always already declaring itself to be plain? That question has long haunted modern criticism of Jonson as well, whether written from inside the circle (often at Stanford) by learned, latter-day members of the tribe, valuing the ethical or moral imperatives of the plain style, or from outside by ideologically motivated critics suspicious of Jonson's exclusionary practices.

As Gregerson suggests, word turning was the very thing Jonson opposed, interested as he was in the idea of communicating without an interpreter, in founding sturdy lineal connections to antiquity, and in sculpting out "essences" of the social, not metaphysical kind. But Gregerson also writes from the critical perspective of someone on the edge of the circle: from Stanford, too, as mentioned earlier but as a "daughter of Ben," as she whimsically identified herself in an email. She walks the line, as it were, seeing what does and does not happen in a Jonson lyric, attending to the "interested" nature of praise yet with nuanced sympathy toward the poet's "craft." That word retains for her some of the formalist attraction it had for Pound when he "quoted" from Jonson's "Celebration of Charis" in the Pisan Cantos, as Gregerson elegantly notes. But it includes, too, recognition of a more controlling but ultimately self-limiting ambition on Jonson's part: a strenuous resistance to change that also produced a lyric "at once virtuosic and strangely, savagely vacated."

As the first of the essays devoted to single authors in *Green Thoughts,* "Ben Jonson and the Loathèd Word" helps to explain, not explain away, problems this important literary figure has frequently posed for modern readers, especially for those coming to Jonson after Donne, which was often the case in the immediate aftermath of Eliot. Calvin Bedient's "Donne's Sovereignty," on the other hand, is "pitched"—the verb is happily unavoidable—toward recovering a poet who has perhaps suffered from too much criticism. With only slight exaggeration, it might be said that in the latter part of the twentieth century Donne came to lead something of a double life. Scholarly criticism of him waned, inevitably perhaps, to the point that his earlier "canonization" by New Critics has become itself one of the most active points of interest among academics. But in the classroom, and for readers coming to him afresh or for the first time, and now in the theater as well in Margaret Edson's *W;t,* Donne remains an explosive force, a high-wire act of the first order. He is the bel canto of metaphysical poets.

The theatrical metaphors are inescapable, and I take an important consequence of "Donne's Sovereignty" to be the dramatic play that comes when criticism is concerned less with responding to designated areas of research than with assaying an immediate response to the verse. To re-phrase the matter in light of the previous paragraph: if Donne's originality is perhaps most available now in the fluid spaces of classroom and theater, so it best continues on the page as part of a passionately analytic dialogue between poet and reader. Play seeks to have play, as much as love wants to find love or danger meet with danger. For the (diso)bedient critic, Donne's sovereignty is liberating, not constraining—as it can sometimes seem in the hands of scholars who fail to take the monarchical as meta-phorical. With Donne's most innovative collection of lyrics, *The Songs and Sonnets,* the games going on "inside" the poems invite those on the "outside" to join the fun, to cross the boundary separating author from reader, to write back. And as presented, or rather enacted, by a reader as critically acute as Bedient, this responsive situation is also not as fancifully anachronistic as it might first appear. For it was in the writings of the poets around him, in a Herbert, King, or Carew, that Donne's initial impact was also most sharply registered.

Donne and Jonson, Jonson and Donne: these near contemporaries can seem, at times, the alpha and omega (not the Rosencrantz and Guilden-stern) of seventeenth-century poetry, and it is probably only right that the two essays on them should figure near the center of *Green Thoughts.* But as the vigorous printing history of *The Temple* testifies, now nearly four centuries old, George Herbert was far more than an afterthought of Donne. A descendent of the Sidney family, Herbert was the most formally gifted poet of his era, indeed probably of any era: the very incarnation of the Renaissance courtier, who turned poetry to the worship of God and filled his temple with almost every shape and kind of lyric then imaginable (but not a sestina, as it happens). But Herbert is sotto voce next to Donne. Intimacy of a "confessional" order has, paradoxically, never seemed more natural than in the verse of this most sophisticated, much analyzed poet; and a striking feature of Carl Phillips's essay, the anomaly of "Anomaly, Conundrum, *Thy-Will-Be-Done:* On the Poetry of George Herbert," lies in how the intimate experience of reading Herbert everywhere informs the act of criticism itself. Phillips records a "private" reading, so to speak, of the "private record" he so prizes in *The Temple.* I don't mean to suggest that regarding *The Temple* as a "private record" is necessarily unusual. Nor does Phillips slight formal analysis in the process of listening to the "ear-nest" voice he so values. But in the critical literature of late, of which there is a vast amount, there have been few instances of so concentrated an encounter between poet and reader, one that increases in intimacy, moreover, over time: a concentration registered not simply by the critic's attempt to listen alone to the voice on the page but also through a syntax adequate to the difficult uncertainties, the conundrums, presented by the anomalous subject of Herbert's verse.

Yes, anomalies all. "The lyric poet is almost by definition a traitor to his own people," writes Charles Simic darkly. "He is the stranger who speaks the harsh truth that only individual lives are unique and therefore sacred."[2] Some anomalies, however, have had to wait longer than others to be spotted. As much drawn to the English Renaissance as she was, Virginia Woolf had trouble with Margaret Cavendish; and Cavendish's contemporary Anne Bradstreet was beyond her ken altogether. And beyond that of her later countryman and "fellow" poet, John Berryman, as Eavan Boland notes at the outset of her moving essay, "Finding Anne Bradstreet." And, it must be added, she remains beyond most literary histories of the English lyric even though the case might easily be made that no female poet writing in English in the seventeenth century has proven more important or more readable.

Of all the essays collected here, Boland's most worries the problem of reading past poets largely, simply, or only in light of present needs and personal preferences. The concern is not hers alone, but, foregrounded and rock solid, it adds a chastening note to the idea of reading without sufficient respect for historical difference. For the contingencies of time that mark out and differentiate as much one reader from another as one poet from the pack also challenge the easy, untroubled lope of canonical literary history—the unhobbled version of Ashbery's "Grand Galop," as recalled by Peter Sacks. Bradstreet rendered by Berryman is yet another object lesson for Boland. But the lesson is not just the usual one about masculine usurpation. It is also a reminder, to Boland, of her own problematic relation to dominant poetic traditions, even, or rather especially, the one that initially nurtured and in a different key later sustained Bradstreet. But that is also not the final lesson because the historical distance that is difficult to surmount is, again for Boland, the thing that helps to preserve Bradstreet's separateness, her anomalous status as a poet. "The truth is, I cannot afford not to see Anne Bradstreet," writes Boland: not, however, because the two are alike but because they are different, and their difference ensures the possibility that one can question the other.

I'm not sure how Eavan Boland would evaluate Alice Fulton's "Unordinary Passions: Margaret Cavendish, the Duchess of Newcastle." From the beginning, Fulton makes no bones about the emotive basis of her response to the duchess and her verse: "I've been a poet for twenty-three years, and I don't cry easily." Then again, Bradstreet is an "established" figure; her poems now appear on Advanced Placement exams for American high school students. She doesn't require excessive "defending," whereas Cavendish remains closeted off as one of nature's freaks, her 1653 *Poems and Fancies* once reprinted but still never edited. "What a vision of loneliness and riot the thought of Margaret brings to mind," wrote Woolf in *A Room of One's Own,* "as if some giant cucumber had spread itself over all the roses and carnations in the world." The response is one of many quoted by Fulton, who, along with admitting to having developed a "crush" on Cavendish, is also most scrupulous about not misrepresenting either the often jaundiced circumstances surrounding Cavendish's reception, slightly improved of late, or what, clear and dry eyed, she most values in the poetry: its eccentric marriage of verbal gusto with moral acuity. Cavendish's "unordinary thoughts" query "standard measures of intelligence," Fulton emphasizes, especially those of the masculine sort, as the duchess demonstrates sympathy toward things scarcely imaginable in her age.

It would be wrong to give away in an introduction what poem of Cavendish's first moved her reader to tears. But unless I miss my bet, Fulton's essay will help to do for Cavendish what Adrienne Rich's did for Bradstreet: spur on the interested reader and perhaps a modern edition of her poems as well. The remaining three essays return us to familiar, now well-edited, if not readily domesticated, poets: Marvell because he's too slippery; Rochester because he's too indecent; and Taylor because he's too distant from the beaten path. These are, of course, precisely reasons to read each poet. But from the ample perspective supplied by literary history, it is also possible to argue that these three poets represent the outer reach of traditions that underlie, and in the right hands intermingle and animate, much lyric poetry written in English from 1500 to 1700: the metaphysical, the courtly, and the devotional. At various moments each poet has been credited with holding the palm at the end of one of these lines.

But exactly which palm is an issue that mercurial Marvell alone seems to have imagined, as Stephen Yenser implies through the selection of poems he chooses to analyze in " 'How coy a Figure': Marvelry." Among other poems that figure into Yenser's essay, "The Garden" is often thought a metaphysical poem for its elegant play of wit in the service, especially, of describing the soul's ascent. "The Gallery" is consciously courtly, that is, until one looks closely, as Yenser does, at some of the images. And

"The Coronet," of course, is manifestly artful and problematically devotional. But distinctions in Marvell, of whatever order (including the political and theological), are most often observed in order to be complicated and elided or "sublated," to borrow Yenser's term for describing Marvell's habit of negating an element in a dialectical process that is then partially preserved in a synthesis. Like the two rivers (or is it four?) imagined in Bishop's "Santarém," Marvell is the bane of either/or thinking. But for a wry reader like Yenser, who revels in what is concentrated, elegant, and off balance, Marvell is an absolute delight: the poet's metamorphic variety, his "vegetable love," a source, perhaps the source, of his strange, inexhaustible energy.

Marvell has his "Clora," a possible figure for the muse, as Yenser neatly intimates. Rochester, who admired the satirical Marvell, has his "Cloris" (and his Corinna and Phillis) but also his "Signior Dildo." The two poets poked fun at some of the same people at the Restoration court—to put the matter mildly; but it was Rochester, not Marvell, who made sex central to his poetry (to put the matter even more mildly). Today's critics still demonstrate their discomfort with Rochester's verse in any number of ways. I'm unsure myself which poems of his to present to undergraduates and even less sure, at times, which need glossing; Rochester still belongs mostly to my private reading. Thom Gunn's "Saint John the Rake: Rochester's Poetry" has the quietly revelatory virtue of addressing Rochester's verse evaluatively, sympathetically, and directly, Gunn's manifestly careful prose serving to illuminate, by contrast, Rochester's sensationally explicit subject. Besides a sense of relief that can accompany such evenhanded, levelheaded criticism—aren't we all just a little (but perhaps only a little) tired of heated discussions of pornography?—his essay provides perhaps the best introduction to Rochester's poetry available. But a poet's introduction, to be sure. Gunn listens to the verse, calculates exactly the shocks and surprises, notes the difference between simple and complex effects, gets close to his subject—a poet knowingly excited over, sometimes exhausted by, but also seeking freedom in and from sex.

There's little doubt about what kind of poems Edward Taylor wrote. Almost all are resolutely devotional. The vast majority belong to two lengthy "series" Taylor designated "Preparatory Meditations," and with the rest of his verse these lay in manuscript form until their initial publication in 1937. But just what Taylor was up to as a poet is a more vexing issue, one that has troubled professional and initial readers of Taylor alike, and the question lies at the heart of Robert Hass's searching (and occasionally bemused) exploration into Taylor's place in the strange wonder world of late Renaissance words and religious thought.

For Hass, Taylor is very much, although not exclusively, a poet of delightful exuberance, of lexical profusion and surprise—an instance of what Austin Warren once called the "Colonial Baroque." The phrase invites us to regard this early "American" writer as part of a broader European tradition somehow ending up in Westfield, Massachusetts, the poet with his Leicestershire diction intact, as Hass emphasizes, somehow untransmuted by the journey across the Atlantic. At one point we are reminded that Taylor's poem "Thy Good Ointment" is "a sort of homemade verbal equivalent to a Bernini fountain, sweetly eschatological, and Calvinist to the core." The phrasing is characteristically generous and evocative, but keeping Bernini and Calvin in balance is no mean feat for poet or critic; and if, figuratively speaking, Calvin usually wins out at the poem's end, Taylor's middles, as Hass beautifully shows—that portion of the formal meditative structure, in which understanding (and imagination) have their greatest opportunities for flight—belong more often to Bernini.

Arriving belatedly as he did, Taylor serves in many respects as a logical terminal point for this collection, and part of the value of Hass's essay is to illuminate continuities as well as differences between Taylor and the meditative traditions and poets, like Donne and Herbert, that nurtured his thinking. But there is also, for Hass, another Taylor (just as for all the poets writing here, there is always another poet peeking out between the lines and looking forward). One might think of this figure as part of the Calvinist core, the legacy of meditative and personal solitude, that Taylor carried with him into the New World, one that also, paradoxically, links him to a poetic future that he could only in small measure have been responsible for creating. As Hass scrupulously notes early on: "the only thing that seems American about him—presciently so—is this strange absence of a social context for his work. He seems—as Anne Bradstreet does in her private and unpublished poems—an early instance of the solitariness, self-sufficiency, and peculiarity of the American imagination." And then, at the end of the essay, Hass broaches again the subject of Taylor's prescience but from a slightly different angle, with Dickinson's "There's a certain slant of light" and Stevens's "The Poems of Our Climate" in mind. And elsewhere too, I might add, for readers wishing to close one book and pick up another: in his own "Meditation at Lagunitas." *Green thoughts, green shades.*

This introduction has been written by someone whose academic home is more in the early modern than the modern or postmodern periods, and with little claim to having written a line of verse since college. The perspective is perhaps one, however, that allows a small window into what, at the moment, is so evidently missing in much criticism of one of the more lyrically inventive moments in English—and a long moment at that: the sense of exhilaration and joy (and power) enabled by the poetry itself. Or almost by itself. Matters of aesthetics have been largely abandoned in many academic quarters, or they reappear theoretically, sometimes wearing the face of revenge, or in provocative counterblasts, most frequently and urgently from the pen of Harold Bloom. The caricatures from both sides can be amusing as well as disorienting. After once telling a colleague about having spent two hours teaching Jonson's difficult and moving Pindaric ode "To the Immortal Memory and Friendship of That Noble Pair, Sir Lucius Cary and Sir H. Morison," I was told in turn, "How quaint," as if that poem (and by extension poetry in general) no longer had any place in the universe, let alone in a university curriculum, even though it is also my experience that students remain receptive readers of poetry if given half a chance.

I don't mean to misrepresent the authors in *Green Thoughts* by suggesting that their studies are part of a program of aesthetic retrenchment. In the relative weight given to theoretical and cultural interests—to the "world" never annihilated by green thoughts but only made more unusual—the authors differ in this as in so many things, but I take as exemplary the double admission made by Peter Sacks in his essay: that the origins of his study date from a personal moment of excited discovery (shared with another reader, Frank Bidart) about a particular poem, and that the process of further exploration led him in a number of directions as well, inclusive of Renaissance new historicism. I take the difference, moreover, between Sacks's admission, made near the beginning of *Green Thoughts,* that understanding moves outward, discovering contexts as these seem relevant, and the following truculent remark made by Thom Gunn near the end of the collection, to be a difference of degree rather than kind: "I have unashamedly used this word [*complexity*] as a term of appreciation, fully aware that many readers may find it old-fashioned, reminding them of midcentury critics. So I should state, with my own defiance, that two of the most interesting pursuits I can find in literature are the expression of energy and the exploration of complexity within that energy." The world would hardly seem any less complex now than half a century ago. Nor, in the time between, has the poetry written in the early modern period become suddenly transparent, that is, less reflective of our own condition. To enlist Bishop for one last time, it took then, as it takes now, "an infinite number of things coming together, forgotten, or almost forgotten, books, last night's dream, experiences past and present—to make a poem."[3] The essays in *Green Thoughts, Green Shades* bear witness, individually and collectively, to this simple, complicating truth.

NOTES

1. C. S. Lewis, *A Preface to Paradise Lost* (London: Oxford University Press, 1942), 9.

2. Charles Simic, "Elegy in a Spider's Web," in his *The Unemployed Fortune Teller: Essays and Memoirs* (Ann Arbor: University of Michigan Press, 1994), 38.

3. Elizabeth Bishop, *One Art: Letters,* ed. Robert Giroux (New York: Farrar, Straus and Giroux, 1994), 621. The letter disputes what Bishop took to be an excessively learned reading of her poems by Jerome Mazzaro; at the same time, however, she allows plenty of room for complexity in her verse, as the quotation indicates.

ONE

The Face of the Sonnet

Wyatt and Some Early Features of the Tradition

PETER SACKS

IN JOHN ASHBERY'S "GRAND GALOP" the speaker listens back across more than four hundred years to what he goes on to call "that still-moist garden where the tooting originates."[1]

> It drifts away in fragments.
> And one is left sitting in the yard
> To try to write poetry
> Using what Wyatt and Surrey left around,
> Took up and put down again
> Like so much gorgeous raw material.[2]

Green sounds? Herbage of pre-Elizabethan songs and sonnets drifting through late-twentieth-century New York? And who is this ever-later, still-prospective poet? Ashbery's impersonal pronoun conjures *one* whose language, if *one* succeeds, will not be *one*'s "own" but rather that used by Wyatt and Surrey. Nor do the displacements stop there, despite the word *originates*. Poetic language belonged to the individual early Renaissance forebears no more exclusively than it does to *one*self: "Took up and put down again / Like so much gorgeous raw material." And by choosing poets (two rather than one) whose signature originations (the first English sonnets, hence some of the early poetic representations of voiced subjectivity in modern English language) arose as *translations* of prior Italian sonnets (so that the voices and the formal actions behind the "I" in their first sonnets are less their own than Petrarch's), Ashbery helps us to recognize that one of the salient features of the English sonnet may be the form's way of confronting head-on, so to speak—while also developing thematic entailments and analogues for—a more general lyric venture: the impersonating of an individuality whose very means of expression impugn any claim for unique self-possession.[3] Indeed Ashbery's earlier "Sonnet," whose twelfth line reads, "Traffic is the reader's pictured face," has no first-person singular at all.[4]

Just as there may be no person without impersonation, no persona without the word's reference to an actor's facial mask, we may come to wonder whether the sonnet's weirdly consistent attentiveness to the image of the "pictured face" may enable it to surpass other poetic forms, or any philosophical or sociological discourse, in pressing us to suspect that there may never be a face (sonnet or no sonnet, poetry or no poetry) that isn't a picture—something *made* up, as the word *face*'s etymology betrays, and as Petrarch, Wyatt, Shakespeare, and many others have emphasized. Wyatt's first sonnet speaks of a "fayned visage"; his second shows the face invaded by "pretence." Eliot's revisionary love song, whose title and whose first fourteen lines (with their closing couplet's reference to a maker not only of visual art but of love sonnets) indicate no slight relation to the sonnet, has its persona sing, "there will be time / To prepare a face to meet the faces that you meet." Or as James Merrill has the flayed speaker of his eponymous sonnet "Marsyas" describe his fatal insult against Apollo, "I made a face. Then crash!"

Appearing to suggest a new level of intimacy, a close-up on inwardness, the sonnet paradoxically depended on the face, or on what Hamlet called the "haviour of the visage," precisely to constitute, by opposition, the alleged substance of whatever "passeth show." My sense is that this very contingent dependency on surfaces—inseparable from the surface of representation as such—leaves its uneasy mark on the sonnet's obsessive traffic between face and heart and that this traffic exposes the suspicion that the sonnet's language travels between a constructed face mask and an interiority whose alleged harborings or sighing vacancies (so often and uncoincidentally afflicted by desire or grief) can only be guessed at, as if between the song-lorn boughs where "yellow leaves, or none, or few, do hang" or as if beneath the fourteen-runged grate of a drain covered by a fabric of borrowed, fallen, or translated foliage.[5] Beginning his sonnet sequence, Sidney seeks "to paint the blackest face of woe," by "oft turning others' leaves"; and however scornfully he is urged to look into his heart and write, neither this advice nor the figures of the Muse and the legible heart have fallen far from the tree.

In addition to its expressions of praise, its meditations on beauty, love, transience, mortality, or power, and despite its historical, religious, or topographical amplifications in the work of Donne, Milton, Hopkins, Wordsworth, Lowell, and others, the sonnet—from *sonnetto* (little sound) —may therefore involve the relatively small fictional voicing of an appeal for a greater degree of personifiable presence and for some enduring form of acknowledgment of whatever may be said to lie behind the face. Whether directed toward the face of another self, a beloved, a vision of place, a star, a god, or God, that voice usually emerges for us across rather than through a screen whose dubious surface may *give away* the anxiety that whatever seems to remain concealed at the supposed core of personhood may be not simply least representable or enduring but perhaps least substantial, personal, or possessible in the first place.[6]

Also, because the sonnet's address always includes the reader or auditor, even though the speaker faces a prospect or describes a different, admired countenance, the poem is at least two-faced—a condition mirroring or perhaps even projectively aggravating the many accusations of duplicity that Shakespeare's sonnets are not alone in casting on the beloved. If desire, loss, blame, entreaty, or praise are some of the dominant motifs of the English sonnet since Wyatt, it is not surprising, in the face of its giveaways, that some of the form's earliest and most pronounced emotional or thematic entailments turn out to be frustration, betrayal, and *shame,* as well as various attempted acts of persuasion. Evocations either of a mediator or of the fugitive beloved's presence (seldom separable from self-presence) consequently often solicit at best a hoped-for image of cosmic or cosmetic redress. Hopkins's Petrarchan sonnet "As Kingfishers Catch Fire, Dragonflies Draw Flame" ends: "For Christ plays in ten thousand places, / Lovely in limbs, and lovely in eyes not his / To the Father through the features of men's faces." Quoting Wyatt ("how like you this?"), Heaney's final Glanmore sonnet concludes with "The respite in our dewy dreaming faces."[7]

"Look in my face." The imperative opens one of the final sonnets in D. G. Rossetti's *The House of Life.* Perhaps designed to speak as the image of a face might speak, sonnets as objects conform more closely than any other lyric to the proportions of the human visage—and the *pictura* for its *poesis* may indeed be that of a person's countenance.

In beginning to focus on the poetic image of the face, and in thinking about *any* image-making in poetry, I am indebted to Elaine Scarry's inspiring account of mental imaging at large. In particular, it would have been impossible for me to contemplate as fully the properties of the sonnet as an object—one that is both the occasion and product of poetic imaging—were it not for the precision with which Scarry analyzes how the size and other attributes of certain objects, such as a flower, affect the ease and degree of vividness with which they may be imaged in the mind. Revealing, for example, that a blossom can be imaged more readily than can a life-sized face, partly because it better fits within "the small bowl of space in front of one's eyes," Scarry's argument could also lead us to recognize that a sonnet may be perceived not as seeking literally to mirror a face but rather to construct an object within whose dimensions a face may be more poetically envisioned. Viewing the flower as an object exemplarily equipped to supply what she calls a "template" for mental imaging, Scarry shows how the mind may in turn build the image of a face on that of a blossom (the flower becomes "the work table on which imaginative life gets processed"), and although the sonnet lacks several but not all of the attributes of a flower, it is in this sophisticated and powerful sense that the sonnet may be said to accommodate a proportionately modeled image of a face.[8]

Assuming this linkage between sonnet and imagined face, it is no coincidence that the conventions of the sonnet form emerged—via the work of Guittone d'Arezzo, Guinizelli, Cavalcanti, Dante, and others—during the thirteenth century, just as Giotto and other painters were beginning to depict more realistically expressive faces than those of Byzantine or Gothic icons. Cimabue was in fashion then, as Dante says, Giotto now.[9] Giotto painted a portrait of Dante, as did Signorelli and others. And during the 1340s, by which time Petrarch had secured and would lend his name to the Italian form, one of the laureate's sonnets actually celebrates his friend Simone Martini, the great painter who "portrayed [Laura] on paper, to attest down here to her lovely face." In the following century the sonnet evolved throughout northern and southern Europe alongside the quattrocento refinement of personal portraiture (Memling, Van Eyck, Parmigianino, Antonello da Messina), appearing in England by the 1530s, soon after Dürer and Leonardo had begun deliberately to theorize the formal representation of the face so as to negotiate between ideal and mimetically accurate depictions not merely of individual features but of what Leonardo called "the motions of the mind." It is more than fortuitous that Holbein drew his unforgettable portrait of Wyatt's face during the very years that Wyatt inaugurated the English sonnet.[10]

Before turning to the substance of particular sonnets, we could continue to speculate on the formal exchanges between sonnet and face, pointing out frequent references to reading a face and to its attendant semiotics. (Is it a coincidence that the Italian *volta,* used to describe the turn to the sestet, is scarcely distinguishable from the word *volto,* often used by Petrarch and others to mean the face, the part of us that turns and signifies with the most expressiveness?)[11] At the outset of the *Vita Nuova* Dante confesses, "I spoke of Love because I bore on my face (*nel viso*) so many of his signs (*insegne*) that it could not be concealed." *Insegne* will show up in the forehead (*fronte*) of the very sonnet of Petrarch to which we will soon see Wyatt and Surrey turn; and Petrarch spells it out repetitively as in *e'l cor negli occhi et ne la fronte o scritto* (and my heart is inscribed in my eyes and on my brow). To take one of many examples from Shakespeare's sonnets:

> so love's face
> May still seem love to me, though altered new,
> Thy looks with me, thy heart in other place.
>
> .   .   .   .
>
> In many's looks, the false heart's history
> Is writ in moods and frowns and wrinkles strange
> But heaven in thy creation did decree
> That in thy face sweet love should ever dwell.
>   *(Sonnet 93)*

As if moving in the other direction, Sonnet 86 ends: "But when your countenance filled up his line, / Then lacked I matter; that enfeebled mine."[12]

Quite literally, we could add that the measured way in which many Renaissance sonnets about the loved face descend from eyes to mouth is closely matched by facial proportions as depicted in several contemporary works by Dürer, Leonardo, Holbein, Titian, and others—in which the ratio between the distances (1) from the top of the forehead across the eyes down to the tip of the nose and (2) from the tip of the nose across the mouth to the bottom of the chin, is that of eight to six.[13] Anatomizing one of the fourteen-line sections of his first canzone, Dante writes: "This second part divides in two; for in one I speak of her eyes, which are the source of love; in the second I speak of her mouth, which is the end of love." Regarding a further sonnet, he comments: "This sonnet has three parts: in the first I tell how this lady reduces this potentiality to act in consequence of the very noble part which are her eyes; and in the third

I say the same in consequence of the very noble part which is her mouth; and in between these two is a particle that is a quasi-petitioner of aid for the previous and subsequent parts, and it begins: *Help me, ladies.*"[14]

But the sonnet is yet more deeply implicated with representations of the human face. From Niccolo Degli Abbizi, Dante, Boccaccio, Petrarch, Wyatt, Shakespeare, Milton, and Sor Juana Inés de la Cruz to Rimbaud, Ashbery, Heaney, and Merrill, the form reiterates a fascination both with the explicit image of the face and with what occurs there.[15] If such a focus seems superficial, I hope to show how many inner lineaments of the tradition it may reveal and how the very positings of depth or inwardness greatly depend on the sonnet's ambivalent facial poetics. Without the image of the personal face the sonnet would be less equipped to generate its images of a mind behind the face; still more opposingly, it would not be as equipped to suggest the hidden depths of the heart.

Skipping a fuller account of this matter in *Vita Nuova* and *Rime Sparse,* I want to recall three lines from what might be Wyatt's first sonnet, a translation of Petrarch 102: "So chaunceth it oft that every passion / The mynde hideth, by colour contrary, / With fayned visage, now sad, now mery." If this is a critique of dissembling, in which the face serves as a medium for the mind's misrepresentation of the passions, we may wonder what would happen if the face were to reveal the true "colour" of the heart: what response would it elicit, and to what extent could such an appearance, however "honest," serve the inner life it is supposed to lay bare? These questions take us to Wyatt's sonnet "The longe love," rendered from Petrarch 140:

> The longe love, that in my thought doeth harbar
>   And in myn hert doeth kepe his residence,
>   Into my face preseth with bolde pretence,
>   And therin campeth, spreding his baner.
> She that me lerneth to love and suffre,
>   And willes that my trust and lustes negligence
>   Be rayned by reason, shame and reverence,
>   With his hardines taketh displeasur.
> Wherewithall, vnto the hertes forrest he fleith,
>   Leving his entreprise with payn and cry;
>   And ther him hideth, and not appereth.
> What may I do when my maister fereth
>   But in the feld with him to lyve and dye?
>   For goode is the liff, ending faithfully.[16]

Because one can't read the first lines without noticing it, and because it distinguishes Wyatt from Petrarch, from Surrey, and from almost everyone after, we might begin by taking in some of the characteristic irregularity of Wyatt's prosody, whose every ripple or rift in the abstract metrical principle of iambic pentameter is loaded with expressive ore. Not surprisingly, there is a strong tie between Wyatt's rhythmic idiosyncrasies and his departures from literal translation. Neither Petrarch nor Surrey says anything directly about the length of love's residency. With two immediately consecutive strong accents ("The longe love, that"), involving a reversed, and caesura-severed, second foot, Wyatt literally stresses his aberrant modifying of love's temporality. (Contrast Surrey's immediate march, after the first foot, into the lockstep of normative iambic pentameter—"Love, that doth reign and live within my thought"; or how anemic it would have been merely to introduce an adjective with the same meaning but without syncopation—"The lengthy love that in my heart doth keep." So, too, Petrarch and Surrey have no *harbar:* Wyatt draws attention to his use of the word by making it a trochee despite its final position in the line.)

Wyatt's initial modifier, *longe,* proves crucial on many counts. As most poets, especially the honorary Proust, have known, one of the more effective ways to construct the semblance of subjectivity is to summon interior time, usually by "remembrance of things past." Although Wyatt's index of duration augments the inwardness that will prove so at odds with an acceptable facial expression, it also highlights the contrast between the length of love and the brief social moment in which it will be made manifest in an actual face-to-face situation.[17] Charging the impending flare of self-exposure, Wyatt's stressed temporality also gives a far more loaded arc of pathos to the whole poem's carefully scored movement through time, a movement that falls cadentially toward the ultimate lift and drop of "For good is the life ending faithfully."[18] After all, this final stress-losing rhythm of the final line—in its poignant contrast to the stress-charged opening of the poem, and in its prosodically recessive demurral against the line's own semantically upbeat rationalization—this rhythm does more than mark a purely *aesthetic* ending: like the pulse of a faltering heart it carries the speaker, however faithfully, toward death.

Great prosody is seldom extricable from syntactic genius. Petrarch ends his sonnet on the word *more* (dies). Surrey has "Sweet is the death that taketh end by love." Wyatt's adverb *faithfully* (neither Petrarch nor Surrey mentions faith) trails its verb dependently, as if to evince yet posthumously gainsay the truth of *ending*. Even the reverse-stressed word, *ending*, is internally complicated by the manner in which its weak syllable dangles from a stem whose accented *end-* (made yet more emphatic by irregularly succeeding the strong-stressed *liff,* as well as by the severe preceding caesura) the participial suffix prods out of its noun-like inertia into a verb that now lingers in an ongoing present tense. It is to this persisting action that the adverb can then add faith.

Prosody and syntax conspire equally well in staging the poem's initial crisis. Stripped to a skeleton of subject plus verb, the main clause of the first quatrain-sentence would simply be "love preseth." With his first caesura and with a barrier of interpositional clauses, Wyatt pens love into its chambers (spatially matching the temporal construction of inwardness) while literally blocking the agent from its main act of predication. Creating what we might call syntactic desire and its frustration, Wyatt builds up the pressure that will give actual force to the word *preseth*. And we can't help noticing that the last and therefore most pressured membrane between love and *preseth* is the syntactically flushed or engorged face:

> The longe love, that in my thought doeth harbar
>   And in myn hert doeth kepe his residence,
>   Into my face preseth with bolde pretence,
>   And therin campeth, spreding his baner.

The impatient energy of the main verb furthers itself by linear position, grammar, and rhythm. First note how the three verb forms (subordinate, subordinate, main) in the opening three lines migrate ever-leftward toward the front. Petrarch's choice from his inventory of words for face here is *fronte;* and given the subsequent language of battle we might say love is moving toward the front lines. Now add the difference between *doeth harbar, doeth kepe,* and *preseth*. Whereas *harbar* and *kepe* (both verbs of stasis) are deferentially led by the auxiliary *doeth,* the kinetic *preseth* pushes any intermediary out of the way—a grammatical microchip of the sonnet's way of dramatizing the problem of mediation at large. All this importunacy is irregularly *front*-loaded by the trochee of *preseth,* a prosodic rush in which the strong stress refuses to wait for its normatively weak intercessor, just as the verb presses one syllable nearer to the front. (Contrast the relative inertia of Surrey's "Oft in my face he doth his banner rest"—there being no word for pressing in Petrarch.) And to keep the sonic capillaries in play, the sound and action continue by a kind of alliterative and assonantal blushing out to the very end of the line, where the word *pretence* emerges, only to be transfused yet further in the next line by the very word *spreding,* as the whole invasion takes possession of the quatrain and of the sonnet thus far.[19]

Two remarks before turning to the second quatrain. First, *pretence* literally stretches—its etymons associate it with the taut string of a musical instrument—between the meaning of extending a claim (as in pretender to the throne, no light matter in Wyatt's time) and that of disguise (the kind of hypocritical courtliness Wyatt despised). Whereas Wyatt's *pretence* is here tilted more toward revealed feeling than to its opposite, the word is uncomfortably close to its counterfeature—the sense of fakery for which Sor Juana's early-seventeenth-century Petrarchan sonnet, scoring the falsification inherent in her painted self-portrait, uses the Spanish *pretendido.*

Second, and more to the issue of disempowerment, there is no personal agency at work thus far within the represented action. Everything is love's doing, not the speaker's. This abeyance is intensified by the next quatrain, where instead of meeting the speaker's attempt to regain control, love encounters and is soon overwhelmed by the beloved's disdain. Syntactically, as well as thematically, *She* dominates the second quatrain-sentence, as he (love) had dominated the first. The speaker is in the object, or even *abject,* position (he has yet to use the word *I*). Not even a principal combatant, he is an increasingly passive amalgam: a suffering student, a site of occupation and contest, a servant of love the loser.

Regarding the language of the second quatrain, a quick scan takes in *wills,* a verb that works its way through so many Shakespeare sonnets, just as *shame, trust, lust* all appear in Sonnet 129. But nuances of Wyatt's language in this second quatrain call for renewed attention:

> She that me lerneth to love and suffre,
>   And willes that my trust and lustes negligence
>   Be rayned by reason, shame and reverence,
>   With his hardines taketh displeasur.

In terms of diction "lustes negligence" dramatizes its meaning by the clash of Anglo-Saxon and Latinate vocabulary (almost as if he says *lust,* she says *negligence,* he says "lustes negligence"). *Hardines* has its witty vascular relation to the spreading banner and lies nicely alongside the negation of whatever pleasure it might have offered. (Thanks to this quatrain, I now know—as one might have suspected from the context—that the suffix *-nes* is from Old English, whereas *-ence* is Latinate, so the sonnet could almost be seen as a struggle, enmeshed with translation itself, between the two, aligned as they are with a native impulse colliding with an external code.) The line *Be rayned by reason, shame and reverence* takes up the Platonic figure of reined horsepower, melding it with the language of chivalric pursuit. But as we shall see, the particular triad of reason, shame, and reverence invites a more extended reflection, particularly in the light of the volta, which now pivots about the flag of *displeasur*—whose syntactic and linear position formally displaces that of love's *baner*.

> Wherewithal, vnto the hertes forrest he fleith,
> Leving his entreprise with payn and cry;
> And ther him hideth, and not appereth.

Given love's precipitous retreat and concealment, and given the absence of implicit or explicit reverence for the beloved, we may assume that *shame* was not casually centered between its apparently less operative companions. Indeed shame (Petrarch's *vergogna* and Wyatt's *shame* occupy as central a position within the *entire* sonnet as one can practically achieve) may be as central a feature of the sonnet tradition as the face itself, with which this feeling is so closely associated, even to the point of the word *shamefaced.* Surrey used "with shamefast look" in his translation, and Tottel lifted the word in titling Wyatt's poem for his 1557 *Miscellany:* "The lover for shamefastnesse hideth his desire within his faithful heart."

As cultural historians and philosophers from E. R. Dodds to Bernard Williams have recognized, shame involves not just a sense of exposure but *a loss of face.* And if sonnets engage with the imaging of faces, it is hardly surprising that they have a pronounced interest in this kind of loss. This essay cannot go into the cultural evolution of shame in general, but we should recall that one of its origins was in the field of warfare. Williams quotes Homer's Ajax: "What countenance can I show my father Telamon? / How will he bear the sight of me / If I come before him naked, without any glory?" And it is Ajax who exhorts: "Dear friends, be men; let shame be in your hearts." There's no lack of fusion in the *Iliad* between military and erotic conquest, but it was the engine of chivalry that most transferred the values of warfare into those of eroticized contest and allegiance. The military tropes are clearly at work in Petrarch and Wyatt (who was a champion jouster, as well as a heroic soldier). But whereas Petrarch's and Surrey's love wears enough armor (*talor armato / Clad in the arms*) to shield its libido, Wyatt drops the figure of defensive armor altogether, while adding both *preseth* and *hardines.*[20]

The sexual element in shame is present as early as the ancient Greek term itself. Bernard Williams points out that "*aidoia,* a derivative of *aidos,* 'shame,' is a standard Greek word for the genitals."[21] Although Williams mentions that "similar terms are found in other languages," he focuses exclusively on Greek origins, thereby missing or perhaps taking for granted how intensely the linkage of shame and sexual exposure drives one of the most foundational moments in *Genesis,* where the fall from being "unashamed" at nakedness (2.25) to the sensation of shame leads both to the first-ever act of hiding ("among the trees of the garden"— Wyatt's forest?) and to the first human artifactual making of any kind: the sewing together of leaves to make a covering for what thereby becomes both concealed and private.[22] Perhaps shame is a two-faced instrument, operating not just for normative control but for the very production of inwardness?

Rather than map the dense prehistory of the Italian sonnet's engagement with shame, let us stay with Wyatt's demonstration of shame in action. *Hideth* is what we do when ashamed. "The reaction is to cover oneself or to hide" (Williams, 78). In a move that is paradigmatic for so many sonnets, Wyatt's love turns away from the face, back into the heart—withdrawing from circulation, so to speak (a circuit that may only be renewed via the displacement from blood to ink and by the subsequent circulation of the poem). For the poem to advance its action, however, and to deepen its construction of inwardness, love can't simply go back to where it was in the first two lines. It can no longer occupy a harbor or residence. In fact, only now do we learn that the heart has a *forest*— unbuilt, uncultivated, the *selvaggio/*savage region of obscurity where Dante's pilgrimage begins.[23] Love *flees* (a frequent verb in Wyatt); and the image of the heart thereby grows to include interior wilderness. There can be no direct speech within such wilds, which is why love's *entreprise* (with its faint echo of *preseth*) is left "with payn and cry." We hear no words. Certainly Wyatt's poem is the "cry of its occasion"; but because neither pain nor a pure cry *have* words—think of Bishop's "*oh!* of pain"— the little sound of his *sonnetto* must translate itself not just out of Petrarch but (as if all translation must stage a reentry to language itself) into human speech.

My guess is that part of the overall occasion of the cry in Wyatt's poem is a variously redoubled shame: the shame of exposure; the humiliation of defeat and loss of face; the speaker's shame at his tortuously passive relation to a baffled love that he can serve but cannot quite claim as his own. Shame probably feeds on itself—aggravated by the hiding that it provokes, deepened by disclaimers of self-possession or of primary agency.

Hence one may be ashamed at feeling shame because one feels the intensified lack of whatever inner sufficiency might have allowed one to outface the world. Many sonnets beyond Petrarch's and Wyatt's may come into being in large part to construct or repair enough sense of interiority, enough of some otherwise unmanifested capacity of another kind, so that they can address and maybe redress whatever has shamed them into being. They need to save face via a detour behind and beneath the face—usually toward the heart.[24]

Closing the poem's third sentence, line 11 thus reaches inward to the furthest reaches of the heart's privacy and privation. In a poem about the very problem of coming into appearance and of (self-)representation, the truest counterlimit from which strength (or nourishment, as Petrarch said) may be drawn is that of disappearance (*and not appereth* will be made to rhyme with *fereth*). It is only now that the speaker begins to regain ground—or rather to regain territory *on other grounds:*

> What may I do when my maister fereth
> But in the feld with him to lyve and dye?
> For goode is the liff, ending faithfully.

For the first time (but very much at last!) the speaker uses the word *I.* And although he presents it as a question, the issue is precisely one of agency: *What may I do?* The most crucial thing to notice here is not the fact that he goes on to answer his own question—an answer whose strength is somewhat vitiated by its claim that there is little choice—but rather that he poses the question at all. Why? Because the turn to the question of agency (a turn here constituting the shift from a given present to a possible future) is made inseparable from an explicit turn toward the reader.

In other words, having broached the wilder regions of interiority, the speaker compensates for the disappearing act of love by putting himself forward, as an "I," into the more overtly summoned presence of the reader. This is in large part what he *can* do. This is what he *does.* Certainly he departs with his master, but first he remains to tell us what he is choosing and the grounds on which he makes the choice. In a sense he makes up for the loss of face by facing us—by acknowledging that he has been addressing us all along. By occupying a third position offered by poetry, he has found a way to step outside the binary face-off between love and the lady. (We can register the subtle shift even in topography as the forest leads back out to the exposure of the field.) Admonished by reason and reverence, preoccupied by love and then by shame, he has counterclaimed harbor and residence within the sonnet—a form whose independently fixed dimensions suit it for this provision of some other, stable premises. Having fallen out with the beloved, the speaker falls in with an array of possible appellants, just as Dante began the poetry of *Vita Nuova* by literally sending his first sonnet to "a number of poets" and by internally orienting that sonnet so as to "greet all Love's faithful servants." Falling toward and beyond death, Wyatt's speaker falls forward across time and space into the present and presence of ourselves.

This action is, I believe, what lends conviction to the final line, even to the point of its final word. For having hoisted the *I,* having raised the question of agency and choice that invests that *I* with ethical identity, having summoned the reader into this very terrain of relation and present choice—having done all this within the increasingly secured precincts of the poem (now extended to the penultimate line of its own life)—the speaker can perform his final action: the making and declaring of a judgment. Not just any judgment but a judgment *and conferral* of value.

If the experience of shame and hiding recapitulated the primal fall, there is something astounding in Wyatt's now reiterating the archetypal first judgment *"that it was good."*[25] (He even brings it transformatively into the present tense: "For good *is.*") The sequence has moved from human shame to an echo of divine benediction—a step up—as if a ladder had been found leaning against the tree of the knowledge of good and evil.

Intriguingly the action of judgment (sealed and given a heightened claim on our attention by its position as the fourteenth of fourteen lines) reinforces the way in which the question *What may I do?* had begun to bind the inside and outside of the poem. I don't mean that it does so simply by a literal framing action. The judgment faces the *feld* of impending death (to lyve *and* dye), while facing out to that indeterminate but nonterminating field of readers on whose attendance the question had called and *within* whose poetically mediated presence an evaluative claim is now made. Instead of the loss of a singular face, the poem has produced the potential for many faces—its own repeating face and (to return to Ashbery) the prospect of many readers' pictured faces.

"Traffic" indeed. As in exchange or trade. By a final breathtaking yet breath-giving turn, Wyatt follows the phrase "lyve and dye" with the verbal resurrection of *liff.* And although he cannot save that life, he can as we have seen revise and indefinitely defer the nature of its end. If there be an actual end achieved here at all, it is form that will accomplish and enforce it.

Which leaves us with the poem's last word. *Faithfully* has more than syntactic and prosodic interest, more even than that of its significance as a term qualifying the previously opposed forces of reason and emotion or as an attribute that substantiates the recent judgment of goodness. I would propose briefly that Wyatt's assertion of faithfulness takes on trenchancy and purpose in the political and cultural context of the 1530s. Wyatt's poem at large has responded to perils of appearance, shame, concealment, loyalty—all increasingly problematic in the intrigue-ridden, centralized court culture that was emerging out of the ruins of a feudal world. Wyatt's father had been tortured by Richard III for his feudal loyalty to Henry Tudor. According to the Wyatts' domestic chronicler, the exchange went as follows. Richard: "Wyat why are thou such a foole? thou servest for moonshine in the water, A beggarly fugitive, forsake him, and become mine, who can reward thee." To which Henry Wyatt: "If I had first chosen you for my Master, thus faithfull would I have been to you, if you should have needed it, but the Earle, poor and unhappy, tho he be, is my Master, and no discouragement or allurement shall ever drive, or draw me from him, by Gods grace."[26]

Many of Thomas Wyatt's poems contest the "strange fashion of forsaking." Behind this thrust is the urgent work of preserving continuity itself in an age of unprecedented disruption: here again the sonnet's relative constancy to its own formal imperatives, and to its own cross-cultural and extratemporal community of writers and readers, makes it ideally equipped for such work, even as its brevity makes it ever aware of "ending." The cultural and literary historian David Wallace has recently proposed the year 1536—marked by the execution, possibly witnessed by Wyatt from his cell in the Tower, of the poet's ex-lover, Queen Anne Boleyn—as one of the most dramatic points of rupture between two entire world orders in England.[27] Despite the primarily secular context for Wyatt's final word, we might bear in mind the degree to which the Henrician Reformation made faith itself a matter of lethal personal, national, and international conflict. Or we may recall Henry Wyatt's implicit binding of feudal loyalty to "God's grace."

In addition, then, to Wyatt's repairing to the poetic principle and to the poetic "field" as a realm in which to save face, to mediate between love and the beloved, to construct and conserve an interior as well as exterior image of personhood, to reclaim displaced agency, to provide words for an otherwise wordless cry, to make judgments conferring value, to give voice to an identity that is pitched beyond the orbits of mere reason, shame, lust, or even love—the poet has staked out (at and as the extreme limit of his poetic practice) a last resort for the profession of faithfulness.

Lest we become too flushed by reparation, too excited by Wyatt's mastery in the lists of poetry—in which all English sonnets will bear a trace of his remains—it is worth taking in the word *maister*. Yes it is love. But in order to end faithfully within a sonnet, Wyatt must serve the impersonal, transhistorical orders forwarded to him by the poet whom Puttenham referred to as Wyatt's "maister." Even the question "What may I do when my maister fereth?" takes on cogency when we recall Petrarch's repeated fearfulness within and on behalf of his heart (*che temo del cor*), and Petrarch's allegiance to a poetic form and system associated with Dante's fearful initiatory confrontation with the one who says *Ego dominus tuus* (I am your master) and who then adds *Vide cor tuum* (behold your heart) as he hands over the poet's heart to be eaten by the beloved. If there is mastery here, it is in the art of being mastered.

To break off this swatch of a larger study of Wyatt, and perhaps of the sonnet, I return first to Ashbery—not to his "Sonnet" but to the poem with which I opened, having left the poet imagining someone sitting in the yard waiting to pick up the "gorgeous raw material" left around by Wyatt and Surrey.[28] Twenty-nine lines later Ashbery's speaker turns back (but now also turns directly) to Surrey: "Surrey, your lute is getting an attack of nervous paralysis / But there are, again, things to be sung of / And this is one of them."

What has happened to Wyatt in the intervening lines? Has he disappeared, only to reappear implicitly via his immediate successor, whose principal elegy ("Wyatt resteth here that quicke could never reste") recalled the "visage sterne and mylde" of the nobleman who, although being Surrey's social inferior, had been his poetic master? (Surrey's additional elegiac sonnet for Wyatt ends: "His lively face their breasts how did it freet / Whose cinders yet with envy they do eat.") Or has Wyatt's nature, absorbed into the "gorgeous raw material," become more generally "subdued / To what it work[ed] in, like the dyer's hand" of Shakespeare's Sonnet III? Not just the dyer's hand, we'd have to say—also his face, and heart.

Finally, I turn back to a sonnet writer before Petrarch. I've not tried to find more information on Niccolo Degli Abbizi, other than what Rossetti appended to his translation of a single "prolonged sonnet." He includes Niccolo with one or two other of the earliest sonnet writers, noting,

"These poets, of whom practically nothing is known, flourished in the second half of the thirteenth century." I believe that my initial and delayed responses to this poem led in large part to the writing of this essay.[29]

> *When the Troops Were Returning from Milan*
> If you could see, fair brother, how dead beat
>   The fellows look who come through Rome to-day,—
>   Black yellow smoke-dried visages,—you'd say
> They thought their haste at going all too fleet.
> Their empty victual-waggons up the street
>   Over the bridge dreadfully sound and sway;
>   Their eyes, as hang'd men's, turning the wrong way;
> And nothing on their backs, or heads, or feet.
> One sees the ribs and all the skeletons
>   Of their gaunt horses; and a sorry sight
> Are the torn saddles, cramm'd with straw and stones.
>   They are ashamed, and march throughout the night;
> Stumbling, for hunger, on their marrowbones;
>   Like barrels rolling, jolting, in this plight.
> Their arms are gone, not even their swords are saved;
> And each as silent as a man being shaved.

NOTES

1. John Ashbery, "Grand Galop," in *Self-Portrait in a Convex Mirror* (1972; repr., New York: Penguin, 1976), 20.

2. Ibid., 19.

3. Just to establish the primacy of Wyatt as sonneteer if not translator, I should point out that Chaucer's translation of one of Petrarch's sonnets, embedded within *Troilus and Criseyde,* does not approximate the sonnet form. The material is assimilated to the surrounding rhyme royal septets, an assimilation that involves much padding and a loss of argumentative shape. Nonetheless, it is interesting to notice the degrees of self-conscious literary estrangement built into the presentation of the song: Chaucer breaks to give voice to Troilus, who is given the words of Petrarch in a crazy anachronistic ventriloquism whose dispossessive power reinforces the song's very theme. The narrator's introduction of the song, which he will alienate further by printing its Latin title, "*Canticus Troili,*" reads:

> And of his song naught only the sentence,
> As writ myn auctour called Lollius,
> But pleinly, save oure tonges difference,
> I dar wel seyn, in al that Troilus

Seyde in his song, Loo! every word right thus
As I shal seyn; and whoso list it here,
Loo, next this vers he may it finden here.

It's hard to miss the "whoso list" (Wyatt was an avid reader of Chaucer); and it's worth reading the lines with which Chaucer resumes after the song: "And to the God of Love thus seyde he / With pitous vois, "O lord, now youres is / My spirit." *Troilus and Criseyede* 1.399–420.

4. John Ashbery, "Sonnet," in *Some Trees* (1956; repr., New York: Ecco Press, 1978), 37. Here is the sonnet in full:

Each servant stamps the reader with a look.
After many years he has been brought nothing.
The servant's frown is the reader's patience.
The servant goes to bed.
The patience rambles on
Musing on the library's lofty holes.

His pain is the servant's alive.
It pushes to the top stain of the wall
Its tree-top's head of excitement:
Baskets, birds, beetles, spools.
The light walls collapse next day.
Traffic is the reader's pictured face.
Dear, be the tree your sleep awaits;
Worms be your words, you not safe from ours.

5. Petrarch's contemporary Boccaccio has a sonnet whose octave, as translated by D. G. Rossetti, ends with these lines:

. . . And each had twined a bough to shield
Her lovely face; and the green leaves did yield
    The golden hair their shadow; while the two
    Sweet colours mingled, both blown lightly through
With a soft wind for ever stirr'd and still'd.

The opening lines of the first of Spenser's *Amoretti* sonnets address the leaves of the sonnets themselves: "Happy ye leaves when as those lilly hands, / which hold my life in their dead doing might, / shall handle you"; and thence to the legible "sorrowes of my dying spright."

6. The word *screen* (schermo) appears already among the sonnets and prose of Dante's *Vita Nuova;* but the figure of the sonnet itself as screen is explicit in Rossetti's Petrarchan sonnet sequence, #97, "A Superscription," which begins in the voice of the script, "Look in my face," and which soon confesses itself to be "a shaken shadow intolerable, / Of ultimate things unuttered the frail screen."

Christina Rossetti uses the same figure, along with painted fabric and face, in her own Petrarchan sonnet about her brother, "In an Artist's Studio" (1856):

One face looks out from all his canvases,
  One selfsame figure sits or walks or leans:
  We found her hidden just behind those screens,
That mirror gave back all her loveliness.

. . . . . .

He feeds upon her face by day and night.

7. The ending of the prior Glanmore sonnet sets up the desire for such respite, as the speaker glimpses an ominous image of the beloved's face: ". . . and beyond, inside, your face / Haunts like a new moon glimpsed through tangled glass" (Seamus Heaney, *Opened Ground: Selected Poems 1966–1996* [New York: Farrar, Straus and Giroux, 1998], 164–65).

As is well known, the words *cosmic* and *cosmetic* are practically cognate. The Neoplatonic tradition is not alone in exploring motifs such as that of Macrobius's image of divine emanation as presented "like a countenance reflected in many mirrors arranged in a row." One of the more powerful envisionings of the cosmic face appears in Cabbalistic writings whose dispersal surely nourished the cultural matrix out of which sonnets originated.

8. Elaine Scarry, *Dreaming by the Book* (New York: Farrar, Straus and Giroux, 1999), chap. 4. Originally "Imagining Flowers: Perceptual Mimesis (Particularly Delphinium)," *Representations* 57 (winter 1997). Ranging in discussion from Chaucer to Wordsworth, Rilke, Proust, and Ashbery, Scarry's essay is a brilliant and subtle registration of the interplay among mental imaging, acts of poesis, and (among other elements) the properties of flowers. If the sonnet accommodates the image of a face, and if the image of a face may be modeled on a flower, we may assume an almost overdetermined affinity between the sonnet and the flower. A small chronological sample of sonnet writers who fulfill this relation includes Guido Guinicelli, Dante, Petrarch, Garcilaso de la Vega, Spenser, Shakespeare (at least twenty-two sonnets mention flowers, and sixteen refer to a face), Sor Juana Ines de la Cruz, Andreas Gryphius, Wordsworth, D. G. Rossetti, Wallace Stevens (whose uncollected sonnet sequence of 1899 has a literal anthology of flower images), and Rilke. Scarry's instances of this last poet's work are drawn mostly from the *New Poems* of 1907/8. Although it is tempting to quote one of Rilke's later *Sonnets to Orpheus*, at least nine of which are devoted to flowers, I will reinforce my observation elsewhere of the sonnet's traffic between face and heart by quoting the last three lines of D. G. Rossetti's "Barren Spring": "Nay, for these Spring-flowers, turn thy face from them, / Nor gaze till on the year's last lily-stem / the white cup shrivels round the golden heart."

9. For Cimabue and Giotto see *Purgatorio* 11. The *Vita Nuova* tells of the poet's attempt to draw the faces of angels, with that of his beloved in mind. D. G. Rossetti has a painting of Dante as he is imagined to be making this drawing.

Although the sonnet is not a mirror for the face, but rather a scaled down image-rendering device, it is worth noting that the thirteenth century did see the introduction of newly accurate flat mirrors into Europe. See S. Edgerton, *The Renaissance Rediscovery of Linear Perspective* (New York: Basic Books, 1975).

10. Although his face is seen in a fully frontal position, Wyatt's eyes gaze off to his right, passing off beyond our left. Because it is this withdrawn yet far-seeing horizontal action that suggests something otherwise unrepresentably in reserve (or yet another face held in Wyatt's view or in mind), the viewer's uneasy factoring in of a lateral, as well as an up-and-down, engagement with the face makes it more like an act of reading. Like the sonnets, the portrait addresses itself in addition to someone who is only virtually present.

11. Petrarch's sonnet in *Rime Sparse* (18) begins: *Quand'io son tutto volto in quella parte / ove'l bel viso di Madonna luce* (When I am turned [facing] completely toward that place where my lady's face shines). To stray from the sonnet proper for a powerful example of the facial turn in Donne, see "Good Friday, 1613. Riding Westward," which ends: "Restore Thine image so much, by Thy grace, / That thou may'st know me, and I'll turn my face." In the light of this ending I see that although the poem is written in heroic couplets, it comprises three argumentatively articulated sections of fourteen lines.

And to return to the sonnet (and to Italian poetry), we might recall Montale's translations of Shakespeare's sonnets during the 1940s, along with his own sonnet adaptations written during this period. The final seven lines from one of these, "*Serenata indiana,*" focus precisely on the *volto:* however desperate, the grappling with issues of dispossession (and ink) evinces a deep intuition about the forces as well as features of the genre:

> Fosse tua vita quella che mi tiene
> sulle soglie—e potrei prestarti un volto,
> vaneggiarti figura. Ma non è,
>
> non è così. Il polipo che insinua
> tentacoli d'inchiostro tra gli scogli
> può servirsi di te. Tu gli appartieni
> e non lo sai. Sei lui, ti credi te.

> Were it your life that stalls me at the threshold—
> and I could lend a face to you,
> imagine you a form. But no,
>
> it's not that way. The octopus that works
> inky tentacles among the shoals
> knows how to use you. You belong to him
> unwittingly. You're him; you think you're you.

Eugenio Montale, *Collected Poems 1920–1954,* trans. Jonathan Galassi (New York: Farrar, Straus and Giroux, 1998), 276–77.

12. Shakespeare's sonnet sequence begins by focusing on the face of the beloved, turning to the question of how that face may come to generate other faces rather than falling into extinction. There is no shortage of legible faces in the plays. To take only the play that is set in a city associated with Petrarch, and that includes and is framed by sonnets (the first of which contains both the words *traffic* and *patient* found in Ashbery's "Sonnet"), we might recall Lady Capulet's instruction to Juliet: "Read o'er the volume of young Paris' face, / And find delight writ there with beauty's pen; / Examine every married lineament, / And see how one another lends content" (*Romeo and Juliet,* in *The Riverside Shakespeare,* ed. G. Blakemore Evans et al. [Boston: Houghton Mifflin, 1974], 1.3.81–84). The immediately preceding cue comes from the Nurse: "Nay he's a flower; in faith, a very flower" (1.3.78).

13. My admittedly amateurish measurements derive from Dürer's *Self-Portrait,* Holbein's portraits of Henry VIII and of Wyatt, Leonardo's *La Belle Ferroniere,* Titian's *Young Englishman.* The subject of the latter portrait would have been a contemporary of Wyatt's, and Titian and Wyatt might have met while at the court of Charles V.

14. *Vita Nuova,* ed. Dino Cervigni and Edward Vasta (Notre Dame: University of Notre Dame Press, 1995), 91.

15. Milton's great sonnet "Methought I saw my late espoused saint" oscillates tragically within three lines between a "[veiled] face" and "no face." Of the poets listed above, the iconoclastic Rimbaud may come least readily to mind, yet despite Rimbaud's revolutionary impulses, the sonnet portrait of "Venus Anadyomene" has the traditional motifs; and the editorial note to the Petrarchan sonnet "Rages de Cesars" reads: "Rimbaud traite son sujet comme sil s'agissait d'expliquer un dessin. Les sentiments de Napoleon III ne sont que conjectures d'apres les traits de son visage." *Oeuvres Completes* (Paris: Gallimard, 1972), 867. Even less predictable, given his disruptive poetic form, is Paul Celan's translation of Shakespeare's Sonnet 137, with its exercised clash of face and fakery. Like Montale's, these translations were made during the 1940s. Since writing this essay I have found a sonnet-face linkage (together with a traditional allusion to unrepresentable inwardness) more recent even than those mentioned in the work of Ashbery, Heaney, or Merrill. In the second of four sonnets making up his "Self-Portrait as Four Styles of Pompeian Wall Painting," Henri Cole writes, as if in the voice of the sonnet-fresco itself: "My face is a little Roman theater / in perfect perspective—with colonnades / and landscapes— making illusionistic / reference to feelings I cannot admit." *The Visible Man* (New York: Knopf, 1998), 4. See also the first and fifth sonnets in the sequence *Apollo.*

Although the sonnet might be less usefully associated with the hand (the palm of which has, of course, been read for centuries), Giusto de' Conti did write an entire book of sonnets regarding a "beautiful hand." In the visual arts Dürer has several self-portraits in which the face is partially covered and measured by the hand; and as Ashbery's *Self-Portrait in a Convex Mirror* begins by noticing, Parmigianino's painting literally foregrounds the relation of hand to face. Just as Parmigianino's portrait manneristically extends or distends the conventional Renaissance portrait, so Ashbery's elongated meditation far exceeds the dimensions of the sonnet.

16. Although R. A. Rebholz's edition of *The Complete Poems* is the more comprehensive text, I cite from the more readily available selection by W. S. Merwin, *The Essential Wyatt* (New York: Ecco Press, 1989). I recommend this edition not only for Merwin's introduction but also for his having chosen to conserve the earlier character of Wyatt's diction and spelling.

The Petrarch reads as follows:

> Amor, che nel penser mio vive et regna
> e'l suo seggio maggior nel mio cor tene,
> talor armato ne la fronte vene;
> ivi si loca et ivi pon sua insegna.
>
> Quella ch'amare et sofferir ne'nsegna
> e vol che'l gran desio, l'accesa spene
> ragion, vergogna, et reverenza affrene,
> di nostro ardir fra se stessa si sdegna.
>
> Onde Amor paventoso fugge al core,
> lasciando ogni sua impresa, et piange et trema;
> ivi s'asconde et non appar piu fore.
>
> Che poss'io far, temendo il mio signore,
> se non star seco infin a l'ora estrema?
> che bel fin fa chi ben amando more.

Petrarch's Lyric Poems, trans. and ed. Robert M. Durling (Cambridge, Mass.: Harvard University Press, 1976), 285.

Because I refer to Surrey's version, I include it here:

> Love, that doth reign and live within my thought,
> And built his seat within my captive breast,
> Clad in the arms wherein with me he fought,
> Oft in my face he doth his banner rest.
> But she that taught me love and suffer pain,
> My doubtful hope and eke my hot desire
> With shamefast look to shadow and refrain,
> Her smiling grace converteth straight to ire.
> And coward Love, then, to the heart apace
> Taketh his flight, where he doth lurk and plain,
> His purpose lost, and dare not show his face.
> For my lord's guilt thus faultless bide I pain,
> Yet from my lord shall not my foot remove:
> Sweet is the death that taketh end by love.

17. Governed by its relative brevity, the sonnet's sensitivity to the mismatch of duration and instant not only drives the argument of individual poems (Rossetti's "The sonnet is a moment's monument") but surely impels the phenomenon of the sonnet sequence, a phenomenon enduring well into the late twentieth century, as works by Berryman, Lowell, Heaney, and others attest. Almost anything briefer than an individual sonnet would be short enough to write on a gravestone, and I would suggest that the sonnet seems formally and expressly designed to subsume the epitaphic mode.

18. Compare the similarly falling rhythm of dactyl-plus-trochee in "Faynting I follow," which introduces line seven of "Whoso List to Hunt." I am not claiming that the so-called falling of all trochees and dactyls is *necessarily* attenuative; there is an obvious semantic component at work in all cases, such as in the contrastively importunate effect of *preseth*.

19. Cf. Spenser's Sonnet 5: "and her faire countenance like a goodly banner, / Spreds in defiaunce of all enemies." Wyatt's physiopoetic blush predates by almost a century William Harvey's discovery of the circulation of the blood.

20. This is the only truly digressive endnote. It concerns Spain's foremost early translator of Petrarch into Spanish sonnets, Garcilaso de la Vega. "In 1536, at only age thirty-five, the courtier and knight of the Order of Santiago died heroically in the presence of his king as a result of leading an assault, unhelmeted, up a ladder on a tower near Fréjus in France" (Willis Barnstone, *Six Masters of the Spanish Sonnet* [Carbondale, Ill.: Southern Illinois University Press, 1993], 4). Barnstone translates the first four lines of de la Vega's Sonnet 23 as follows: "While there is still the color of the rose / and lily in your face, and your bright gaze / in its sincerity can set ablaze / a heart, and yet control the flame it shows." In 1537 Wyatt, age thirty-three, became ambassador to Spain, hence to the court of de la Vega's king, Charles V, patron of Titian. Five years later he himself would die in royal service, having become overheated and feverish from a furious ride on horseback to welcome the imperial Spanish envoy to England.

21. Bernard Williams, *Shame and Necessity* (Berkeley: University of California Press, 1993), 78.

22. From the now only apparently unlikely jointure of shame and leaves, we might sympathize further with the speaker of Shakespeare's Sonnet 73. As his yellow leaves thin out, is he not merely anxious but also slightly ashamed about his increasingly exposed old-age in the presence of his lover? As the season turns to darker days, as the sun gives way to utter night, and as the firelight expires, there may be some unlooked-for compensation in the "sealing" darkness out of which he expresses his concluding hope, or claim.

23. Given Dante's immediate journey from the *selva oscura* into hell, it is not surprising that Shakespeare's paroxysm of shame in Sonnet 129 ends, "To shun the heaven that leads men to this hell," nor that one of the elements of

almost suspenseful interest throughout the *Inferno* is the degree of shame or shamelessness the pilgrim encounters in each inmate.

24. Petrarch's prefatory sonnet to the entire *Rime Sparse* reads:

> Voi ch'ascoltate in rime sparse il suono
> di quei sospirir on'io nudriva'l core
> in sul mio primo giovenile errore,
> quant'era in parte altr' uom da quel ch' i' sono:
>
> del vario stile in ch' io piango et ragiono
> fra le vane speranze e'l van dolore,
> ove sia chi per prova intenda amore
> spero trovar pieta, non che perdono.
>
> Ma ben veggio or si come al popol tutto
> favola fui gran tempo, onde sovente
> di me medesmo meco mi vergogno;
> et del mio vaneggiar vergogna e'l frutto,
> e'l pentersi, e'l conoscer chiaramente
> che quanto piace al mondo e breve sogno.

In Durling's prose translation: You who hear in scattered rhymes the sound of those sighs with which I nourished my heart during my first youthful error, when I was in part another man from what I am now: // for the varied style in which I weep and speak between vain hopes and vain sorrow, where there is anyone who understands love through experience, I hope to find pity, not only pardon. // But now I see well how for a long time I was the talk of the crowd, for which often I am ashamed of myself within; // and of my raving, shame is the fruit, and repentance, and the clear knowledge that whatever pleases in the world is a brief dream (Durling, *Petrarch's Lyric Poems,* 36–37).

25. How significant is it for us to be told that before God judged anything, before he *made* anything other than heaven and earth, before he said "Let there be light"—before all of this—"darkness was upon the face of the deep. And the Spirit of God moved upon the face of the waters"?

26. Quoted in Patricia Thomson, *Sir Thomas Wyatt and His Background* (Stanford: Stanford University Press, 1964), 4.

27. David Wallace, *Chaucerian Polity: Absolutist Lineages and Associational Forms in England and Italy* (Stanford: Stanford University Press, 1997), 378.

I should add here that I have benefited from the studies of Wyatt by Stephen Greenblatt and Jonathan Crewe. Their respective chapters on Wyatt in *Renaissance Self-Fashioning from More to Shakespeare* (Chicago: University of Chicago Press, 1980) and in *Trials of Authorship: Anterior Forms and Poetic Reconstruction from Wyatt to Shakespeare* (Berkeley: University of California Press, 1991) reinforce my sense that there would be considerable value in initiating a specific account of the relation between the origins and emerging prevalence of the English sonnet as a form, and the kinds of political, cultural, psychological, and theological provocations that Greenblatt, Crewe, and others have investigated. See also Anne Ferry, *The "Inward" Language: Sonnets of Wyatt, Sidney, Shakespeare, Donne* (Chicago: University of Chicago Press, 1983). Although not a new historicist account, Ferry's study has been important to my understanding of Wyatt and the sonnet.

28. Sidney, having attributed the dawning of a truly refined English poetry to the era of Wyatt and Surrey, wondered how much the "evill[y] apparrelled" work of preceding poets such as Chaucer might have been enhanced had it been "trymmed in . . . gorgeous eloquence" (Patricia Thomson, ed., *Wyatt: The Critical Heritage* [London: Routledge, 1974], 6).

29. My Everyman edition of Rossetti's poems and translations has no date, but it is probably from the 1910s. Niccolo's sonnet is on pp. 234–35. It was Frank Bidart who introduced me to this poem, simply by reading Rossetti's translation aloud—one poet's giving voice to another's translation of yet another's sonnet, which begins by appealing to a brother addressee, pictured as "fair," and which takes as its subject the faces of shame and the compassionate, perhaps even ashamed, attempt to say something about what might be felt behind the intensified silence of those faces as they are then more generally (but still more closely, and singularly) imagined under the exposing, cleansing, yet potentially bloody action of the razor.

TWO

Sidney and the Sestina

ANTHONY HECHT

AMONG THE MANY CHARMS of the fourteenth edition of the *Encyclopædia Britannica,* few can match the pleasure of pure surprise elicited by the bold, unequivocal assertion: "The earliest sestina in English was published in 1877 by Edmund Gosse."[1] In *The Countess of Pembroke's Arcadia* (1593) Sir Philip Sidney, usually credited with being the first to employ the form in English, introduces three sestinas, each distinctly different from the others. The first, beginning "Since wailing is a bud of causefull sorowe," is formally the most conventional, disposing its terminal words according to what have become orthodox permutations.[2] Invention of this established form is commonly attributed to the troubadour poet Arnaut Daniel and was quickly imitated by, among others, Dante, whose sestina "to the 'stony lady, Pietra,'" is a superb example of the form. William A. Ringler Jr., editor of the Clarendon Press edition of Sidney's *Poems,* remarks that "the monotonous sevenfold repetition [if the final tercet is taken into account] of the same six words is appropriate to a song of mourning, though Puttenham, the only Elizabethan critic to recognize the form, commented that 'to make the dittie sensible will try the makers cunning'" (416).

I take these two points to be of the greatest importance and potentially self-contradictory. The sevenfold repetition of the same terminal words does indeed invite a monotony that best accompanies a dolorous, de- spairing, and melancholy mood, such as would possess Dante's forlorn lover in his stony sestina. The repeated words, inexorable in their order, seem designed to convey a state of obsession, and of gloomy obsession especially. But what Puttenham calls "the makers cunning" may refuse to yield to that mood of solitary and redundant woe or may at the very least wish to vary it through the "cunning" of art. "To make the dittie sensible" is presumably to put those redundancies in a meaningful and effective order; but it may also mean "to create something that is acutely felt; markedly painful or pleasurable." And a number of poets have taken up the challenge of composing sestinas that defy the mood of desolation seemingly imposed by the rigid monotony of terminal repetition. One such poem is Pound's bravura "Sestina: Altaforte," which gleefully rejoices in violence and sanguinary enthusiasm; another is Ashbery's comic "Farm Implements and Rutabagas in a Landscape." Such poems specifically repudiate the more familiar and lugubrious music of most sestinas.

Of Sidney's two remaining sestinas in the *Arcadia*, the one beginning "Farewell Ô Sunn, *Arcadia*'s clearest light" departs from canonical form by employing rhymes, its first stanza's terminal words deployed in this order: *light, treasure, might, pleasure, direction, affection.* The subsequent stanzas redeploy these words according to the canonical system of sestinas, and the poem, in keeping with tradition, is mournful and valedictory throughout. T. S. Eliot, too, wrote a rhymed sestina, although his rhyming links, unlike Sidney's, did not occur within the limits of a single stanza. In "The Dry Salvages," third of the *Four Quartets*, Eliot rhymes all the first lines of his six stanzas with one another, and proceeds to do the same with the terminal words of the five remaining lines. Again, the poem is mournful, even dirgelike.

Possibly inspired by Sidney's example, Spenser, in the month of August in *The Shepherd's Calendar*, included a sestina of his own, although he varies the permutations of the terminal words in an original and unexceptionable order of his own. Both in its music and its substance, Spenser's poem seems to owe much to Sidney's pioneering efforts in the field, as Spenser's first stanza makes clear:

Ye wasteful woods! bear witness to my woe,
Wherein my plaints did oftentimes resound:
Ye careless birds are privy to my cries,
Which in your songs were wont to make a part:
Thou, pleasant spring, hast lulled me oft asleep,
Whose streams my trickling tears did oft augment.

The following stanzas faultlessly pursue the doleful tone that had become the ensign of sestinas and at which both Sidney and Dante had excelled. But as his scholiast, E.K., tells us, Spenser's August eclogue is indebted to another tradition as well, one that derives from Theocritus and Virgil, not because the classical poets wrote sestinas (which they did not) but because they wrote poems in the form either of debates or contests between competing shepherds, the competition sometimes judged by a third. In Virgil's Third Eclogue Damoetas and Menalcas compete in a singing contest judged by Palaemon, and in the Fifth Eclogue Mopsus and Menalcas compete in mourning for Daphnis. In the Eighth Eclogue Damon pines for Nysa ("Farewell, O / my woods. I'll hurl me into the sea / From yonder peak"),[3] while Alphesiboeus pines for Daphnis. Theocritus, too, in his Sixth, Eighth, and Ninth Eclogues, presents competitions in song and in lyric devotion to a lost or absent loved one.

These independent traditions, of sometimes lighthearted and cheerful rivalry and competition between shepherds for excellence at song, and the other, melancholy and painful song of lament that seemed especially to belong to the sestina, are surpassingly braided, musically and dramatically intertwined in Sidney's masterful and brilliant double sestina, "Yee Goteheard Gods . . . ," one of the greatest achievements of English Renaissance poetry.

Strephon   Klaius

Strephon.   Yee Gote-heard Gods, that love the grassie mountaines,
Yee Nimphes which haunt the springs in pleasant vallies,
Ye Satyrs joyde with free and quiet forrests,
Vouchsafe your silent eares to playning musique,
Which to my woes gives still an early morning:
And draws the dolor on till wery evening.

Klaius.   O *Mercurie,* foregoer to the evening,
O heavenlie huntresse of the savage mountaines,
O lovelie starre, entitled of the morning,
While that my voice doth fill these wofull vallies,
Vouchsafe your silent eares to plaining musique,
Which oft hath *Echo* tir'd in secret forrests.

Strephon.   I that was once free-burges of the forrests,
Where shade from Sunne, and sport I sought in evening,
I that was once esteem'd for pleasant musique,
Am banisht now among the monstrous mountaines

Of huge despaire, and foule affliction's vallies,
Am growne a shrich-owle to my selfe each morning.

Klaius.   I that was once delighted every morning,
Hunting the wilde inhabiters of forrests,
I that was once the musique of these vallies,
So darkened am, that all my day is evening,
Hart-broken so, that molehilles seeme high mountaines,
And fill the vales with cries in steed of musique.

Strephon.   Long since alas, my deadly Swannish musique
Hath made it selfe a crier of the morning,
And hath with wailing strength clim'd highest mountaines:
Long since my thoughts more desert be then forrests:
Long since I see my joyes come to their evening,
And state throwen downe to over-troden vallies.

Klaius.   Long since the happie dwellers of these vallies,
Have praide me leave my strange exclaiming musique,
Which troubles their daye's worke, and joyes of evening:
Long since I hate the night, more hate the morning:
Long since my thoughts chase me like beasts in forrests,
And make me wish my selfe layd under mountaines.

Strephon.   Me seemes I see the high and stately mountaines,
Transforme themselves to lowe dejected vallies:
Me seemes I heare in these ill-changed forrests,
The Nightingales doo learne of Owles their musique:
Me seemes I feele the comfort of the morning
Turnde to the mortal serene of an evening.

Klaius.   Me seemes I see a filthie clowdie evening,
As soon as Sunne begins to clime the mountaines:
Me seemes I feele a noysome sent, the morning
When I doe smell the flowers of these vallies:
Me seemes I heare, when I doo heare sweete musique,
The dreadfull cries of murdred men in forrests.

Strephon.   I wish to fire the trees of all these forrests;
I give the Sunne a last farewell each evening;
I curse the fidling finders out of Musicke:
With envie I doo hate the loftie mountaines;
And with despite despise the humble vallies:
I doo detest night, evening, day, and morning.

Klaius.   Curse to my selfe my prayer is, the morning:
My fire is more, then can be made with forrests:

My state more base, then are the basest vallies:
I wish no evenings more to see, each evening;
Shamed I hate my selfe in sight of mountaines,
And stoppe mine eares, lest I growe mad with Musicke.

Strephon.   For she, whose parts maintainde a perfect musique,
Whose beawties shin'de more then the blushing morning,
Who much did passe in state the stately mountaines,
In straightnes past the Cedars of the forrests,
Hath cast me, wretch, into eternall evening,
By taking her two Sunnes from these darke vallies.

Klaius.   For she, with whom compar'd, the Alpes are vallies,
She whose lest word brings from the spheares their musique,
At whose approach the Sunne rase in the evening,
Who, where she went, bare in her forhead morning,
Is gone, is gone from these our spoyled forrests,
Turning to desarts our best pastur'de mountaines.

Strephon.   These mountaines witnesse shall, so shall these vallies,

Klaius.   These forrests eke, made wretched by our musique,
Our morning hymne this is, and song at evening.

Sidney's was not the first double sestina. He had for a model one pub-
lished by Sannazaro in his *Arcadia* of 1502, as David Kalstone reminds us
in his excellent book, *Sidney's Poetry,* where, among other valuable obser-
vations, he remarks, "Sidney has seen the possibilities in Sannazaro's or-
ganization of the sestina as a dialogue, employing pairs of stanzas, state-
ment and response."[4] And explaining the dramatic context in which
Sidney's Strephon and Klaius render their joint poem, Kalstone declares,
"The only shepherds not native to Arcadia, they are clearly to be distin-
guished from the rustics of the eclogues. They have come to the seacoast
to mourn the departure of Urania for the island of 'Cithera'" (72). Ac-
cording to Ringler, "Strephon and his older friend Klaius" were in fact
"two gentlemen who had become shepherds because of their love for a
maiden named Urania, 'thought a Shepherdes Daughter, but in deede of
farr greater byrthe.' She never returned their affection, and some months
previously had departed from Arcadia, leaving orders that they should
remain there until they received written instructions from her" (416). It
is of supreme importance that the island of Cythera was reckoned as
"sacred to the goddess Venus, who was from thence surnamed *Cytheraea,*
and who rose, as some suppose, from the sea near its coasts," near Laconia
in Peloponnesus.[5] The island was traditionally supposed to be joyfully

devoted to the rites of Venus and to be home to a continuous festival of erotic pleasures. Strephon and Klaius, therefore, have specifically been denied entrance into the sacred domain of requited love.

Cythera, that realm of "gratified desire," to use Blake's words, has played a long and troubled role in the human imagination. It figures in a famous painting (or rather in two versions of one painting) by Jean-Antoine Watteau, called *Departure for the Island of Cythera.* One commentator, Michael Schwarz, notes:

> For the *Departure* Watteau brightened his palette, using pastel shades of pink and pale blue. Thin clouds and diaphanous veils of mist spread across the picture, increasing the delicacy of the pastel shades and making them glow even more intensely. Pairs of happy lovers are grouped around the boat. One cavalier is helping his lady to embark while she coquettishly tucks up her skirt. They are joined by a second couple, who go arm-in-arm, while others, who are seen approaching the boat, are indulging in friendly or amorous banter. The boat itself, which is enveloped in haze and surrounded by numerous putti, looks almost as if it had descended from the roseate heavens. These putti, the charming envoys of Venus, rise up high into the air as they sport and play with one another. The sailors, who were seen straining on their oars in the first painting of the *Departure,* were omitted from the later version so as not to mar the perfect serenity of the arcadian setting. In this work, ancient mythology and eighteenth-century custom combine to form a world that appeared entirely real to Watteau's contemporaries. They themselves become dream figures and in Watteau's paintings they were able to enter into the lofty regions of the supernatural world previously denied to them. By daring to rise to these heights, by entering into this world of the imagination, they were able to transfigure their own everyday world. But would not this illusion be followed by profound melancholy? There is a hint of melancholy in all of Watteau's painting; it is one of the characteristic features of his style.[6]

The melancholy of which the critic speaks regarding Watteau is probably implicit in any vision of amorous perfection, whether in painting or in such a drama as Sidney presents.

In his brilliant and precocious survey of the tonal inflections and molecular linkages of English poetry, *Seven Types of Ambiguity,* William Empson has set down with remarkable compression some of the wisest and most probing comments on Sidney's double sestina:

The poem beats, however rich its orchestration, with a wailing and immovable monotony, for ever upon the same doors in vain. *Mountaines, vallies, forrests; musique, evening, morning;* it is at these words only that Klaius and Strephon pause in their cries; these words circumscribe their world; these are the bones of their situation; and in tracing their lovelorn pastoral tedium through thirteen repetitions, with something of the aimless multitudinousness of the sea on a rock, we seem to extract all the meaning possible from these notions.[7]

He proceeds to show how richly and emotionally equivocal are those six terminal nouns, colored in each case by the speaker's state of mind, as they might reflect a former state of happiness or a present state of deprivation. *Mountaines,* for example, can be great challenges to feats of strength but also a weight beneath which one would be crushed to extinction. They can also become metaphorical "mountaines / Of huge despair," and their metamorphosis from the literal to the figurative provides one of the most unnerving elements in the poem, as the distracted minds of the speakers seem to approach an almost suicidal phantasmagoria. In the same way, *vallies* are protected and secure yet cut off from other, and perhaps better, kinds of life. Their lowness befits humility but also the status of the unworthy. *Forrests* are places of danger but a welcome challenge to the courageous hunter, a place where stately cedars grow, where the mixed *musique* of both nightingale and owl is to be heard. *Morning* is the time of rising and hopefulness, unless one is so depressed that it can only renew the misery of the day before. *Evening* ought to bring rest after the labors of the day, and the serenity of sleep after waking hours of misery; but evening is also a fading of light and of hope as well, and Strephon claims that he has been cast "into eternal evening."

I have summarized here, far too briskly, the analysis Empson bestows on these six crucial nouns, demonstrating how slippery and unstable they become in a troubled mind. It is worth noting also that of the six, four are naturally mated pairs: morning is matched with evening, mountains with valleys. (Forests and music are not natural mates except by a pastoral extension; forests are places where shepherds dwell and, according to tradition, sing their songs to one another; music belongs to those pastoral songs but also to the more musical creatures of the forests, the nightingales. Used ironically, music is applied to the cacophony of owls or the painful groans of the tormented lovers.)

But there is something about this beautiful work of Sidney's that calls for further comment and, in my view, seems to challenge all the criticisms brought against it under the heading of "monotony." Not that such a claim is baseless. Ringler, Empson, and I have used the word, which, given the mandatory repetition of six terminal words in an inflexible order, seems hard to avoid. But clearly one of the first resolves of any poet who sits down to compose a sestina must be the evasion, by whatever cunning available, of that imposition of monotony. The poet's job is somehow to divert us by drama, pathos, a crescendo of emotional forces and to encourage us to feel that in one way or another each succeeding stanza will provide some novelty or a wholly new perspective. Few readers have any patience for monotonous poetry, and good poets, of whom Sidney was certainly one, are perfectly aware of this.

We may usefully return to David Kalstone's observation that "Sidney has seen the possibilities in Sannazaro's organization of the sestina as a dialogue, employing pairs of stanzas, statement and response." Nothing, it seems to me, so characterizes Sidney's double sestina as the careful (one may say "musical") parallelisms of its paired stanzas, and there cannot be the least doubt that Sidney expected this to be noticed and appreciated. The first two paired stanzas contain the same line, "Vouchsafe your silent eares to playning musique," which serves as a link between the speakers, Strephon and Klaius; but in each case the addressee is different. Strephon addresses the earth deities, Pan, Priapus, nymphs, and satyrs, whereas Klaius addresses the celestial deities, including Diana, who is, poignantly, both goddess of the hunt, and thus protectress of the shepherds, and also goddess of chastity, and thus enemy of the love they both profess. The fact that one addresses earthly and the other heavenly deities may be seen as divisive but more probably as complementary aspects of prayer that together embrace the entire cosmos.

The second pair of stanzas begins with identical wording: "I that was once." They also contain two lines that, although not identical, bear a close resemblance to one another. The third line of the first of these two stanzas ("I that was once esteem'd for pleasant musique") resembles the third line of the next stanza ("I that was once the musique of these vallies"). The two stanzas, moreover, describe the transformation of the two speakers from a former freedom, happiness, and capacity for musical performance to a present state of utter despondency, wretchedness, and complete remove from that realm of music that belonged to the pastoral life and betokened the harmonies of nature and of love. The parallels are worth pursuing. The second speaker, always Klaius, does not seem intent on besting his companion in misery by outstripping Strephon in the severity of his complaints. This is not a competition in who suffers most or in who can utter the most miserable complaint. The paired stanzas are instead like musical variations on each other, and the parallelisms can suggest that Klaius quite humbly takes his cue from the speech of Strephon that precedes his own. This will be especially striking in the next two stanzas.

The first, fourth, and fifth lines of the fifth and sixth stanzas begin, "Long since . . ."; and both speakers are now concerned to explain that they have been languishing in the depths of misery for some time. Strephon's music has turned "deadly" and "Swannish," indicating his expectation of imminent death but also indicating that one who was "once esteem'd for pleasant musique" is now incapable of anything but unmelodious complaint. Klaius, too, confesses that "the happie dwellers of these vallies, / Have praide me leave my strange exclaiming musique." The two pastoral swains have lost possession of the one art that most characterized their profession. It is just possible that Sidney is making a subtle joke at his own expense—or at the expense of the traditional dolorous monotony of sestina writers. In any case these two stanzas have become profoundly more "inward" and describe states of mind that are neurotic, self-tormenting, and virtually suicidal. They are preparing us for the even more hallucinatory stanzas that immediately follow.

The seventh and eighth stanzas are rich in parallelism. The first, third, and fifth lines of both stanzas begin with almost identical phrases. The first of the stanzas offers them as "Me seemes I see . . . ," "Me seemes I heare . . . ," and "Me seemes I feele . . . ," and the following stanza alters the sequence to "see," "feele," and "heare." These stanzas are morbidly surrealistic, reminding one of the weird and primitive terrors in the paintings of Piero di Cosimo. All the familiar values have been transvalued; nothing is stable or familiar; the minds of Strephon and Klaius are profoundly disoriented and given over to a morbidity that is the more frightening in that we have seen it grow in intensity right before our eyes in the course of the poem.

The ninth and tenth stanzas are the most violent in their self-condemnation. The first line of the ninth ("I wish to fire the trees of all these forrests") is echoed but altered in the tenth's second line ("My fire is more, then can be made with forrests"). The ninth's second line ("I give the Sunne a last farewell each evening") is restated in other terms in the tenth stanza's fourth line ("I wish no evenings more to see, each evening"). These two stanzas are, in their way, more terrible than the immediately preceding ones, because they have abandoned the protective devices of hallucination and are now coldly and self-condemningly analytical. Someone who can say unflinchingly, "I doo detest night, evening, day, and morning," has covered all possibilities and has nowhere to exist. And someone who says I "stoppe mine eares, lest I growe mad with Musicke" has acknowledged that the single most powerful and celestial cure for the soul not only avails nothing but drives the poet to further disorder. This important reference to music as that harmonious and reconciling power that was thought to operate throughout the universe, presented as unavailing at the end of the tenth stanza, leads now to the unfolding of the mystery: the revelation in the final two full stanzas of the source and cause of all this disorder.

Both Strephon and Klaius begin, "For she . . ."; but Strephon continues with the musical metaphor that closed the previous stanza: "For she, whose parts maintainde a perfect musique." Her "parts" are certainly bodily parts, assembled in a perfect proportion. They are also her attainments, as "a woman of parts." But they are of course the musical parts of a composition scored for the interweaving and combination of several musical "parts," as in a madrigal or motet. Both Strephon and Klaius, in praise of their departed mistress, return once again to images of utter perfection, to the very sovereign "music of the spheres," but only at the end to contrast that perfection to the desolation in which both of them now must, as it seems, forever abide.

I should like to claim that the poem escapes, at least to some degree, the charges of tedium and monotony by virtue of the intensifying psychological drama it presents and through the pairing, yet distinct separateness, of the two speakers, who seem to take cues from one another, to enhance and embroider one another's statements. No doubt this point must not be made too forcefully. The terminal words are, if anything, more insistently repetitive in a double sestina than in a single one, yet I can't imagine anyone wishing this poem shorter than it is. It fills out all its stanzas with richness and variety; its tone is not merely dolorous but also terrifying, unbalanced, and in fact not so remote from that self-disgust that characterizes certain late-nineteenth- and early-twentieth-century poems.

But if this poem, and some other sestinas, can be defended against accusations of monotony, it is more difficult, I think, to protect them from the claim that they tend to be dramatically static. They present a frame of mind, sometimes an interestingly disturbed frame of mind, but usually an obsessed one that tends to harp on the same sad theme, varying it in certain ways but never departing from it, bound to it by the shackles of those six terminal words. Indeed, something about those compulsory repetitions seems to prohibit the possibility of a sestina developing in the way other kinds of poems do. A familiar lyric freedom is curtailed; richly detailed descriptions are pretty firmly excluded; narrative development, above all, is difficult to accommodate. The resources of the sestina seem astonishingly circumscribed.

But if these seem to be characteristic limitations imposed by the form itself, we are entitled to be the more delighted, impressed, and gratified when we find some poet intelligent and ingenious enough to overcome them. And such triumph over the form has been attained not once but twice by Elizabeth Bishop in two sestinas that otherwise bear very little resemblance to one another.

A Miracle for Breakfast
At six o'clock we were waiting for coffee,
waiting for coffee and the charitable crumb
that was going to be served from a certain balcony,
—like kings of old, or like a miracle.
It was still dark. One foot of the sun
steadied itself on a long ripple in the river.

The first ferry of the day had just crossed the river.
It was so cold we hoped that the coffee
would be very hot, seeing that the sun
was not going to warm us; and that the crumb
would be a loaf each, buttered by a miracle.
At seven a man stepped out on the balcony.

He stood for a minute alone on the balcony
looking over our heads toward the river.
A servant handed him the makings of a miracle,
consisting of one lone cup of coffee
and one roll, which he proceeded to crumb,
his head, so to speak, in the clouds—along with the sun.

Was the man crazy? What under the sun
was he trying to do, up there on his balcony!
Each man received one rather hard crumb,
which some flicked scornfully into the river,
and, in a cup, one drop of the coffee.
Some of us stood around, waiting for the miracle.

I can tell what I saw next; it was not a miracle.
A beautiful villa stood in the sun

and from its doors came the smell of hot coffee.
In front, a baroque white plaster balcony
added by birds, who nest along the river,
—I saw it with one eye close to the crumb—

and galleries and marble chambers. My crumb
my mansion, made for me by a miracle,
through ages, by insects, birds, and the river
working the stone. Every day, in the sun,
at breakfast time I sit on my balcony
with my feet up, and drink gallons of coffee.

We licked up the crumb and swallowed the coffee.
A window across the river caught the sun
as if the miracle were working, on the wrong balcony.[8]

This extraordinary, elusive but mesmerizing poem has something of the
nature of a parable about it. Shy of making anything that might be taken
for grandiose religious claims, Bishop once wryly referred to it at a poetry
reading as "my Depression, or Bread Line poem." But however much it
may apply to enfeebled social programs for the poor, it also clearly seems
like a secular equivalent of the Feeding of the Multitudes and of the
Eucharist. The mystery of the poem (an analogy, perhaps, to the mystery
of the Feeding or the Eucharist) resides in that completely unexpected
vision of wealth and comfort embodied in the "beautiful villa [that] stood
in the sun." Its "galleries and marble chambers," its "baroque white plaster
balcony" make it sound positively Spanish or Italian in its luxury and
altogether alien from the vague, unspecified, but generally bleak setting
of the rest of the poem. The "vision," for that's what it is, of a palatial
glamour is attained by the minute, close-up inspection of a crumb of
bread that was handed out in the breadline. As I have commented else-
where, "The complex intricacies of the 'architecture' of the risen dough,
its baroque perforations, corridors, its struts, ribs and spans of support,
all form the 'beautiful villa' with its 'white plaster balcony.' And this bread,
and the vision it provides, have come into existence by the miraculous
and infinitely patient workings of that evolutionary process that Darwin
(one of Miss Bishop's favorite writers) and other naturalists have so pains-
takingly recorded. The process itself is awesome enough to be character-
ized, not improperly, as a 'miracle.'"[9] But the chief point about this sestina
is that it is composed as a kind of narrative. It begins at six o'clock in the
morning; a crowd has gathered, waiting to be fed; the first ferry of the
day had only just crossed the river. It is depressingly cold out. At seven a

man appears on the balcony; a servant joins him, handing him "the makings of a miracle." The man proceeds to distribute individual crumbs and drops of coffee. How are we to make sense of the dispensing of these Loaves and Fishes? In any case action is going on by specific stages, as in a religious ritual. And this action precipitates a "vision" and concludes on a note of cheerful, contented comfort and serenity. The familiar bane of "monotony" and "stasis" has been triumphantly overcome. As it is once again in another Bishop sestina.

Sestina

September rain falls on the house.
In the failing light, the old grandmother
sits in the kitchen with the child
beside the Little Marvel Stove,
reading the jokes in the almanac,
laughing and talking to hide her tears.

She thinks that her equinoctial tears
and the rain that beats on the roof of the house
were both foretold in the almanac,
but only known to a grandmother.
The iron kettle sings on the stove.
She cuts some bread and says to the child,

It's time for tea now; but the child
is watching the teakettle's small hard tears
dance like mad on the hot black stove,
the way the rain must dance on the house.
Tidying up, the old grandmother
hangs up the clever almanac

on its string. Birdlike, the almanac
hovers half open above the child,
hovers above the old grandmother
and her teacup full of dark brown tears.
She shivers and says she thinks the house
feels chilly, and puts more wood in the stove.

It was to be, says the Marvel Stove.
I know what I know, says the almanac.
With crayons the child draws a rigid house
and a winding pathway. Then the child
puts in a man with buttons like tears
and shows it proudly to the grandmother.

But secretly, while the grandmother
busies herself about the stove,
the little moons fall down like tears
from between the pages of the almanac
into the flower bed the child
has carefully placed in front of the house.

Time to plant tears, says the almanac.
The grandmother sings to the marvellous stove
and the child draws another inscrutable house.[10]

Superficially, nothing much happens in this little drama with its two characters who don't interact in any dynamic way on the wet September afternoon they share. But their situation and their setting is laden with omens. The grandmother not only weeps in the very first stanza but must struggle to conceal her tears from the child. Something predestined governs the season of the tears, as of the rainy weather, and the recurrent cycles of the year return annually to the anniversaries of past events. Conspicuous by its absence from this poem is the intervening generation between child and grandmother; where are the parents? The drawing of a house by a child is regarded as an expression of a desire for security, although this child seems touchingly unaware that anything is out of order. The almanac prophesies tears to come, presumably when the child is old enough to understand what the grandmother already knows and is trying to conceal. The drama is the more poignant and terrible for being so carefully understated and evaded. Were the parents killed in some accident? How long ago? Did they die in some other terrible way? The poem allows us a terrifying latitude in which to let our imaginations range. The almanac, half open, is even likened to a bird, traditionally a prophetic creature. The drama is the more eloquent for its spareness. But the point is that a story has been unfolded in a way that is not usually to be found in a sestina.

We may take the story as a poetic fiction, and it stands up with perfect form and as much clarity as the situation permits. But biographers have been diligent in pointing out that Elizabeth Bishop's father died in 1911, when she was eight months old. His death so deeply disoriented his wife, the poet's mother, that she was in and out of hospitals and rest homes for the next five years, after which, in 1916, she was permanently hospitalized in Nova Scotia. Elizabeth never saw her mother again, although her mother lingered on as a patient until 1934. There was a time when I felt that this documentary information was required for a full understanding of the poem. I no longer think so. The poet has created a heartrending drama, from which she has deftly removed herself except as the artificer of the work. And it remains to be said that the challenge she has set for herself is the more demanding in that this poem is composed in tetrameter, rather than pentameter, thus making even tighter than usual the constrictions of the six-linked chain of terminal words she has bound herself with.

Let me cite one more example, this one by James Merrill, that clearly defies the lugubrious, monotonous, static condition usually associated with sestinas.

Tomorrows

The question was an academic one.
Andrey Sergeyvitch, rising sharp at two,
Would finally write that letter to his three
Sisters still in the country. Stop at four,
Drink tea, dress elegantly and, by five,
Be losing money at the Club des Six.

In Pakistan a band of outraged Sikhs
Would storm an embassy (the wrong one)
And spend the next week cooling off in five
Adjacent cells. These clearly were but two
Vital details—though nobody cared much for
The future by that time, except us three.

You, Andrée Meraviglia, not quite three,
Left Heidelberg. Year, 1936.
That same decade you, Lo Ping, came to the fore
In the Spiritual Olympics, which you won.
My old black self I crave indulgence to
Withhold from limelight, acting on a belief I've

Lived by no less, no more, than by my five
Senses. Enough that circus music (BOOM-two-three)
Coursed through my veins. I saw how Timbuctoo
Would suffer from an undue rainfall, 2.6
Inches. How in all Fairbanks, won-
der of wonders, no polkas would be danced, or for

That matter no waltzes or rumbas, although four
Librarians, each on her first French 75,
Would do a maxixe (and a snappy one).
How, when on Lucca's greenest ramparts, three-

fold emotion prompting Renzo to choose from six
Older girls the blondest, call her *tu,*

It would be these blind eyes hers looked into
Widening in brief astonishment before
Love drugged her nerves with blossoms drawn from classics
Of Arab draughtsmanship—small, ink-red, five-
Petaled blossoms blooming in clusters of three.
How she would want to show them to someone!

But one by one they're fading. I am too.
These three times thirteen lines I'll write down for
Fun, some May morning between five and six.[11]

There can be no denying that this brilliant, quasi-inebriated poem is crowded with incident: so much for the charge that sestinas are doomed to be static. Just what all the activities add up to is open to some conjecture, although apparently the speaker regards himself as someone gifted with "second-sight" and concludes by foretelling the composition of the poem he has just finished. There is a wonderful mixture of milieux, events, of the fictive and the seemingly factual, astonishingly disparate and unrelated characters (we learn no more of Andrée Meraviglia, Lo Ping, or Renzo than of Eliot's Mr. Silvero, Madame de Tornquist, or Fräulein von Kulp) as if in a sort of hashish trance yet with enough tantalizing detail (the Chekhovian particulars of the first stanza seem comfortingly familiar) to persuade us, however briefly, that we are in a world we ought to recognize. This is emphasized by the curious historical context provided for some of the events, dates, and statistics urged on us. And these historical and factual details have a bearing, however obscure, on the whole notion of futurity (the poem is titled "Tomorrows"), of "second-sight," and the significance of all events, whether large or small, real or fictive, because even fictive worlds are made to resemble the one we commonly think of as "real." All this is accomplished with a bravura sense of ridiculousness, although not, I would claim, with frivolity. The question of how much we think we understand our lives and the lives of others and the course of history itself lurks among the interstices of this poem.

It hardly seems necessary to defend the poem against the charge of lugubriousness, so I turn directly to the indictment of monotony, commonly brought against sestinas because of the inexorable repetitions of the terminal words. Merrill has ingeniously taken the first six ordinals for this purpose but has escaped his fetters by the sparkling use of homophones, homonyms, word fragments, and hyphenation and various other sorts of wordplay. In the last line of the third stanza he forms the sound of *five* by borrowing the *f* at the end of *belief* and joining it to *I've*. This is neither unprecedented nor irresponsible. In the thirty-second stanza of Hopkins's great and deeply serious poem, "The Wreck of the Deutschland," the poet rhymes "unconfessed of them," with "the breast of the" and borrows the needed *m* sound from the word that begins the following line, *Maiden.* To be sure, when Hopkins takes this kind of "liberty," it is done on behalf of the pulse and pressure entailed by a lyrical rapidity of action and meditation, which makes use of free-flowing enjambments.[12] Merrill, too, has his enjambments ("won- / der of wonders"), but they are dictated by easy colloquial speech rather than by Hopkins's kind of agitation. No doubt a certain lightness of tone and intention is a necessary ingredient in Merrill's versatility, but it may be claimed that he has for once emancipated the sestina from some of the bondage traditionally imposed on it. He serves cheerfully to remind such commentators as Ringler, Empson, and others that monotony, obsession, and gloom are not the destined trademarks of all sestinas.

At the same time, the possibilities Merrill discovers in no way offer disrespect to the still more virtuosic achievements of Sidney's great double sestina. Sidney's world in the *Arcadia* was a world he shared in part with Ariosto and many other writers of pastoral romance, in which the lament of the forlorn lover enjoys a long and honorable history. The "tradition" of frustrated and unreciprocated love was popular in the Middle Ages and is to be found in Wyatt and Surrey, as well as in the belated "Definition of Love" by Marvell. Great as was the pain described by these poets, it was thought to confer the spiritual benefits of mortification, and "the poets of the circle of Charles d'Orléans," Huizinga tells us, "compared their amorous sadness to the sufferings of the ascetic and the martyr. They called themselves 'les amoureux de l'observance,' alluding to the severe reforms which the Franciscan order had just undergone."[13] Writing of this tradition from its medieval origins, Maurice Valency observes,

> Love was . . . a special hazard of the poet's trade, for it was chiefly out of
> the pain of love that poetry was made. The symptoms of love-illness,
> *hereos,* Chaucer called it, were often described; from the *Viaticum* of
> Constantinus Africanus in the eleventh century to Burton's *Anatomy* in
> the seventeenth, the love-syndrome varied little. In the initial stages
> the symptoms were not unbecoming—sleeplessness, loss of appetite, loss
> of flesh, and the characteristic pallor of the lover, together with love of
> solitude and a tendency to weep, particularly when music was played.

But, we are told, unless the disease was cured, it became dangerous—the lover might pass into a melancholy, waste away, and die.[14]

And these are the perils to which, in his *Arcadia,* Sidney exposes Strephon and Klaius. They were the perils of an abundant literature.

NOTES

1. *Encyclopædia Britannica,* 14th ed., s.v. "sestina."

2. *The Poems of Sir Philip Sidney,* ed. William A. Ringler Jr. (Oxford: Clarendon Press, 1962), 108. Further references to Sidney's poetry are to this edition.

3. *The Eclogues and Georgics of Virgil,* trans. C. Day Lewis (1947; repr., New York: Doubleday, 1964).

4. David Kalstone, *Sidney's Poetry* (Cambridge, Mass.: Harvard University Press, 1965), 77.

5. *Lempriere's Classical Dictionary* (London: Routledge and Kegan Paul, 1951), s.v. "Cytherea."

6. Michael Schwarz, *The Age of the Rococo* (New York: Praeger, 1971), 14–15.

7. William Empson, *Seven Types of Ambiguity* (London: Chatto and Windus, 1947), 36–37.

8. Elizabeth Bishop, *The Complete Poems, 1927–1979* (New York: Farrar, Straus and Giroux, 1983), 18–19.

9. Anthony Hecht, *Obbligati: Essays in Criticism* (New York: Atheneum, 1986), 123–24.

10. Bishop, *Complete Poems,* 123–24.

11. James Merrill, *Collected Poems,* ed. J. D. McClatchy and Stephen Yenser (New York: Alfred A. Knopf, 2001), 759–60.

12. In my essay "On Rhyme" (*Yale Review* 87 [1999]: 77) I discuss rove-over rhymes in Hopkins, and specifically in stanza 31 of "The Wreck of the Deutschland," but I do not in that essay compare these Hopkins techniques to any Merrill works.

13. Johan Huizinga, *The Waning of the Middle Ages* (1924; repr., New York: Doubleday, 1954), 111.

14. Maurice Valency, *In Praise of Love* (1958; repr., New York: Macmillan, 1961), 154.

THREE

Naked Numbers
A Curve from Wyatt to Rochester

HEATHER McHUGH

Thou knew'st this *papyr,* when it was
Meer *seed,* and after that but *grass;*
Before 'twas *drest* or *spun,* and when
Made *linen,* who did *wear* it then . . .

HENRY VAUGHAN
"The Book"

COVERS ARE ABOUT BOOKS. But when you find books about covers, well, then you have wandered into a paradoxer's paradise, a place where a sensualist's eye might at any moment be turned on its own holdings, a literalist's eye on the unsettled literary premises themselves, and an analyst's eye on content's uncontainability. In such regards the sixteenth and seventeenth centuries in English poetry resemble our own era. Materialists, students of sensation, these poets knew how to redden a reader, inflame a page.

Cover: the wild beast hides his hide under it, fills his belly with it. The cover he consumes may sleeken his skin for the volumes of his own consumers (those arguably lesser beasts whose books—leather-bound or not—have boards and leaves). In other words: a guise can expose; a hide can reveal.

A name is itself a kind of cover, and in the English literary tradition of the time, poetry went under the name of numbers—numbers not only configured poetry's events but transfigured them, too. Numbers as an incarnation of mystery may seem to today's computer-whizzing,

59

digit-crunching public less immediately plausible than they would have seemed to a people across whose lives the powers of theology and numerology cast larger shadows than they do now. The power in divine arithmetic lay in its capacity to transcend (not merely to calibrate) the commerces of men.

According to a bon mot of La Rochefoucauld (a shrewd late-seventeenth-century figure himself), the true use of speech is to conceal our thoughts. His is a sentiment congenial to the spirit of materialism. (It should be noted that "the spirit of materialism" is no oxymoron in such an era.) One might equally say, since Vesalius, that the true use of flesh is to conceal our nakedness. A poem's content no less than its form can be a cover: *what* it means may reveal less than *how* it is seen *through*.

If I am drawn to the poems of the English literary Renaissance and its vicinity, it is partly because the era lavished such attention on containers as to enrich any notion about content. Here paradoxes abound. Here even scatologies are scrupulous: and the era's poetic precisions put to shame our own time's casual (or automated) forms of ravishing and lavishing: these poems pose rich linguistic alternatives to our feedback mechanisms, our wasting of the infinite on a mere regress. Full of outlaws and intricacies, the best sixteenth- and seventeenth-century English poetry proposed a more capacious means for meaning. I mean a language able to mean in more than ordinary ways, a language that proliferates and enriches (rather than hones to a point) the meaning of meaning.

Look back at Henry Vaughan's "The Book" (from which this essay takes its epigraph). The material of the poem and the poem on materials are mutually interpenetrating. Down to the word *wear,* the poem cannot be said at any moment to refer exclusively to either possible topic (robe or tome). The word *meaning* itself seems mean at such moments, for the meanings of such poems have something in common with those of spirit: they aren't to be *contained* (the way, for example, a pint of beer's contained). Shot glass, looking glass, eyeglass, isinglass: poetry drinks them all in and is drunk from them all—the lowest flows and the quickest sands of language.

John Wilmot, earl of Rochester, is a case in point. Given both to exposés and to impersonations, "he took pleasure to disguise himself, as a Porter, or as a Beggar; sometimes to follow some mean Amours, which, for the variety of them, he affected. At other times, meerly for diversion, *he would go about in odd shapes* . . . [my italics!]."[1] Lover of lingoes, chameleon of culture, connoisseur of senses, the poet seeks out a luxuriance in covers (and sometimes even under them). In his tenure as a quack physician he set up shop under the name of Alexander Bendo[2] (and in that incarnation even issued a mock mountebank bill)—all this apparently to escape a period of disgrace at Court. (Rochester's father, in his own day, evaded imprisonment precisely by dint of such undercover talents.)

Some impersonations actually work *as* exposés. Rochester savaged his rival Sir Carr Scroope by mocking Scroope's courtship of Cary Frazier (daughter of the king's physician and a dresser of the queen). The haplessly monikered Scroope had the further misfortune to have undertaken his courtship in verse. (Publishing love poems, one makes a bed one may not later like to lie in.) One of Scroope's amorous efforts went like this:

> I cannot change as others do,
>   Though you unjustly scorn,
> Since that poor swain that sighs for you
>   For you alone was born.
> No, Phyllis, no, your heart to move,
>   A surer way I'll try,
> And to revenge my slighted love,
>   Will still love on, will still love on, and die.
>
> When killed with grief Amyntas lies
>   And you to mind shall call
> The sighs that now unpitied rise,
>   The tears that vainly fall,
> That welcome hour that ends his smart
>   Will then begin your pain,
> For such a faithful, tender heart
>   Can never break, can never break in vain.[3]

Rochester's burlesque of it fairly seethes with mimic malice:

> *The Mock Song*
> "I swive as well as others do;
>   I'm young, not yet deformed;
> My tender heart, sincere and true,
>   Deserves not to be scorned.

Why, Phyllis, then, why will you swive
    With forty lovers more?"
"Can I," said she, "with nature strive?
    Alas I am, alas I am a whore!

"Were all my body larded o'er
    With darts of love, so thick
That you might find in every pore
    A well-stuck standing prick,
Whilst yet my eyes alone were free,
    My heart would never doubt,
In amorous rage and ecstasy,
    To wish those eyes, to wish those eyes fucked out."[4]

Never would "blind" love earn its adjective more painfully! The poem's craft is turned with exquisite malevolence, sinister adroitness. Its refinements connive with its crudity, and the poem's venal virtues haven't been tamed by time: a reader is every bit as astonished today as readers must have been in Rochester's, caught in the cross fire between such a diction and such a dick. Mere sexual explicitness is not so sharp a point (as much of pornography attests), but the skill and savage wit involved in this particular lady's larding-over make for a masterpiece of nastiness. In Rochester's version of the lay, the only one lewder than the layman is the lady who's so ludicrously laid. (*Lewd* comes from *lay,* and *lay* from *unlearned* or *ignorant.* And *laid* she'd be—forgive my French—as ugly as they come, under such heavings of *schlag.*) The lady in question is, of course, only an excuse for the humiliation of her lover. The grossness of that larding is deepened by the precisions of those "well-stuck standing prick[s]," the stand-ins, so to speak, for the slings and arrows of Rochester's assault on Scroope's own "tender heart." No presumption to delicacy could fail to be offended, and Scroope's delicacy will surely now go down in poetic history as a presumption. It seems writing well is, after all, the best revenge.

Around the same time, Thomas Carew was admonishing his Celia:

Let fooles thy mystique formes adore,
    I'le know thee in thy mortall state;
Wise Poets that wrap't Truth in tales,
Knew her themselves, through all her vailes.[5]

That the mortal could be presented as the naked state, and the "mystic forms" as the veils that obscure it, reverses the substantive conventions.

The sheer materiality one encounters in poets of the seventeenth century celebrates both senses of the sheer and the material, of spirit and of flesh: and when the body's the figure of truth, nakedness can suddenly seem a virtuous transparency. Reminding the lover that her immortality was, after all, conferred by his poems, Carew goes on in the poem's final figure to claim to *know* the naked truth, the figure underneath the veils, and so entertains a flash of knowing's carnal sense: that Truth is not, for all its mystic forms, unfuckable by lovers nor unlovable by fuckers.

Do poets honor or besmirch the truth in so claiming to know her? Neither Carew's construction nor our own age's skepticism will permit an exclusively sweetened reading. (Thank whatever heavens you revere.) Perhaps more apparently than in any other poetic era, what matters is the fabric of the felt, the material of the meant.

Full of spit and spunk, of pricks and pranks, at one time or another Rochester pitted himself against a number of the literary figures of the age—including Dryden. His history is prolifically appointed with stabbings and pikings and—over the course of a lifelong marriage he began by means of an abduction—the rakeries of a roué. Even his writing swaggers. Look for instance at this advice to a mistress:

Song
By all love's soft, yet mighty powers,
    It is a thing unfit
That men should fuck in time of flowers,
    Or when the smock's beshit.

Fair nasty nymph, be clean and kind,
    And all my joys restore
By using paper still behind
    And spunges for before.

My spotless flames can ne'er decay
    If after every close,
My smoking prick escape the fray
    Without a bloody nose.

If thou wouldst have me true, be wise
    And take to cleanly sinning;
None but fresh lovers' pricks can rise
    At Phyllis in foul linen.[6]

The sensual intelligence of such a piece of work makes of the mind a most convincing member. His ear (and nose) are in top form, his humors as hilarious as bilious. "My smoking prick"—now there's a pistol! And "its bloody nose"? A reluctant casualty of the love wars. Rochester's is a happy capacity to deflate the hot airs of romance with a twist of smear, a wicked prick. Intimated in this poem's exquisite economies are the arts and vices of a gentleman's engagement in a fray—and also the lady's signature of menstrual anointing (or loss of virginity, if you prefer: given a phrase like "fuck in time of flowers" neither the young nor the mature woman escapes, and the fore and aft of foulness in this poem are writ in time as well as space).

There's a lot of literary subtlety in the pen that takes to task—for their "freshness"! (or inexperience)—lovers insouciant of Phyllis's lack of it. The rhetorical balance of fresh and foul expands on "cleanly sinning['s]" oxymoron. And if linen content can inform a page, the poem can be taken as a kind of ars poetica.[7] Rochester entertains no more staleness in the love of forms than in the forms of love.[8] It's a low goad he uses but a high style: malevolence alone is not the point. The point's a skillful prick, a sharpened wit, a tended craft. No Betty Boop or Sir Carr Scroope escapes.

Of all the examples of a sartorial poetic tradition in English, the instance that comes most readily to mind may be the venerable "Greensleeves." Its full length contains a mind-boggling number of bodily baubles, bedeckings with which the lover woos (and fails to win) his lady. In order of appearance, each in its stanza, they include kirchers (kerchiefs), peticotes (petticoats), "jewels for thy chest," a "smock of silk," a "girdle of gold," purse and pincase ("no better wore the Burgesse wives"), crimson stockings, "pumps as white as was the milk," gown "of the grassie green," "sleeves of Satten," and "garters fringed with the golde." One can't read such poetry without becoming luxuriantly aware of how materialistic are its love bargains. In the poetry of a Sir Philip Sidney even nature will be rendered as "rich tapestry." As David Norbrook remarks, "To post-Romantic readers, for whom poets are expected to disguise their art, there may seem something shameless about the Elizabethan poets' conspicuous consumption of artifice."[9] Of course, sexual *ex*pressiveness can be every bit as shameless as sartorial *im*pressiveness—and it's the coefficiency of the two (redress in undress, snake in weeds) that makes these poetries so sly and so astonishing. The fashioner of such enchantments, the maker of such materials, covers his discoveries with ever more expert insinuation, ever nicer needling. He's aiming for the ultimate understory.

Her Muffe

1

'Twas not for some calm blessing to receive,
Thou didst thy polish'd hands in shagg'd furs weave;
 It were no blessing thus obtain'd,
 Thou rather would'st a curse have gain'd,
  Then let thy warm driven snow be ever stain'd.

2

Not that you feared the discolo'ring cold,
Might alchymize their Silver into Gold;
 Nor could your ten white Nuns so sin
 That you should thus pennance them in
Each in her course hair smock of Discipline.

3

Nor *Hero*-like, who on their crest still wore
A Lyon, Panther, Leopard or a Bore,
 To look their Enemies in their Herse;
 Thou would'st thy hand should deeper pierce,
And, in its softness rough, appear more fierce.

4

No, no, *Lucasta,* destiny Decreed
That Beasts to thee a sacrifice should bleed,
 And strip themselves to make you gay;
 For ne'er yet Herald did display,
A Coat, where *Sables* upon *Ermin* lay.

5

This for Lay-Lovers, that must stand at dore,
Salute the threshold, and admire no more:
 But I, in my Invention tough,
 Rate not this outward bliss enough,
But still contemplate must the hidden Muffe.[10]

Hide and *hide,* some furs removed, some furs revealed! (Coats even of arms have venereal symbols, and Lovelace's hunt comes right into the bedchamber.) All these half-draped, half-naked elaborations make for tantalizing sport. After a giveaway like "lay-lovers" (lovers of women, like lovers of poetry, are lovers of linen content), that "hidden muff" won't need much glossing; rather, let's say, it glosses itself. To love less can mean to love lace; this less is more. And to the question "What's under the underthings?" there is no end of answers.

Thus do clothes make the woman; and the more transparent the better. These muffs and cuffs and scarves are more than mere accessories: like the fan and sword of sexual archetype in Asian art, or the cross and arrow on the biological signs of the sexes, they become incarnations of character. Their chemises and charades expose as much as they disguise. In the work of a poet like Rochester, the distinction between *sartor* and *satyr* is virtually annihilated. Producing most of his best work between the ages of twenty-seven and thirty-three, he survives in all his priapic rancors and tart misanthropies[11] from the late edge of his larger era into the leading edge of ours precisely because so fine a fastidiousness informs the fucking: not everyone who executes such "larding[s] o'er"—is scrupulous down to the "pore." Rochester is. He understands the erotic charge that arises between delirium and discipline. The carnal connoisseur is no anarchist: the body of his work is bound; his liberties are lashed.

———

From the works of Sir Thomas Wyatt to those of the earl of Rochester, there's a curve in the flesh—but the flesh of poems is, of course, the poetic cloth itself. And poetic material, of all literary materials, is peculiarly designed to be torn. Between the death of Wyatt and the birth of John Wilmot lay a century of sensual *chirage*. One of the first poems I ever heard heartily loved by a professor was this one:

> They fle from me that sometyme did me seke
>   with naked fote stalking in my chambre
>   I have sene theim gentill tame and meke
>   that nowe are wyld and do not remember
>   that sometyme they put theimself in daunger
>   to take bred at my hand and nowe they raunge
>   besely seking with a continuell chaunge
> Thancked be fortune it hath ben othrewise
>   twenty tymes better but ons in speciall
>   in thyn arraye after a pleasaunt gyse
>   When her lose gowne from her shoulders did fall

and she me caught in her armes long and small
therewithall swetely did me kysse
and softely said dere hert howe like you this
It was no dreme I lay brode waking
but all is torned thorough my gentilnes
into a straunge fasshion of forsaking
and I have leve to goo of her goodenes
and she also to use new fangilnes
but syns that I so kyndely ame served
I would fain knowe what she hath deserved[12]

And now it's my lot to love it.

Separated from his wife only a few years after they married, Wyatt was arrested and banished in 1536 (probably for amorous relations with Anne Boleyn, about to marry Henry the VIII); he was tried again in 1541 and ordered (on pain of death) to abstain from further infidelities. Throughout his adult life Wyatt lived under the suspicion of adultery. Indeed, the lives of almost all the poets I'm treating here (under the cover of covers) have in common some uncommon concupiscences. Wyatt's "deer" are severally venereal, irresistibly homonymal. Under the marksman's rubric Wyatt remembers Venus's complicity in the aristocratic hunting grounds and figures forth the dangers of encounters there.[13]

The greatness in the poem "They fle from me that sometyme did me seke" lies in the marriage of candor and cover, the cooperation of thematics and rhetoric. The poem's numbers trace the course of amorous diminishment through its pronouns and time markings: from a third-person plural account of encounters in general, through the memory of an episode "ons in speciall" between two lovers (a switch from the generic to the specific that creates an effect breathtakingly erotic), and finally to the poet's solitude at the mercy of her particular leave, her "new fangilnes." The poem thus moves through three social states (three passages marked by capitalizations): first of loves at a remove (in the pronominal *them*); then of a single her (who says "you" and so brings the crowd down to a company of two); and finally of a self relegated to forsakenness. So "Torned . . . into a straunge fasshion" is the story of the poem's own numbers: there's an amorous arithmetic according to which what was given is now taken away: what he was served, she has now *de*served. In all fairness, to wish her the same would be to wish her "torned" as well. And so a verse is turned.

The question of kind so deftly raised in the poem's penultimate line is a question of several species because how kind or "gentill" either lover was is precisely what's at issue in the lines preceding. If all can be turned—*or* torn—through gentleness, then even a goodness could wound. Thanks to a host of likenesses and links at work in the linguistic fabric of the poem, the lovers are torn in turn, torn in kind, turned foreign, turned alike, and torn apart. And the dressing of the entire poem in terms of the seduction of wild animals (the taming of the unicorn being a conventional sexual motif) makes the usual unhappy destiny of the hunted animal haunt the poem's last line. She has deserted, or failed to serve, her lover: "what she deserves," then, in this welter of cognates, conflates the predatory and protective gestures. ("Cover me," says the friend who runs, to the friend with the gun. He wishes to be kept in sights, covered in auspices.)

——

The necessity for great poetry to garb itself in musical recurrences or regularities is equaled only by the compulsion of great poetry to tear through conventional ties and binds: to find its founding breathlessness again. And that compounding of compulsions is itself an amorous figure.

Pyramus and Thisbe
Two, by themselves, each other, love and fear
Slain, cruel friends, by parting have joined here.[14]

A neglected little piece by John Donne, this couplet reminds us how literal the love of numbers can become—and how uncontainable the implications of the epigram. "Each" and "other," in this poem's sixteen words, are not only slain but do the slaying, not only rejoined but do the rejoining. Syntactically speaking, this little couplet is a most compacted feat. It's something of an enjoining, too. "By themselves" is at once the sign of each's solitude—and of both's suiciding. The lovers live by themselves and are killed by themselves. (In the myth, you'll recall, one lover thinks the other dead and so kills himself, and then the other, seeing HE is dead, kills herself in consequence.) The lovers are together yet by themselves, parted yet by themselves—you see the ramifying properties of the phrase "by themselves," not only grammatically but philosophically, as it operates in different syntactical connections, different senses of agency. The two lines of the couplet, like the two persons of a couple, are able to stand complete and apart. (Were the couplet split by a period—or Dickinsonian dash—instead of only the line break's passing hint at discouplement, then "two people when left alone will love and fear each other" would be a perfectly legitimate intact reading for line 1, and for line 2, "hard-hearted lovers, killed, have come together here by being separated there.") Yet every comma or breath-turn marks a chance for recombining: in some blinks of the combining eye, "love" and "fear" can switch from verb to noun, and back, as elements of both lines are indispensably interwoven then rewoven. Each of the two is half of one, yet each of the two is an all. Love and death are the grounds on which such paradoxes most can move us—they are the surprises of our lives.

Grammatically speaking the "two" who begin this poem *become* the very love and fear that do them in. The syntactical deftness needed to keep so many meanings in simultaneous operation is the measure of the poet's art. Great syntactical economy is required to keep this poem's little mechanism self-escaping: all its counterpoises (male and female, love and fear, parting and joining, themselves and each other, friendly ones and cruel) must be able to shift grammatical functions in different readings. Where every single noun can operate either as a subject or an object, the usual dynamics of mutual exclusion have to be suspended. Conspiring is expiring's counterpart, and the cooperation of opposites prevails over their distinction. Measuring, as they may, "self-life's infinity to a span, nay to an inch," most critics reading Donne seek to reduce a generosity of possibilities to a proper exclusivity. Donne "did unite but not confound . . . in seeking secrets"—a fashion of mind that befits his readers as well. The syntactical coil is as animating to Renaissance love-numbers as is the genetic coil to contemporary microbiology. (DNA is, after all, a backreader's conjunction! And the slash of metaconjunction in any "and/or"—a slash that has always implicitly cast an extra *or* across our hermeneutic landscape—that slash ought, for the most capacious reading, to be refigured as an *and*. Such a sewing up of the slash might manage to redress [with love] a critical insufficiency, given that "and *and* or" will comprehend the two at once, whereas "and *or* or" means always only one alone.)

The phrase "cruel friends" condenses the coil of conspiring opposites into the simultaneous positive and negative of oxymoron. The ones who kill themselves rob each other of love, for love, and so are themselves each other's "cruel friends." But in another reading, it is we, the readers, thusly addressed—we who think ourselves beyond the story yet are implicated in it; we who bestow such far-off favor on the poem's centuries-old act.

We may bring to a classic literary work our readerly fire—but always in the cool of a here-and-now forever relegated to the poem's hereafter. Four hundred years ago John Donne entered the service of Sir Thomas Egerton, the lord keeper; he was dismissed when his secret marriage to Lady Egerton's niece was exposed. Later he'd become a clergyman, but John Donne the poet continues to weigh love's *and*s and *or*s, conjunctions and compunctions. Numbers are poems, but Donne goes us one better, giving us numbers *in* numbers; for he actually alludes to enumeration inside the poem, counting up love's tallies, counting down love's tolls.

"The Triple Fool," for example, explicitly turns the meaning of numbers into a number of meanings.

The Triple Fool
    I am two fools, I know,
For loving, and for saying so
    In whining poetry;
But where's that wiseman, that would not be I,
    If she would not deny?
Then as th'earth's inward narrow crooked lanes
Do purge sea water's fretful salt away,
    I thought, if I could draw my pains
Through rhyme's vexation, I should them allay.
Grief brought to numbers cannot be so fierce,
For, he tames it, that fetters it in verse.

    But when I have done so,
Some man, his art and voice to show,
    Doth set and sing my pain,
And, by delighting many, frees again
    Grief, which verse did restrain.
To love and grief tribute of verse belongs,
But not of such as pleases when 'tis read,
    Both are increased by such songs:
For both their triumphs so are published,
And I, which was two fools, do so grow three;
Who are a little wise, the best fools be.
                          (Smith, 81)

Like "Pyramus and Thisbe" this poem drives the lover's computation all the way to its poetic destiny in oxymoron—two oxymorons, to be exact:

"a little wise" and "best fools." As a double oxymoron it works deepeningly: the one who remained a little wise (that is, who stopped short of poetry and wound up married) would be the best (or biggest) fool. The numbers game is evident enough as it piles up the lover's foolishnesses. But it reaches a self-reflexive peak in the line "Grief brought to numbers cannot be so fierce," a line variously readable to mean "the woes of love are allayed when turned into poems" or "unhappiness shared among many is diminished in intensity." (Paraphrase confirms, by contrast, the generous grace of a poem's parsimonies!) In fact, of course, the verse that attracts reciters tends to spread—rather than fetter—feeling, and Donne has hidden in the folds of the poem's apparent humbleness a secret self-love: he has written a poem so good the world won't be able to stop singing it back. It's not only the singer's modesty that's at issue here. To have allayed the pain, never to have turned it into poetry, to have won the beloved, and so been a "little wise" or the "best fool" (rather than the writerly kind), can, in retrospect, hardly be whole-heartedly desirable. The wish to share one's heart is, by this token, consanguineous with the wish to diminish it; and to give of one's heart, one has to break it. A sensitive reader will catch in Donne's fancy footwork the sorrow's underlying joke: while tallying up his fooldoms the poet-figure is also reminding us with what gifts of numbers (what numbers of gifts!) he outpaced the mixed condition of the oxymoron, or the marriage. The foolscap is a cover for poetic immortality.

There's another undercover delight to be had in this skeptic's sachet. Do a double-take at that penultimate line. Even as numbers are mentioned, they are also metrically encoded: as the poet's foolhoods multiply, his solitudes are reinscribed. Look at the line's first foot ("And I"). It appears, in the context of the poem's overall iambic pentameter, simply to be a regular iamb. But what follows can be said to tear away the regular stitch work of the iambic habit: two unstressed syllables ("which was") themselves followed in turn by two stressed ones ("two fools"), and then, only a quick beat later, three stresses in a row ("so grow three")—to my ear, a prominent derangement of the metrical expectation. Jonson once remarked that Donne, "for not keeping of accent, deserved hanging." (Among the Talmudic tales and rabbinical lore is recorded a similarly horrifying judgment: that of the rabbi who declares that any scholar who looks up from his studies even for a moment—if only to admire a tree!—deserves to die!) But scholars may, at such times, miss the bewitchment that Herrick knows cannot inhere "when Art / is too precise."

For although the final line of "The Triple Fool" will return us to a rea-
sonably regular iambic lope, it does so only after having alerted us to the
possibilities of an extraordinary stress pattern: whenever a number is men-
tioned, it is also beaten out in code. The thought of three fools makes a
mimicking molossos in the metric; the thought of two is spelled out too,
in spondee. (If an iamb is a normal heartbeat, then a spondee is a heart
in trouble—and a molossos is a cardiac emergency, a heart a beat or two
away from fatal overstress. What rhythmical disfiguring could better fit
this poem's amorous disconsolation?)

Best of all, when we work our way backward through the penultimate
line to admire how the metrics underscore the meaning, we wind up
considering the first metrical foot in a new light. For now it seems to
contain, by token of its numerical code, the "one" that would inform its
single stress: a one in the form of that first-person singular pronoun. The
iamb "and I" contains a pronoun that, as we go backward, could only
count down to loneliness and a conjunction that brings us back not to
any "you" but only to the speaker's solitude. This one is ciphered, so to
speak, as soon as deciphered.

—

The Expiration
So, so, break off this last lamenting kiss,
    Which sucks two souls, and vapours both away,
Turn thou ghost that way, and let me turn this,
    And let ourselves benight our happiest day,
We asked none leave to love; nor will we owe
    Any, so cheap a death, as saying, Go;

Go; and if that word have not quite killed thee,
    Ease me with death, by bidding me go too.
Oh, if it have, let my word work on me,
    And a just office on a murderer do.
Except it be too late, to kill me so,
    Being double dead, going, and bidding, go.
                                    (Smith, 56)

The intelligence of poems is a carnal matter. The word gives life, and it
can kill; an amour is a little death, and a bidding (or a forbidding) may
double an undoing. "So, so" the poem begins. But, later, at its heart, a
similarly rhyming pair is severed: "Go" is drastically removed from "Go"

and the whole poem broken in half. The saying and the doing are two things, not one, and that's why deaths (like vows) can come in numbers. The amorous math involved may bemuse us, because it doubles nothing and dilates (twice each!) upon the two who die.

It's important that the numbers remain irreducible to solutions, critically speaking. By that I mean to say that the poems would remain lesser puzzles, mere dead tricks, if their formulae were more apparently resolvable. Each dance of dualities spawns its third; and threes resolve back into ones, as in the Christian mysteries. All of Donne's numbers are enlisted in love's battle, a battle to the thing it battles against: the big cipher, that is, death. Lovers are those who wish to multiply; and would-be multipliers know that nothing (and only nothing) conquers all.

> Study me then, you who shall lovers be
> At the next world, that is, at the next spring:
> > For I am every dead thing,
> > In whom love wrought new alchemy.
> > > For his art did express
> A quintessence even from nothingness,
> From dull privations, and lean emptiness
> He ruined me, and I am re-begot
> Of absence, darkness, death; things which are not.

> All others, from all things, draw all that's good,
> Life, soul, form, spirit, whence they being have;
> > I, by love's limbeck, am the grave
> > Of all, that's nothing. Oft a flood
> > > Have we two wept, and so
> Drowned the whole world, us two; oft did we grow
> To be two chaoses, when we did show
> Care to aught else; and often absences
> Withdrew our souls, and made us carcases.

> But I am by her death (which word wrongs her)
> Of the first nothing, the elixir grown;
> > Were I a man, that I were one,
> > I needs must know; I should prefer,
> > > If I were any beast,
> Some ends, some means; yea plants, yea stones detest,
> And love; all, all some properties invest;
> If I an ordinary nothing were,
> As shadow, a light, and body must be here.

> But I am none. . . .[15]

Here too the lovers are figured (in one breath!) both as agents ("we two") and as objects ("us two") of their own destruction. Much of one's pleasure in reading John Donne arises from his capacity to melt with such exactitude the very lock of numbers he has forged, to liberate into heartening irreducibility his means and matters.

> *The Computation*
> For the first twenty years, since yesterday,
>   I scarce believed, thou couldst be gone away,
> For forty more, I fed on favours past,
>   And forty on hopes, that thou wouldst, they might last.
> Tears drowned one hundred, and sighs blew out two,
>   A thousand, I did neither think, nor do,
>   Or not divide, all being one thought of you;
>   Or in a thousand more, forgot that too.
> Yet call not this long life; but think that I
> Am, by being dead, immortal; can ghosts die?
>
> *(Smith, 49)*

One gains a respect for the complexity of poetic numbers when one tries to sort out the syntax of lines 6 and 7. Any attempt to simplify can only deepen the mystery—yet there's no murk in this work. If I attempt some paraphrases here, you have to keep in mind what any good reader keeps in mind: that the poem means no one of these readings; it means them all.

For a thousand years I neither thought nor did anything, nor did I divide the years. . . . I neither thought up a thousand years, nor made (nor multiplied) them; I did not divide them either. . . . I neither thought a thousand years in the past, nor do I think a thousand years in the present; nor do I divide millennium from millennium—all eons being one when thought in your connection. . . . All being is one thought about you. All being is one thought of yours. . . .

It's no accident that "The Computation" ends, as do so many other Donnean numbers, in an oxymoron—in this case, in a dead immortal (or dead ghost); for comprehended opposites (one as all) are the natural crown of a Donnean proof. (The poem "Lovers' Infiniteness" ends "we shall / Be one, and one another's all.") "Batter my heart," too, is rich with paradoxes and oxymorons. One could say it is a prayer for a violent inspiring. Unlike our contemporary American versions of good works, Donne's religious petition has no reverential pallor or mere politeness about it. No one could mistake his metamorphiliac forms for mere formulae. Like Rochester, he equips his love lyre with a whip:

> Batter my heart, three-personed God; for, you
> As yet but knock, breathe, shine, and seek to mend;
> That I may rise, and stand, o'erthrow me, and bend
> Your force, to break, blow, burn and make me new.
> I, like an usurped town, to another due,
> Labor to admit you, but oh, to no end,
> Reason your viceroy in me, me should defend,
> But is captived, and proves weak or untrue,
> Yet dearly I love you, and would be loved fain,
> But am betrothed unto your enemy,
> Divorce me, untie, or break that knot again,
> Take me to you, imprison me, for I
> Except you enthral me, never shall be free,
> Nor ever chaste, except you ravish me.
>   *(Smith, 314–15)*

The four onslaughts of line 2 seeming to the petitioner too weak, each verb is scrupulously deepened a screw's turn or two in line 4. In the last four lines the poet wants of God something unholy—a divorce, and then a rape. He conceives freedom as a thralldom, chasteness as God's ravishment—and in so doing, makes four hundred years of readers (—and counting!—) breathe a little faster.

If mere good intentions are insufficient token of poetic genius (a fact much of contemporary America's "celebration" of poetry overlooks), so too is reason insufficient to poetic proof. The usually antithetical realms (of carnal and spiritual passion) are indivisible in the work of a writer like Donne (who, as eventual dean of St. Paul's, was as passionate a lover of God as of women and for whom the subtext of all carnal multiplication is God's triune arithmetic).

The Trinity
>   O Blessed glorious Trinity,
> Bones to philosophy, but milk to faith,
>   Which, as wise serpents, diversely
> Most slipperiness, yet most entanglings hath,
>   As you distinguished undistinct
>   By power, love, knowledge be,
> Give me a such self different instinct,

Of these let all me elemented be,
Of power, to love, to know, you unnumbered three.

(Smith, 318)

That jolt of odd yoked opposites (and tri-posites!) in Donne can still compel and shock us, even out of postmodernism's natural indifference to gods and absolutes—not least because through the eye slits even of our casual oversight we can still, as animal beings, recognize the structure (that is, the rhetoric and patterns) of a stunning understanding. We gasp at the literary and spiritual audacity that would admire God's slippery entanglements (God the wise serpent! Now there's a hell of a celestial oxymoron!), the mind that would speak of "self-difference" or make the very syntax of divine distinction "undistinct." (One finds oneself trying vainly to sort out the syntactical strands: distinguished in Himself? or by ourselves? Distinguished by virtue of his own power and love and knowledge, all of them inseparable?—Or distinguished as easily by exertions of our power as by exertions of our love or our knowledge? or . . .). Or. Or. Therein lies the gold: we can't distinguish ourselves, much less distinguish God.

And of course our ramifying questions must remain unreduced, for the answers are not mutually exclusive if God is to be in us or we in God. In this poem's scrupulous illimitability, the ultimate negotiation is between an "all me" and a "you three." But just what kind of being is that "all me"? A compound self or a sum of individuations? (The answer to that question is best left at "yes.") And as for "you three"—are they the aforementioned capacities of power, loving, and knowing (conveniently more or less synonymous with Father, Son, and Holy Ghost)? Overall, we have a negotiation, clearly, between a first-person "me" and a three-personed second person ("you")—but how many is that, all together? two? four?

It's all one, to Donne. And all (at last) "unnumbered"!!

The One (or "unnumbered three") the poem addresses is countless: it's what cannot be contained by reason, what cannot be held by (or to) lesser forms of love. Its provenance is neither time nor poems. (God, says Meister Eckhart, is neither good nor true. I take that to mean that God is not to be submitted to our moral scales, that God is not susceptible of comparison insofar as the divine is no mere nominal, much less adjectival matter.)

In such paradoxes the usual laws of scale and separation don't obtain: parts of speech (or laws of lesser logic) can't contain the Logos. Readers

sensitive to such pervasive insecurities at the source must keep relinquish-
ing their grasp if they wish to accommodate, rather than merely resolve,
the comprehensive grammars at work here. It's not clear (ultimately, in
this poem's course) whether "unnumbered" doesn't shift from adjective
to verb (just as "distinguished" seemed to shift from verb to adjective).
No parser may lord it over what passeth understanding. The Word may
move in ways mysterious—but never imprecise.

Numbers *will* be brought to grief, for we are mortal. But Donne's own
spunky capacity to free poetic numbers from their merely quantitative
senses represents an abiding mortal need. That "inner muff" of Lovelace's
is a ludicrous profanity that harbors something serious. As Dickinson
would put it two hundred years later, "The Outer—from the Inner /
Derives its magnitude."[16] We may strip ourselves naked and still not have
discovered ourselves.

Formal eccentricities (Jonson blasted Donne for them) were what made
Dickinson's first readers so uneasy. The bulk of John Donne's work was
not to be published in his lifetime, nor was the bulk of Dickinson's in
hers. The greatest writers may not find their readers for some generations;
the greatest works work proleptically to create their readers, over time
(". . . for till thou heare us, Lord / We know not what to say").[17] Among
the pleasures of the best poetry (or the best criticism) in any era are what
the conventionally hidebound reader dismisses as quirk or idiosyncrasy—
lines that leap out at us now for the same reason they could not lie down
then; images unseen theretofore, or since; peculiarities promenaded, ex-
cesses intimated, stripes of a species of one:

> The piller pearisht is whearto I Lent
> the strongest staye of myne unquyet mynde
> The lyke of it no man agayne can fynde
> From East to west still seking thoughe he went
> To myne unhappe for happe away hath rent
> Of all my joye the vearye bark and rynde
> And I (alas) by chaunce am thus assynde
> Dearlye to moorne till death do it relent
> but syns that thus it is by destenye
> What can I more but have a wofull hart
> My penne in playnt, my voyce in wofull crye

My mynde in woe, my bodye full of smart
And I my self, my self alwayes to hate
Till dreadfull death, do ease my dolefull state[18]

In this little poem by Sir Thomas Wyatt there's an obsessively repetitive element that might well be deemable disbalanced or disorderly were it not earned by the appealing pealing of the poem (as, in "The Triple Fool," Donne's piled-up stresses actually count). By *pealing* I mean the way the tolling pailfuls of the poem's woe are doled out, especially in the last six lines, as they turn us from the past's mainstay and pillar toward the singer's destiny in something desperate, disquieting, sung.

Someone once told me a story I stole for a poem—the story of Giordano Bruno burned at the stake for believing God moved in all things, worked as a force rather than a figure. In this account of Bruno's life he was burned in an iron mask (his captors fearing his eloquence would incite the crowd). The man who told me this story ended it by saying, "Poetry is what he thought, but did not say." In the silence after (that other man's account of) that other man's story, audiences are often struck dumb; every time I've told the story publicly, some people actually weep. And into just such a silence, in a crowded auditorium a couple of years ago, a Seattle interviewer chirped up, overquick, with the question: "Are you comfortable with that, I mean as a definition of poetry?"

I suffered, for a long moment, my own speechlessness. Then I told her. The answer is no. Comfort is decidedly beside the point. Because poetry is not there to make you feel good—although it may make you feel exquisitely. The impaler's pike is more to the point—and I mean God (not Vlad) the Impaler; I mean the one who *always* makes us die, and for whom we may never presume to speak. Donne's violent figures in "Batter my heart" arise from a mortal combat with the received forms of religious reverence, forms that reduce the Logos to an iterable human word. But God, if granted to be beyond our ken, neither good nor true, a Lord essentially unspeakable, can thoroughly be loved (read: believed in) only at great cost to comfort. Such a work requires one's life. It's an aesthetic necessity: not an anaesthetic one.

It was, remember, an "unquyet mynde" that Wyatt's pillar stabilized. That pillar gone, disquietude floods forth in words. Even the pen fills with pain. Maybe only one other poem in English mourns so relentlessly, so materially; so recalls to mind the dulling of meaning by keening, and so knows sorrow's way of overflowing a human ken with drone. (Misery loving company, it should find the poem by Edward Thomas called "Rain" and read it aloud.)[19] These lamentations fill the ear with unrelieved reiteration: they dress the mind in weeds. Wyatt asks, What else could I do? Inventively recalled, any failure of invention is an occasion for the mind to catch itself in the act, become the very ill to which, and through which, it itself refers. In Wyatt's mental misery the word *smart* refers less to wits than whippings. Self-hate wells in, where love of another is lost (—for that "pearisht" pillar must once have been animate). And because self's destiny seems to be written unrevisably, in inks of fate, the pen grows ill as well, the voice woe-choked. Woe fills every receptacle, and so (since woe is me, and I hate woe) I hate myself. The mind full of itself, the body of itself, the self of self, always itself (because *always* is operative not only as adverb but as noun) and always itself to hate—under such conditions immortality is hell. Only what is dreaded by health can bring ease at last out of disease and take this world (of self and all its words) away. (Cioran: a book is a suicide postponed.)

The poem was surely as odd a song in its own time as in ours, giving such obsessive *voice* to its senses of disquietude. The very mind's a moan, the mouth mucked up. In Wyatt's lament the scope of hope is closed right down; the freedom to seek outward, freely east and west, is shrunk to the scale of a self-absorption, self as a hell of echoes. If sounds close down (an ear pressed only to its own head), we shouldn't wonder, for a sound in a solitude makes only its own sense. Here in a lone soul's lamentation at the loss of love, and love's lamentation at the loss of life, is dramatic evidence that although solitude may greaten grief, numbers greaten it unbearably too. The sheer repeating of a same sound, mere resounding of reminding, empties the material of meaning—in itself a kind of enchantment. For poetic corroboration look at Stein or Stevens. Mere meaning seems, by comparison with such tones and moanings, mean.

The stuff of poetry: no transparency moves us like a slippered foot; no naked thought achieves the heft or depth of a maul sunk in mud. Time can be tricked by a trochee, spirit lifted with a scarf. No wonder surprise is better registered in quaverings and quirks than in a lexicon: the heart of poetry may long and legally go iambing along—but it will leap sooner or later again, at hopes and hurts. And the convention of the poem establishes its proprieties of line precisely in order to have something *against which* to get out of line. All the ties that bind a poem, its strings attached, its threads, invite undoing. Poetry can think in spunk, expose the human guises in a gaze, find mind in matter, and love wilderness with wit—that's what these writers remind us. They come to their senses not in cozy securities and comforters but in rippable, or ripple-able, veils.

And we today have Renaissance England's same instrument, the shafted, shining, language with which we could still so finely deepen understandings (or hurl out curses). Were America to care for its linguistic heritage, it could find good company in such complexities. Take Herrick, last but far from least, going about town in a fever of forms, tweaking what he needs, reminding us that nothing perfect lives and breathes, and giving us a lot of latitude for the imagination. Herrick was trained as a goldsmith—and ordained as a priest. Contemporary readers, whatever their jaunty irreverence, may find that combination rather more unholy than their Renaissance counterparts did, when "men of the cloth" did not take the profession's fabric to be merely figurative, and the wealth of religious institutions was emphatically worldly. For all the gulfs between our eras, life as lived in the sixteenth and seventeenth centuries surely felt as full of force and fear, of power and peril, of diverse slipperiness and entanglings, as it feels to us, in us, today. And its arts of elegant innuendo have plenty of pleasures to offer a modern sensualist.

The Silken Snake
For sport my *Julia* threw a Lace
Of silke and silver at my face:
Watchet the silke was; and did make
A shew, as if 't'ad been a snake:
The suddenness did me affright;
But though it scar'd, it did not bite.[20]

How gloss the silver on that silk? What did that fabric cover? (What it covered may well bite, if Julia's data are dentata.) Perhaps all ingenuities take delight in balancing opposing claims (certainly these poets seem to). That we wind up once again in oxymoron shouldn't seem surprising— or should seem both inevitable and surprising. Language itself being our material (our cover, as I've styled it here), we come to love it down to the numbered hairs. Our harried human hides (those covert things!) had best delight in numbers—numbers in the olden sense, of poetry, whatever keeps measures apprised of timelessness, sensualities of proportion, politics of oxymoron, overcoats of underwear, and design of all it couldn't quite control.

Delight in Disorder

A sweet disorder in the dresse
Kindles in cloathes a wantonnesse:
A Lawne about the shoulders thrown
Into a fine distraction:
An erring Lace, which here and there
Enthralls the Crimson Stomacher:
A Cuffe neglectfull, and thereby
Ribbands to flow confusedly:
A winning wave (deserving Note)
In the tempestuous petticote:
A carelesse shooe-string, in whose tye
I see a wilde civility:
Doe more bewitch me, then when Art
Is too precise in every part.[21]

What Herrick sees in a careless tie is worked for us into a golden phrase—a "wilde civility." (How he would have loved the vagrant strand of DNA, its revelation through the sharp contemporary eye of an electron microscope! Instruments may change, but the big picture still beguiles and escapes the mind. Watched it is, and makes a show, indeed! In the face of such mysteries, inner and outer, it is faith [only another name for the imagination] we must still rely on.)

As for that "Crimson Stomacher," in the sartorial terminology of the time it's a kind of cummerbund (that's fine enough, with *come* and *bond* both bound inside the word!), but I bet there's something of the reddened upright member also connoted there. And what but a well-fired mind would ever think up "kindle," for disorder's verb? The "lawne" that meant fine linen could also, even in those days, suggest a cultivated man's backyard. A cuff's a careless blow, as surely as a portion of a sleeve; and what would flow from it in ribbands might well attend deflowerings, once a "crimson stomacher" is involved. Whose winning do you suppose that is, there in the petticoat? (Subjective or objective genitive?) What temp or temper here is turned into a tempest? Herrick has given us a song entirely animated by the tie's undoneness, naughtiness unknotted. If the woman is not mistress of her fate, neither is fate's master any man, the likes of whom his lover may "bewitch." As poets know, the knot that's tied is always also language's. And the fiancée, the lady in the golden braid, is always also one of the daughters of Mnemosyne.

We burn for a pure indicative or superlative, but we live forever, finally, only in the comparative, that ladder or scale or ziggurat of means without end. The reason spirit can be made out in matter is this: matter is essentially mysterious, despite our ever-sharper beams upon it.

That our poetry's scansion can't be doled out in perfect certitudes—that the language is less angled than it is anglish, less susceptible of the geometer's rule than of the forms of fire, the fluencies of air, the curves of earth (whose humus gives the human its etymological ground)—is occasion not for lament but elation. It is in the very nature of poetic numbers to supply literary content with grounds for uncontainability. Measure informs (rather than reforms) a poem, and numbers aren't merely the girdle, grid, or girth of poetry—they are its body and soul. Numbers aren't just the silk; they are its silver rivulets. They are the ravishment itself, the kindling of civility, the spotlessness of flame, the cry in the voice, the self that burns or floods its I. They are the carnal weave in which all spirit must be implicated, or we never know it. ("In a nett I seke to hold the wynde," or so the airs of Wyatt have it.) Reading the greatest poems in English, we feel we've caught (but not to keep!) something of the world's stuff—a gown of sounds, the flow in the flower, a fluency in numbers, play of scopes and scales. A caress of the recognized comes as all the more precious for having been licked with unpredictabilities. We are mortal men and women: naked flesh *is* our tearable garb.

And where do we go from there? Words aren't only a cover. They are the discovery. Quick with quirks, acquainted with unkept accents and apparently careless ties, their artful negligees may gape, but when they do, they intimate ultimate things; they reveal what they re-veil: everdeepening senses of the material.

NOTES

1. Burnet, "Some Passages," 54.
2. One of the undercover pleasures of the name *Bendo* is the anagrammatical double duty it can do, in the service either of chastity or of cheat, depending on whether you read it to suggest "no bed" or "on bed."
3. Vieth, *Complete Poems of John Wilmot*, 136.

4. Ibid., 136–37. Elsewhere Rochester would etch his memorial to Cary Frazier in even more economical caustics:

> *On Cary Frazier*
> Her father gave her dildoes six;
> > Her mother made 'em up a score;
> But she loves nought but living pricks,
> > And swears by God she'll frig no more.
> > > *(Ibid., 137)*

5. "Ingrateful Beauty Threatened," in Woudhuysen, *Penguin Book of Renaissance Verse,* 354–55.

6. Vieth, *Complete Poems of John Wilmot,* 139.

7. For a bawdy joke on the *arse* poetica, worthy of a Wilmotian temper, consider X. J. Kennedy's little poem "Ars Poetica":

> The goose that laid the golden egg
> Died looking up its crotch
> To see how well its sphincter worked.
> Would you lay well? Don't watch.
> > (Kennedy, *Cross Ties,* 101)

8. Ovid's amorous escapades and erotic writings would have been well known to, and served as something of a forebear for, such poetries.

9. Woudhuysen, *Penguin Book of Renaissance Verse,* 1.

10. Richard Lovelace, "Her Muffe," in Woudhuysen, *Penguin Book of Renaissance Verse,* 370.

11. Not mere misogynies! His misanthropies are far too broadminded to stop at broads alone.

12. Woudhuysen, *Penguin Book of Renaissance Verse,* 181–82.

13. Consider, for example, this little Wyatt poem:

> Who so list to hount I knowe where is an hynde
> > but as for me helas I may no more
> > the vayne travaill hath weried me so sore
> > I ame of theim that farthest cometh behinde
> > yet may I by no meanes my weried mynde
> > drawe from the Deere but as she fleeth afore
> > faynting I folowe I leve of therefor
> > sethens in a nett I seke to hold the wynde
> Who list her hount I put him owte of dowbte
> > as well as I may spend his tyme in vain
> > and graven with Diamondes in letters plain
> There is written her faier neck rounde abowte
> > noli me tangere for Cesars I ame

and wylde for to hold though I seme tame

(Woudhuysen, *Penguin Book of Renaissance Verse,* 182)

Here the item of adornment cannot be removed, that necklace that, in its status as a mark of imperial possession, recalls the royal dog-collars inscribed, "I am her majesty's dog at Kew. Pray tell me, Sir, whose dog are you?"

The danger is part of the mark of the lord: *danger* and *domain* come from the same root.

14. Smith, *John Donne,* 149. Subsequent quotes from this edition will be referenced parenthetically by page number in the text proper.

15. Donne, "A Nocturnal upon S. Lucy's Day," in ibid., 72.

16. Franklin, *Poems of Emily Dickinson,* no. 450.

17. Smith, *John Donne,* 324.

18. Quoted in Woudhuysen, *Penguin Book of Renaissance Verse,* 85.

19. From R. George Thomas, ed., *Collected Poems of Edward Thomas,* 259:

> *Rain*
>
> Rain, midnight rain, nothing but the wild rain
> On this bleak hut, and solitude, and me
> Remembering again that I shall die
> And neither hear the rain nor give it thanks
> For washing me cleaner than I have been
> Since I was born into this solitude.
> Blessed are the dead that the rain rains upon:
> But here I pray that none whom once I loved
> Is dying tonight or lying still awake
> Solitary, listening to the rain,
> Either in pain or thus in sympathy
> Helpless among the living and the dead,
> Like a cold water among broken reeds,
> Myriads of broken reeds all stiff and stiff,
> Like me who have no love which this wild rain
> Has not dissolved except the love of death,
> If love it be towards what is perfect and
> Cannot, the tempest tells me, disappoint.

20. Woudhuysen, *Penguin Book of Renaissance Verse,* 352. *Watchet* is commonly glossed to mean "blue" or "light green." I can't help adding, from the poet's angle, that the looks of things are implicated. I believe the word *shew* seconds that impression, for his eyes are on her overthrown underthings, which themselves suggest something of the serpentine moves and quickenings to follow.

21. Ibid., 351.

BIBLIOGRAPHY

Burnet, Gilbert. "Some Passages of the Life and Death of Rochester." In *Rochester: The Critical Heritage,* ed. David Farley-Hills. London: Routledge and Kegan Paul, 1972.

Franklin, R. W., ed. *The Poems of Emily Dickinson.* Cambridge, Mass.: Belknap Press at Harvard University Press, 1998.

Kennedy, X. J. *Cross Ties: Selected Poems.* Athens: University of Georgia Press, 1985.

Smith, A. J., ed. *John Donne: The Complete English Poems.* Harmondsworth, Middlesex: Penguin, 1996.

Thomas, R. George, ed. *The Collected Poems of Edward Thomas.* Oxford: Clarendon Press, 1978.

Vieth, David M., ed. *The Complete Poems of John Wilmot, Earl of Rochester.* New Haven: Yale University Press, 1968.

Woudhuysen, H. R., ed. *The Penguin Book of Renaissance Verse, 1509–1659.* Introduction by David Norbrook. Harmondsworth, Middlesex: Penguin, 1992.

FOUR

Ben Jonson and the Loathèd Word

LINDA GREGERSON

"THE PROFIT OF *GRAMMAR*," wrote Ben Jonson in his preface to *The English Grammar*, "is great to Strangers, who are to live in communion, and commerce with us; and, it is honourable to our selves. For, by it we communicate all our labours, studies, profits, without an Interpreter."[1] Jonson's dream of a language impervious to interpretation was at the heart of a lifelong and notorious quarrel with the stage.[2] With the exception, in our own era, of Samuel Beckett,[3] one can scarcely think of a playwright of comparable stature so driven by animus toward the very essence—the collaborative essence—of his craft. What I wish to argue in the present essay is that Jonson's quarrel, while trenchantly enacted in the playhouse and repeatedly rendered in the idioms of the stage, extended well beyond the theater to language itself. In the Jonsonian lyric as in the Jonsonian drama, the word is staged with profound ambivalence: it is the crown of labor and the servant of politics, an accessory to pleasure and an instrument of profit, a hedge against transience, a symptom of transience, the ground of self-sufficiency, the currency of subjection. Jonson's ambition was to craft a self-sufficient word, but the ambition is profoundly paradoxical, as much a death wish as a will to omnipotence. Governed by this paradox, the Jonsonian lyric is at once virtuosic and strangely, savagely vacated.

The seventeenth-century poems we read most easily today tend to be those in which are muted the dynamics of topicality, the circuits of patronage, title, estate, political faction, and literary salon that dominate the overwhelming preponderance of Jonson's lyric production. We favor the Jonson canonized by nineteenth-century anthologists:[4] songs extracted from theatrical context, brief elegies to children, the outpourings of lovers and nymphs who populate *The Under-wood,* "lesser Poems, of later growth,"[5] poems we can flesh out with affective and biographical "story," poems whose conventions have been retrofitted and adapted to so many different historical moments we can tell ourselves they are somehow less bound to history than are the other kind. That other kind, the poems published in the 1616 Folio under authorial supervision and authorial proclamation ("the ripest of my studies"), impress us for the most part as straitened and withholding, unfriendly to readers. Some of our uneven preference has to do with discontinuities in learned community and discomfort with the footnotes that copiously testify to our need for prosthetic assistance. In Epigram 18 ("To My Meere English Censurer") Jonson criticizes his detractors as too ignorant to be capable of discernment: "To thee, my way in *Epigrammes* seemes new, / When both it is the old way, and the true." For *new,* read *dry* or *obscure,* and retain the stinging charge of monolingualism, and we, the great majority of us, find ourselves reproached for failures of learning and attention. It is not pleasant to be chronically reproached.

So we chiefly avoid the lyric Jonson, embarrassed by our reliance on the footnotes, put off by our sense that the poems were written for a body of initiates to which we do not belong, those whose Latin and Greek are larger than our own, those who know the period players, the details of affiliation and ideological controversy, the gossip and competitive ambitions of the age. We are not wrong about the exclusionary dynamic. On the contrary, it is even more sweeping than at first we may imagine. The *Epigrammes* begin with a single cautionary couplet addressed "To the Reader": "Pray thee, take care, that tak'st my booke in hand, / To reade it well: that is, to understand."[6] Stand under: submit. But even granting that submission, who among the general readership can with certainty claim to stand inside the circle Jonson so acidly describes? Describe: to trace the outline of, as with a compass. For the circle has no enumerable contents. Its members are distinguished not by particulars of character or faith or learning or occupation but by essence, which goes without saying. In Jonson the category of virtue cannot be broken down for analysis or inventory. For all their topicality his lyrics systematically eschew distinctive feature and distinctive event. We may arm ourselves with philological and sociohistorical detail, but no amount of filling-in unlocks these poems. The genuinely daunting prospect that opens up behind the foot-notes is that of featureless tautology.

WITHOUT

This morning, timely rapt with holy fire,
   I thought to forme unto my zealous *Muse,*
What kinde of creature I could most desire,
   To honor, serve, and love; as *Poets* use.
I meant to make her faire, and free, and wise,
   Of greatest bloud, and yet more good then great;
I meant the day-starre should not brighter rise,
   Nor lend like influence from his lucent seat.
I meant shee should be curteous, facile, sweet,
   Hating that solemne vice of greatnesse, pride;
I meant each softest vertue, there should meet,
   Fit in that softer bosome to reside.
Onely a learned, and a manly soule
   I purpos'd her; that should, with even powers,
The rock, the spindle, and the sheeres controule
   Of destinie, and spin her owne free houres.
Such when I meant to faine, and wish'd to see,
   My *Muse* bad, *Bedford* write, and that was shee.
(E76, "On Lucy Countesse of Bedford")

Even before the Muse dictates the name that signifies aristocratic blood-line and landed estate, the lady's Christian name glimmers (lucent) just below the surface of the daystar summoned to be her (inadequate) poetic approximation. Her bosom contains all virtues and exceeds them (it is softer) in quality. Fate derives its three parts (the "rock" or distaff, the spindle, the shears) and time its allegorical divisions (the "hours," female divinities who govern the changes of season) from her soul.

Again and again in the first and "ripest" of his lyric collections, Jonson performs the trope of naming as the consummate epigrammatic gesture:

I doe but name thee PEMBROKE, and I find
   It is an *Epigramme,* on all man-kind;
Against the bad, but of, and to the good:
   Both which are ask'd, to have thee understood.
(E102, "To William Earle of Pembroke")

The exemplary patron is an exemplary readership of one. As inspiration and audience, sign and substance, he (elsewhere she) constitutes the poem from every angle. All praise, all showing forth of summary virtue is better achieved in the bare syllables of the patron's name than in the furthest reaches of poetic "feigning." If I, writes the poet, "but say you are / A SYDNEY . . . / My praise is plaine." Indeed, to a percipient reader the name is manifest before it is spoken:

> How well, faire crowne of your faire sexe, might hee,
>   That but the twi-light of your sprite did see,
> And noted for what flesh such soules were fram'd,
>   Know you to be a SYDNEY, though un-named?
>   *(E103, "To Mary Lady Wroth")*

Jonson's teacher, William Camden, had taught him to seek "the reason of the name" or etymological "consonancy . . . between the name of the thing and thing named."[7] One of the foremost educators and historiographers of his time, Camden was also empowered, as Clarenceux King at Arms in the College of Heralds, to grant or withhold the coat of arms to claimants in the English polity. His own power of naming, in other words, contained both philological and legal force. The brute political lesson, however—that certain names might be a force to conjure with—required no special erudition in early modern England. Nor was it an early modern innovation for poets to address their praise and petition to persons of great family. "Stand high, then, HOWARD, high in eyes of men,"

> . . . design'd to be the same thou art,
>   Before thou wert it, in each good mans heart.
> Which, by no lesse confirm'd, then thy kings choice,
>   Proves, that is gods, which was the peoples voice.
>   *(E67, "To Thomas Earle of Suffolke")*

As the poet punned on the light in Lucy, so he puns on height in Howard (whose name, argues Camden in *Remains Concerning Britain,* means "High Warden or Guardian").[8] And in the pun is lodged an etymological forecast. The career conforms to the logic of the name, is fully present in the name before it is enacted in time. Promotion to high position (Lord Treasurer in the Jacobean state, for instance) merely "proves" or illustrates (as in a proof sheet) the aptitude that was inherent all along. Worth and title, royal election and popular opinion, private ambition and providential "design" are coincident. In the *"Epistle* to Katherine, Lady Aubigny" (F13), the poet celebrates the distillate union of "title," "birth," and "vertue," "the beauties of the mind" and "those of FORTUNE" in a single, consummate embodiment. This pattern, the centripetal working of character and fate, is found throughout the lyric encomia.

But what if virtue does not advertise itself in quite so redundant a manner? What if praise must be delivered to one whose origins are more of the middling sort, who has had to be promoted to title, and promoted in a year (the year of James's accession) when titles were suddenly, embarrassingly cheapened? The cheapening Jonson can only sublimely ignore. But the change in outward honors he can seal as a new, corrective paradigm: "Thou . . . mad'st merit know her strength, / And those that lack'd it, to suspect at length, / 'Twas not entayl'd on title." Jonson still wants the feel of airtight homiletic, but now iambic pentameter and the closed circle of rhymed couplet must enlist the aid of chiasmus:

> That bloud not mindes, but mindes did bloud adorne:
>   And to live great, was better, then great borne.
> These were thy knowing arts: which who doth now
>   Vertuously practise must at least allow
> Them in, if not, from thee; or must commit
>   A desperate solœcisme in truth and wit.
>   *(E116, "To Sir William Jephson")*

The poet's wit and the impeccable truth of his verses now rely not merely upon the overdetermined connection of worth and sign but on a manipulated account of derivation: "That bloud not mindes, but mindes did bloud adorne." The ideology is still one of stasis: virtue is still a cipher, absolute rather than relative, given rather than learned, devoid of particular content and measured by its binary opposite, by those outside the knowing circle, those who fail to acknowledge inherent virtue until it is adorned by title or who, intransigent as well as dull, adhere to desperate solecism. The Latin word *soloecismus* derives from the Greek *Soloikos*, which refers to a manner of speaking incorrectly; *Soloikos* derives from *Soloi*, an Athenian colony in Cilicia whose inhabitants spoke a dialect regarded as substandard. *Solecism*, like *barbarian* or *philistine*, is a slur spoken from inside the circle, a symptom (and self-constituting strategy) of sealed community.

Wielded as a paradigm by the versifying stepson of a bricklayer, the closed circle might seem an all too obvious (and self-betraying) piece of snobbery. But it also offers tactical advantages. As a paradigm for benefaction, for example, it can free the petitionary poet from an intolerable burden of indebtedness. For the poet's ability to mirror a worthy patron in his poem itself bespeaks a fully reciprocal worthiness. The benefit is mutual. Indeed, the poet may go so far as to reverse the usual understanding of benefaction "by making the acceptance rather than the granting of the favor the crucial act of judgment."[9] In poems that address the phenomenon of the gift explicitly, like the epigram "To Lucy Countesse of Bedford" (E84) or "An Epistle to Sir *Edward Sacvile,* now Earle of *Dorset*" (U13), Jonson delineates an ideal of instantaneous and prevenient succor, giving that so perfectly anticipates want as to spare the poet both overt petition and the accompanying "blush." So prompt and proximate is the giving that the recipient needn't suffer the smallest conscious interval of being without.

"Be alwayes to thy gather'd selfe the same," the poet counsels Sir Thomas Roe (E98). The circle of self-sufficiency may be expanded beyond the single self and still retain its essence so long as those it embraces are alike in merit. Acts are emanations of essence. Essence is impervious to fortune. All very good for the self-regard of self-identified worthies. But perpetual self-sameness does rather cramp conventional ideals of travel and learning, progressive enlargement, change by any name. When Sir Thomas's cousin William proposes to seek expanded horizons, the poet sends him off on his journey thus:

> Roe (and my joy to name) th'art now, to goe
>   Countries, and climes, manners, and men to know,
> T'extract, and choose the best of all these knowne,
>   And those to turne to bloud, and make thine owne:
> May windes as soft as breath of kissing friends,
>   Attend thee hence; and there, may all thy ends,
> As the beginnings here, prove purely sweet,
>   And perfect in a circle alwayes meet.
> So, when we, blest with thy returne, shall see
>   Thy selfe, with thy first thoughts, brought home by thee,
> We each to other may this voyce enspire;
>   This is that good AENEAS, past through fire,
> Through seas, stormes, tempests: and imbarqu'd for hell,
>   Came backe untouch'd. This man hath travail'd well.
>   *(E128, "To William Roe")*

The poet's epistolary bon voyage is a conspicuous non-sonnet: fourteen lines of couplets locked tight on iamb and masculine rhyme. The travel that prompts the poem is described as a kind of cannibalism: the best of other "climes" and peoples are to be eaten and made incorporate ("turne[d] to bloud") by the traveler. No postcolonial critic could posit the consumerist paradigm more blatantly. But when the poet proposes a corrective wish for the traveler, it does not entail a humbler course of open-minded reciprocity. On the contrary. The "travail" he recommends, a punning composite of labor and geographic distance, is one that shall leave the traveler "untouch'd." As an ethical or ontological proposition, this standard has a certain austere plausibility; it certainly accords with the pervasive logic of Jonsonian encomium. As a mode of proceeding through time, which poems must do as well as men, the paradigm is more problematic.

UNTOUCHED

Jonson was twice thrown into prison for his plays, once for *The Isle of Dogs* and once for *Eastward Ho*. On the second occasion he and his fellow authors were expected to have "their ears cutt & noses."[10] They escaped with ears and noses intact, but Jonson, like all satirists of his age, had vivid reason to establish for himself a margin of deniability. In the lyric poems he prominently names those he praises, whose naming itself secures merit. He omits to name, or names by allegorical pseudonym only, those he heaps with scorn or blame so that any who take offense must themselves assume responsibility for both the sin and the sullying of reputation. In order to charge the poet with slander, an accuser would first have to "own" the vice, by publicly recognizing himself in the satirical portrait.

> GUILTIE, be wise; and though thou know'st the crimes
>   Be thine, I taxe, yet doe not owne my rimes:
> 'Twere madnesse in thee, to betray thy fame,
>   And person to the world; ere I thy name.
>   *(E30, "To Person Guiltie")*

As the poet contrives to remain untouched by imputations of slander, so, in the opposite case, he contrives to remain untouched by the accidents of mere fact. "[If] I have praysed, unfortunately, any one, that doth not deserve . . . I hope it will be forgiven me, that they are no ill pieces, though they be not like the persons" (*Epigrammes*, dedication "To the . . . Earle of Pembroke"). When, halfway into his book of epigrams, the poet falls into disillusion with one who has been the object of his encomia, he at first repudiates his muse: "Away, and leave me, thou thing most abhord, /

That hast betray'd me to a worthlesse lord" (E65, "To My Muse"). But on second thought he finds he can have it both ways; he can disclaim the error and simultaneously preserve the efficacy and intactness of his verse: "But I repent me: Stay. Who e're is rais'd, / For worth he has not, He is tax'd, not prais'd." The verse hits home whether its subject proves worthy or not. In this best of all possible economies, the poet may hold himself blameless (his muse, not his judgment, deceived him), he may retain the credit for high-mindedness (his lord, not he, has failed the test), and he may keep his full store of publishable verse (he can print the retraction right next to the original poems of praise).

Only when the inconvenient accidentals of history overtake his subject from another angle is the poet reduced to the expedient of outright suppression. And even then he contrives to give his canceled lines an afterlife. The "Epistle" he sent to the countess of Rutland some months after her marriage to the earl of Rutland originally ended with the poet's "best" and prophetic wish that the lady bear a son within the year. When the earl was subsequently discovered to be impotent, Jonson simply canceled the last lines of the poem and substituted the disingenuous notation, "*The rest is lost*" (F12, "Epistle to Elizabeth Countesse of Rutland"). The "loss" is not the poet's, of course, and the suppression is as much an act of effrontery as a gesture of delicacy. Many of his readers would have seen— nay, would have possessed—the poem in manuscript and would know very well to what the sudden gap so conspicuously pointed. The gap itself, by the time the poem was published, mimetically reproduced what was missing in the marriage of the earl and his countess.

THE SAME

"[H]e had ane intention to perfect ane Epick Poeme," wrote William Drummond of his conversations with Ben Jonson in 1619; "it is all in Couplets, for he detesteth all other Rimes." Furthermore, "he cursed petrarch for redacting Verses to Sonnets, which he said were like that Tirrants bed, wher some who were too short were racked, others too long cut short" (*Conversations with Drummond*, 132, 133–34). The projected epic never came to fruition, but Jonson's contempt for the lineage of Petrarch appears to have been durable. High-mindedly rejecting the Procrustean bed of the sonnet, which crams all thought and musical phrasing into a single unvarying format of fourteen pentameter lines, Jonson opted instead, and throughout his lyric career, for the couplet, which would later be recognized as the foundation of English neoclassicism. Even the verses of "sonnet length" are overwhelmingly composed in couplets, as if to assert that, although the present poem has happened to achieve its proper fulfillment at fourteen lines, it might easily have stopped at twelve or gone on to sixteen if its matter had so required. On those rare occasions when Jonson produces a sonnet-by-the-book, his relation to the book preserves a considerable margin for irony: the sonnet "On Poet-Ape" (E56) enacts a frank diatribe against poetic hackwork; the dedicatory sonnet to Thomas Wright's *The Passions of the Mind in General* (UV7) grinds to a suspiciously mechanical halt between the octave and the sestet; the tribute sonnet to Lady Mary Wroth's own Petrarchan sequence is conspicuously double-edged:

> I that have beene a lover, and could shew it,
>> Though not in these, in rithmes not wholly dumbe,
>> Since I exscribe your Sonnets, am become
> A better lover, and much better Poët.
>>> (U28, "A Sonnet, To the noble Lady, the Lady Mary Worth" [sic])

Just how the lady's sonnets have effected the alleged improvements (by inoculation perhaps?) is a process left tactfully unspecified. If Jonson's literary assessments (is it a good thing to "over-come / Both braines and hearts" with one's verses?) preserve a sly elusiveness, and if his feminine end-rhymes ("shew it," "poet," "owe it," "know it") smack somewhat of parody, Lady Wroth may take some solace in the fact that her person and her name have fared far better in Jonson's encomia (see E103, E105, and the dedication to *The Alchemist*) than have her poems.

As contrasted to the sonnet, the couplet seems to have commanded Jonson's esteem as the suppler form, more capable of varying response to the varying motions of mind and exigencies of matter. The reader unwilling to take Jonson at his word, of course, might see and hear in the couplet a far more severe, preemptive sameness than ever the sonnet produced. What is it that sameness preempts? Change. And when might sameness seem the better fate? When one sees change as faithlessness. The "*Epistle* to Katherine, Lady Aubigny" (F13) is a "mirror" wherein the lady may view herself. Augmenting this highly conventional conceit is an equally conventional contrast between the present, truthful mirror and the false or superficial mirror of flattery. Although Jonson's poem does not "reject" the ornaments of physical beauty, title, and wealth, it takes as its chief business "the beauties of the mind": the lady's obedience and virtue, her indifference to fashion, her steadfastness in marriage, her retirement from the court. As the poem modulates from a descriptive to a hortatory mode, the reader may remember that in late medieval and early modern usage a mirror might be an instructive exemplar rather than a passive reflecting surface. The reader may also sense some strain. Katherine Clifton's marriage to the Lord D'Aubigny (1609) had been one in a series of forced unions perpetrated by King James in the early years of his English rule. James's idea was to cement the union of his two kingdoms and to provide for the financial ambitions of his Scottish courtiers by means of a single device: by marrying these courtiers off to English heiresses. If the heiresses and their families tried to resist these unhappy matches—and they often tried strenuously indeed—they resisted in vain.[11] Lord Clifton's wealth secured, his daughter is encouraged by the poet Jonson to observe a modest country retirement; her husband, Jonson's patron, was all this time a conspicuous presence at a court well known for its sexual and sumptuary license. But never mind. The ideal is one of stasis that transcends the incidentals of daily life. The poem and its subject are imagined as securing one another and a quasi-Platonic "forme" against the assaults of time:

> *Madame,* be bold to use this truest glasse:
> Wherein, your forme, you still the same shall finde;
> Because nor it can change, nor such a minde.
> *(F13, "Epistle to Katherine, Lady Aubigny")*

If the poet prefers sameness to change, this may be because he thinks of change as a falling off from achieved perfection. Change may reveal the fault lines in the poet's modeled "minde." At the very least, change bodes some limit to the poet's control of his work. "When we doe give, ALPHONSO, to the light, / A worke of ours, we part with our owne right" (E131). These lines "To the Same" cast sameness in several desirable aspects. They address a fellow artist, marking the poet and his dedicatee as persons of similar merit and accomplishment. They reiterate the title and occasion of a previous poem (E130, "To Alphonso Ferrabosco, *on his Booke*"), sealing compliment with ceremonial redundancy. They posit a closed circle of discernment, impervious to the changeable crowd: "Then stand unto thy selfe, not seeke without / For fame, with breath soone kindled, soone blowne out" (E131). One hears in Jonson's tribute "To the Same" a tenor more of consolation than congratulation on the publication of Ferrabosco's work. One senses again and again in the published poems of Jonson that he does not give his own work "to the light" without mixed feelings.

What does this say about compositional and cognitive process? Jonson told William Drummond "that he wrott all his [verses] first in prose, for so his master Cambden had Learned him" (*Conversations with Drummond*, 143). Whatever this means, it would seem to suggest that poetic form is somehow after the fact, that the venerable but arbitrary contract with meter and rhyme, the sometimes disparate, sometimes concordant pacing of syntax and line are add-ons or enhancements rather than foundational strategies for the discovery of affect or idea. If "all" can be rendered first in prose, what work is left for the verses to do? Perhaps they can shut the subject down. Perhaps they can render it immutable, perfected.

Perhaps they can constitute the poet's word as the last word. "BARTAS *doth wish thy* English *now were his*," writes Jonson to the English translator of Du Bartas (E132, "To Mr. Josuah Sylvester"). The telling point is not the assessment of relative merit (Jonson later spoke slightingly of the Sylvester translation)[12] but the ground of the encomium. The translator is imagined as wishing to be told he has outdone, has indeed *become*, "the *originall*" (E132). Compare the author's encomium to Thomas May's translation of Lucan: "What Muse, or rather God of harmony / Taught *Lucan* these true moodes!" (UV29, "To my chosen Friend, *The learned Translator of* Lucan, Thomas May, *Esquire*). This particular portrait of method appears at first to imagine some mediating function for poetry: Phoebus and Hermes, "interpreters twixt godds, and men," are said to have been the Latin poet's teachers. "But who hath them interpreted?" the next line reads, and one thinks for a moment the complex gains and regressions of going between, interpreting, have earned some curious attention at last. But no, for at once: "The selfe same *Genius!* so the worke will say. / The *Sunne* translated, or the Sonne of *May*." The circuits of translation resolve to a tautological pun. The consummate performance, in Sylvester's Du Bartas, in May's Lucan, or rather in Jonson's idealized account of both, is one that *makes no difference*. One recalls at this point how many of Jonson's own poems were built around direct translations of Martial, Horace, Pliny, Seneca, and Catullus. In Jonson's book, to make no difference is by definition to achieve fidelity or truth; what is more, and far more difficult to grasp, the truth one aims for seals an original perfection precisely by exceeding it.

The extended panegyric to Clement Edmonds, translator of Caesar, speaks more explicitly about the nature of writing-as-action:

Not CAESARS deeds, nor all his honors wonne,
   In these west-parts, nor when that warre was done,
The name of POMPEY for an enemie,
   CATO's to boote, *Rome,* and her libertie,
All yeelding to his fortune, nor, the while,
   To have engrav'd these acts, with his owne stile,
And that so strong and deepe, as't might be thought,
   He wrote, with the same spirit that he fought,
Nor that his worke liv'd in the hands of foes,
   Un-argued then, and yet hath fame from those;
Not all these, EDMONDS, or what else put too,
   Can so speake CAESAR, as thy labours doe.
          (E110, "To Clement Edmonds,
          on His Caesars Commentaries observed, and translated*")*

Under the pressure of Edmonds's and then Jonson's reinscription, "style" returns to its source in *stylus* and becomes a weapon for engraving the will upon a yielding table of wax or, which will serve as well, for killing off the competition. Achievement is measured in a sort of double negative, one part grammatical, one part conceptual: not the names of Pompey or Cato (great enemies), not the liberty of Rome (which Caesar defeated by assuming the title of dictator), not even the conversion of foes to agents of posthumous fame can "speak CAESAR" as the current author's labors do. To "speak Caesar" is as much as to proclaim tyrant. Or more: to be as God. Jonson hyperbolically casts the Edmonds translation (mere prose!) as "a new creation" and a miraculous resurrection combined ("restored" to life by Edmonds, Caesar "can dye no more"). English prose (the translation) modulates to English verse (the Jonsonian tribute) and becomes a trump card to Roman imperium. In Jonson's brazen reversal (Caesar takes life from *us*) of the usual hierarchy (we in the conquered "west-parts" are but a barbarous periphery to empire), one may hear a touch of the colonial's revenge.

"To the Same; On the Same" (E111) continues the encomium to Edmonds, focusing this time on the "matter" of his *Observations,* the layered commentary on ancient and modern warfare. The commentary demonstrates, writes Jonson, "that, in action, there is nothing new," that is, that all practitioners of warfare are indebted to a single "master," the Caesar whose mastery Edmonds revives. All excellence in combat is a variation on "the same." As if to prove the point by example, the poet casts his poem as itself an exercise in combat and concludes with a preemptive strike against imagined detractors. To those who would "deprave thee, and thy work," he writes to Edmonds,

> CAESAR stands up, as from his urne late rose,
> By thy great helpe: and doth proclaime by mee,
> They murder him againe, that envie thee.
> *(EIII, "To the Same; On the Same")*

This sounds very like Mark Antony's strategy in his famous funeral oration: there can be no contestation that is not attributable to envy; it is not I who speak but Caesar speaking through me; my speech has the moral force of mouthèd wounds. The airtight circle of authority displays the structure, and the anxious absolutism, of patrilineal pedigree: Caesar by thee by me. It leaves no space for any judgment but "the same." Jonson's subject here is the hypothetical reception of a book, but he does not scruple to conclude with a curse: those who do not like the book are murderers. But whose in fact is the death grip? Hostile to interpretation, suspicious of the reader, construing the publication of his work as parting with his "right" in it (E131), the poet writes his poetry in stone. And stones mark graves. Jonson's starkest confrontation with the circuit of "the same" is the epitaph to Benjamin, his firstborn son.[13]

SWANSDOWN

There is, of course, another Jonson. The Jonson who came to Ezra Pound in his Pisan cage in the closing months of a murderous war was a lifeline, the trace memory of an unspoiled world:[14]

> Hast 'ou seen the rose in the steel dust
>   (or swansdown ever?)
>   *(Canto 74)*

> hast'ou swum in a sea of air strip
>   through an aeon of nothingness
>   *(Canto 80)*

> This wind is lighter than swansdown
> the day moves not at all
>   *(Canto 80)*

Hast 'ou fashioned so airy a mood
   To draw up leaf from the root?
Hast 'ou found   a cloud   so light
   As seemed neither mist nor shade?
                 (Canto 81)[15]

When the world has been hung by its heels in Milan (and its mistress with it) (Canto 74), when the loneliness of death comes upon the bare survivor (Canto 82), when "the mind swings by a grass-blade" (Canto 83), the slightest hint of underlying order arrives like "palpable / Elysium" (Canto 81). It may come in the guise of song: the curve in the bowl of the lute that produces an air that possesses the power to draw up leaf from root. It may come in the concentric pattern a magnet makes in industrial waste: a rose in the steel dust. It may come in the rising rhythm of the anapest, the triple meter that makes a seventeenth-century lyric go lightly on its feet:

Have you seene but a bright Lillie grow,
   Before rude hands have touch'd it?
Have you mark'd but the fall o'the Snow,
   Before the soyle hath smutch'd it?
Have you felt the wooll o' the Bever?
            Or Swans Downe ever?
Or have smelt o'the bud o'the Brier?
            Or the Nard i' the fire?
   Or have tasted the bag o'the Bee?
O so white! O so soft! O so sweet is she!
     (U2.4, "Her Triumph,"
     from *"A Celebration of* CHARIS *in ten Lyrick Peeces")*

In an age of faithlessness the triple meter is a kind of faith. Crosscut with Jonson in the Pisan cantos is the medieval poet Dante, for whom the underlying structure of three, the terza rima, was homage to the holy trinity: a promise, a mnemonic, a ceremonial performance of devotion. Dante's pilgrim moves through the three-part *Comedia,* from hell to paradise, toward the vision of a rose. "[S]o light is the urging," writes Pound in hell, "so ordered the dark petals of iron / we who have passed over Lethe" (Canto 74).

The lightness is remarkable in portions of *The Under-wood.* The dominance of the pentameter couplet is broken to allow for varied stanzas and varied lines; the dominance of epigram and epistle is disrupted to allow for some playful engagement with other genres: the love poem, the dream poem, the pastoral dialogue, the song. We are invited, with equal measures of geniality and rue, to imagine a poet behind the poem:

> Let it not your wonder move,
> Lesse your laughter; that I love.
> Though I now write fiftie yeares,
> I have had, and have, my Peeres.
> *(U2.1, "His Excuse for loving")*

The poet is no longer an unsullied force of intellect. He has a body. He suffers the liabilities of age. He fears that his love "hath seen"

> My hundred of gray haires,
> Told seven and fortie years,
> Read so much wast, as she cannot imbrace
> My mountaine belly, and my rockie face,
> And all these through her eyes, have stopt her eares.
> *(U9, "My Picture Left in Scotland")*

The self-presentation, markedly different from that in the occasional and ceremonial poems, affects a winning informality.

Even women are allowed to speak in *The Under-wood*, albeit in words provided by the poet. When Charis replies to "Ben" in the ninth part of her sequence, she describes "what Man would please me" (U2.9, "Her man described by her owne Dictamen") and makes him, somewhat vengefully, a far cry from her aging, untitled, and importunate poet-suitor. Women are discovered to wield the rapier couplet as well as any man: "For were the worthiest woman curst / To love one man, hee'd leave her first" (U6, "Another. In defence of their Inconstancie. A Song"). Women turn the tables on Petrarchan praise and show that they understand its constitutive fictions, and its power structure, very well. They devise a composite lover out of parcels and scraps (for where could they find a whole one worth wishing for?) and find they like the devising rather better than they like the lover:

> And as a cunning Painter takes
> In any curious peece you see
> More pleasure while the thing he makes

Then when 'tis made, why so will wee.
        (*U5*, *"In the person of Woman-kind.*
        A Song Apologetique")

All this is delightful. And there are more in this vein: the songs in *Cynthia's Revels,* the lover's "Dreame" (U11) that Swinburne so admired,[16] the Donne-like "Houre-glasse" (U8), a universal subject (romantic love) given purchase by means of well-chosen biographical particulars or musical phrasing so ravishing it might be Herrick's. But lest we too readily psychologize the lyric divide, construing one part as calculated or driven by business and one part as "expressive," we would do well to remember the business side of love. In Jonson's era, as in others one might name, poets were required to suffer the afflictions of eros; it came with the territory:

Let me be what I am, as *Virgil* cold;
    As *Horace* fat; or as *Anacreon* old;
No Poets verses yet did ever move,
    Whose Readers did not thinke he was in love.
        (*U42*, *"An Elegie"*)

Does the calculation nullify the lineaments of remembered perfection? The bright lily growing? The swansdown? The snow? Of course not. But the Jonson distilled by Pound to become a precipitating essence of modernist poetics is a Jonson wrested from social and political context to become a secret sharer in very different patterns of affliction and longing, a Jonson carefully stripped of satiric distance, a Jonson estranged from his own most characteristic modes.

NO

Jonson was in some respects estranged from his own era as well. His era was that of the Reformation—a fraught, disorderly, and violent schism in the church that defined itself as universal—and it left him, as a lyricist, remarkably untouched. There are, to be sure, some references to faith in Jonson's poems (I will turn to the rare devotional poems in a moment). Some of these references are downright strained (the "virgin-traine" that consoles a mourning mother for her daughter's death) or disconcertingly pat ("Yet, all heavens gifts, being heavens due, / It makes the father, lesse, to rue") (E22, "On My First Daughter"). Others bring the paradox of

Christian consolation into deliberately straitened focus: "He that feares death, or mournes it, in the just, / Shewes of the resurrection little trust" (E34, "Of Death"). Some hedge the question of faith with taut conditionals, as in the epitaph on Sir John Roe:

> If any pious life ere lifted man
> To heaven; his hath: O happy state! wherein
> Wee, sad for him, may glorie, and not sinne.
> *(E27, "On Sir John Roe")*

That *if* is the weightiest syllable in the poem. For the most part, in Jonson, the gestures of faith are either formulaic or missing altogether.

This odd absence is not somehow "explained" by Jonson's extended rejection of Protestantism (the poet told William Drummond he had been "12 yeares a Papist").[17] As a lyricist, Richard Crashaw was emphatically of his age, and emphatically dominated by the devotional habits of Counter-Reformation Catholicism. Donne's religious verse—the standard by which we measure the age and the genre—is as arguably "Roman" as it is "Reformed." The telling absence in Jonson is not thematic—vast stretches of the Renaissance lyric omit explicit reference to matters of religion—but structural: it is an absence of *process.* Process dominates the lyric poems of Shakespeare, Marvell, Herbert, and Donne and is, I would argue, the chief contribution the Renaissance lyric has made to our tradition. Visible process: a way of getting in conceptual or figurative or syntactical trouble (carried away with metaphorical vehicle, for instance, or with branching modifiers) and needing to invent a way out. Shakespeare, Marvell, Herbert, Donne—regardless of their actual or ostensible subject—cultivate a specific lyric *shape,* an instinct for crux that the poem must discover and without which the poem is merely a series of verses. This crux is the embodied crisis of two competing conceptual demands; it is an abutment discovered in situ; it cannot be rendered in paraphrase. It coincides, I am convinced, with a foundational religious apprehension; it is the working method of those whose governing instinct is that of a chasm between letter and spirit. Milton built his every line upon this chasm, which is why his poems are a culmination of the English Renaissance—the Elizabethan and Jacobean Renaissance—despite the fact that they were written, the greatest of them, after the Restoration.

Jonson, on the other hand, is not a Renaissance poet at all, not in the English sense; he is rather a neoclassical poet *avant la lettre,* one whose method looks forward to the eighteenth century and Enlightenment. The distinguishing feature of England's belated, northerly Renaissance is that in England, as nowhere else, the rediscovery of Roman and Athenian classics coincided with profound ideological hostility to Rome, a *national* hostility that ultimately assured the breakup of the Roman Catholic Church. In England the reinvestment in literary continuity collided with renewed insistence on the ruptures and paradox of the Word. In England the reauthorizing prestige of classical Latin and Greek met head-on with a new and radical authorization of the vernacular. Vernacular Scripture was a centerpiece of the Reformation, but the philological competence and the textual method in which this Scripture was newly grounded were the distinguishing accomplishments of the Renaissance. The English Renaissance poem found its characteristic means in just these disorderly intersections; its crowning achievement was a messy, fecund, investigative vernacular.

The word is not, for Jonson, primarily investigative. The word is a maddening struggle for dominance:

Heare mee, O God!
  A broken heart,
  Is my best part:
Use still thy rod,
  That I may prove
  Therein, thy Love.
        (UI.2, "A Hymne to God the Father")

This second of the three devotional poems that open *The Under-wood* aspires to be very much like a rod itself: thirty-two narrow lines, dimeter throughout, iambic for all but three of its sixty-four feet, it beats its rhythm as the penitent beats his flesh, hoping the chastisement will prove to be from God and thus a sign of God's continuing interest. And like the poems of patronage in *Epigrammes* and elsewhere, this poem to the heavenly patron seeks to seal its logic with a circular after-measure:

That gav'st a Sonne,
To free a slave,
    First made of nought;
    With all since bought.

The sinner looks for reassurance in the price that has been paid for his salvation: worth is measured retroactively, by cost, as a patron may be measured by the verses that praise him or a poet by the virtue his verses attribute to the patron.[18]

"To Heaven" occupies that place in *The Forrest*—the concluding place—often reserved by poets for poetic retraction or palinode, a turning away from the worldliness of all that has gone before. The exculpatory function of the palinode is always equivocal: the poet takes cover and also assures that all he has written remains intact. Jonson forgoes retraction altogether; we have only the site of retraction, and apostrophe to God. "Good, and great GOD," Ben Jonson writes,

> . . . can I not thinke of thee,
>   But it must, straight, my melancholy bee?
> Is it interpreted in me disease,
>   That, laden with my sinnes, I seeke for ease?
> (F15, "To Heaven")

This is a poem about trying to pray. And like the famous effort at prayer in *Hamlet,* the scene in which the prince beholds his uncle on his knees, this effort runs aground on the split between words and thoughts. Like the famous scene in *Hamlet,* this poem turns out to be less about prayer than about misinterpretation. "Good, and great God": the imperfect coincidence of these two terms, *good* and *great,* has been the occasion of much vexed negotiation in the epigrams and epistles to lofty patrons. Perhaps godhead is where the discrepancy can finally be resolved? "[C]an I not think of thee": we may imagine that the melancholy that intrudes its *not* is the affective experience of the poet at prayer. The melancholy impediment would conventionally—in Donne and Herbert, for example—be the poet's conscious immersion in sin. But in line three we learn that melancholy in the present case is not a feeling at all but something mistakenly attributed to the poet, an instance of ungenerous and incorrect *interpretation.*

The Latin *interpretari* (explain, expound, translate, understand) derives from *interpres* (agent, negotiator). The Indo-European root from which both words derive means "to traffic in" or "sell." In addition to *interpret,* the family of *per-* derivatives includes *praise, appreciate,* and *pornography* (G. *pornē,* prostitute; from *pernanai,* to sell). When Shakespeare writes in Sonnet 21, "I will not prayse that purpose not to sell,"[19] he is making an etymological point.

Praise has never been disinterested, never entirely separable from selling.

This was the tarnishing reality that made the poet Jonson so loathe to be interpreted.

> I feele my griefes too, and there scarce is ground,
>   Upon my flesh t'inflict another wound.
> Yet dare I not complaine, or wish for death
>   With holy PAUL, lest it be thought the breath
> Of discontent; or that these prayers bee
>   For wearinesse of life, not love of thee.

The place at which the poet would arrive, at "love of thee," is introduced as a negative within a negative: "I dare not . . . lest it be thought . . . not love of thee." The poet names only those motives he would not be thought to be governed by: melancholy, spiritual disease, weariness, discontent. According to the doctrine of grace, the path to heaven is a *via negativa;* the negative way requires a surrender of will. But Jonson, aware of the doctrine, still favors the path of grammatical and poetic coup. "Where have I beene this while exil'd from thee? / And whither rap'd, now thou but stoup'st to mee?" The answer the poet hopes to extract is the title of his poem. Whither am I raped? "To Heaven." Among religious poets of the early seventeenth century, rape was the classic figure for being seized by God against, or in spite of, one's will. But Jonson wants the rape and wants his will as well. He is determined to storm heaven by sheer force of mind.

His fiercest, and finest, storming begins with a stanza remarkably mild:

> The Sonne of God, th'Eternall King,
> That did us all salvation bring,
>   And freed the soule from danger;
> Hee whom the whole world could not take,
> The Word, which heaven, and earth did make;
>   Was now laid in a Manger.
> (*U1.3, "A Hymne On the Nativitie of my Saviour"*)

The alternating pattern of end-stopped tetrameter and trimeter lines (4 + 4 + 3) is underscored by a pattern of simplest frontal rhyme; the deliberate effect is somewhere between nursery rhyme and ballad. But the stripping-to-essence quickly assumes a nearly unbearable torque:

The Fathers wisedome will'd it so,
The Sonnes obedience knew no No,
    Both wills were in one stature;
And as that wisedome had decreed,
The Word was now made Flesh indeed,
    And tooke on him our Nature.

"The Sonnes obedience knew no No": pressing hard on the boundaries
of nonsense, treading very near epistemological and metaphysical abyss,
Jonson the poet imagines at last a word that would suit him, a word that
puts mystery in its place, a word whose obedience knows "no No." The
word he imagines knows no difference between being and meaning, will
and effect. The word and the creator who speaks it partake of a single
nature. The word secures its poet against change. The word is always and
proleptically subdued.

The human son whose name is also Ben Jonson and is in death a "piece
of *poetrie*" seems to be invested with just such properties:

Farewell, thou child of my right hand, and joy;
    My sinne was too much hope of thee, lov'd boy,
Seven yeeres tho'wert lent to me, and I thee pay,
    Exacted by thy fate, on the just day.
O, could I loose all father, now. For why
    Will man lament the state he should envie?
To have so soone scap'd worlds, and fleshes rage,
    And, if no other miserie, yet age?
Rest in soft peace, and, ask'd, say here doth lye
    BEN. JONSON his best piece of *poetrie*.
For whose sake, hence-forth, all his vowes be such,
    As what he loves may never like too much.
                    (*E45, "On My First Sonne"*)

Readers of the epitaph "On My First Sonne" have generally taken Jonson's
confession of "sinne" as the pertinent key to the final, thorny line of the
poem. That confession may be disingenuous (a sort of inverted boast: I
have loved you too much and swear never to make that mistake again);
it may be real (a sin of pride or worldliness: I have loved you with too
earthly a love); or it may be a mixture of disingenuous and real (I ac-
knowledge too earthly a love but simultaneously protest the religious stric-
tures against such love). What these readings fail to provide is any account
of the mystifying distinction between *love* and *like*; all tend to treat these

words as roughly cognate. If, however, we understand the father as authentically acknowledging a will to reproduce himself, a will to "likeness" that disfigures love in both heavenly and earthly terms, we may at last have a means of construing the sin while preserving the poet's semantic scruple. That scruple is itself a captivating "piece of *poetrie,*" a final, virtuosic gesture that reenacts the sin even while disavowing it.

There is no outside to Jonson's will. It "knows no No," and the knowledge registers as a kind of aphasia. The divine poet may deliver a son to death and suffer no division, as "A Hymne" reminds us. But to wish for such a son, to covet such a word, is for the human poet worse than futile: it is blasphemous. Jonson, to his credit, does not flinch. He knows the price of blasphemy and blasphemes still. And he never stops seeking the word that will transcend the very nature of words, the word so right and final it will accommodate no *No.*

NOTES

1. C. H. Herford, Percy Simpson, and Evelyn Simpson, eds., *Ben Jonson,* 11 vols. (Oxford: Oxford University Press, 1925–52), 8:465.

2. On Jonson's antitheatricality see Jonas Barish, "Jonson and the Loathèd Stage," in *The Antitheatrical Prejudice* (Berkeley: University of California Press, 1981), 132–54.

3. I do not refer to the playwright's tendency to script the very breath patterns, tonal inflections, and eye movements of his actors, to bury them up to the neck in sand, consign them to urns that allow for neither sitting nor standing, or banish them from the stage altogether: these radical forms of play with authorial control, with something that borders on authorial hostility, can be construed in any number of exhilarating ways. I refer to those times when Beckett sought by means of lawsuit to halt productions he judged to take intolerable liberties with his play scripts, as when JoAnne Akalaitis set *Endgame* in a subway tunnel or several directors in several countries staged *Waiting for Godot* with all-female casts. Beckett thought more deeply about the metaphysical premise of performance than any other playwright of his era. Whatever one thinks about the merits of particular stagings, the playwright's effort to police the boundaries of theatrical interpretation is baffling if only because it is doomed by the very nature of the medium.

4. On this question and the broader challenges of annotation, see Ian Donaldson's introduction to his edition of *Ben Jonson* (Oxford: Oxford University Press, 1985), xv.

5. The phrase is Jonson's own, part of his brief foreword to *The Under-wood,* which was not printed in his lifetime but assembled posthumously by Sir Kenelm Digby for the Second Folio.

6. "To the Reader" [Epigram 1], in Herford, Simpson, and Simpson, *Ben Jonson*, 8:27. Subsequent citations from this edition of the lyric poems will be parenthetical and will include brief reference to original publication data: E = *Epigrammes*, F = *The Forrest*, U = *The Under-wood*, UV = *Ungathered Verse*. Except for the silent modernization of *u/v* and *i/j*, original spelling will be observed.

7. David Riggs, *Ben Jonson: A Life* (Cambridge: Harvard University Press, 1989), 16. On Camden and naming see also W. H. Herendeen, "Like a Circle Bounded in Itself: Jonson, Camden, and the Strategies of Praise," *Journal of Medieval and Renaissance Studies* 11, no. 2 (fall 1981): 137–67, esp. 153.

8. Donaldson, *Ben Jonson*, 37n.

9. This formulation is that of Stanley Fish in "Authors-Readers: Jonson's Community of the Same," *Representations* 7 (summer 1984): 26–58. My debts to this superb essay are extensive.

10. *Conversations with Drummond*, in Herford, Simpson, and Simpson, *Ben Jonson*, 1:140. Subsequent citations will, for the most part, be noted parenthetically.

11. See Riggs, *Ben Jonson*, 148–50.

12. See *Conversations with Drummond*, in Herford, Simpson, and Simpson, *Ben Jonson*, 1:133.

13. For a fascinating discussion of the masculinity founded upon the death of the son, see David Lee Miller, "Writing the Specular Son: Jonson, Freud, Lacan, and the (K)not of Masculinity," in *Desire in the Renaissance: Psychoanalysis and Literature*, ed. Valeria Finucci and Regina Schwartz (Princeton: Princeton University Press, 1994), 233–60.

14. The citations that follow are from Ezra Pound, "The Pisan Cantos," in *The Cantos of Ezra Pound* (New York: New Directions, 1970), 449. Subsequent citations will be parenthetical.

15. See also the Jonsonian echo in Pound's draft of Canto 110: "Hast 'ou seen boat's wake on sea-wall." I am certain the *Cantos* bear traces of Jonson that I have not found.

16. See Herford, Simpson, and Simpson, *Ben Jonson*, 11:54.

17. *Conversations with Drummond*, in Herford, Simpson, and Simpson, *Ben Jonson*, 1:139. This period comprised roughly the years 1598 to 1610.

18. On Herbert's use of secular patronage paradigms in the religious poem, see Michael C. Schoenfeldt, *Prayer and Power: George Herbert and Renaissance Courtship* (Chicago: University of Chicago Press, 1991), esp. 57–113.

19. Citation is from the Stephen Booth edition of *Shakespeare's Sonnets* (New Haven: Yale University Press, 1977).

FIVE

Donne's Sovereignty

CALVIN BEDIENT

I HAVE THE SUNSET over a rocky peak on my writing table. No, it's just a red-and-golden dahlia in a black stone vase. No, it's a sunset, if that's what the imagination says it is. All right, it's both.

Poetry is the genre that will have such things both ways. The metaphysical poets of the seventeenth century took this as their unwritten gospel. They indulged metaphor, if with a classical lucidity. They whistled it down to the seed in their hand. What seed? Metaphysics. The inside. The invisible. Come and eat, imaginary concretenesses, or how will we know if the inner life, which seems so renewable, so tender, so real, so immense, is anything but ghostly seed?

The proof was thus circular: essentially Airy figures (since metaphors are only imaginary resemblances—only language) to do the arithmetic of Airy Innerness. Surprising figures, for the substance of the metaphysicals was often sublime emotion, chiefly the miraculous arithmetic of love (both amorous and devout), in which one plus one equals One.

Classical *and,* classical *but,* sublime, John Donne, for instance, may have had all his wits about him—so much so that his wit wore imagination like a dashing great hat (as in the "pose of a Melancholy Lover" in the Lothian portrait of Donne)—yet he wrote like the most fantastical alchemist about a certain Elixir, which he called love, as if the great hat wore *him,* as a great hat may appear to do.

If one crosses classical lucidity with the sublime, the result, of course, if we leave aside Greek tragedy, is a minor sublime, whose name is astonishment and not holy awe or unholy dread. The result is, if you will, playful—a played-with, a played, sublime. This is the great quality in Donne's *Songs and Sonnets,* one that his critics sometimes miss, testing his arguments, as they do, as if they were doctrine, when not misconstruing them as mere cleverness. They circle around his conceited sovereignty with worrying democratic growls. But the *Songs and Sonnets* are, above all, sports, jeux d'esprit, performances. Performances of what? Of roused speech. Not belief, but vigor and astonishment are their metals, their content. Not solutions, but sovereign emotion.

Donne is sovereign in the modern sense: sovereign inside, not over others; sovereign absolutely—if also, for poetic purposes, absolutely playfully. Love can set a person up in that way, as can laughter, beauty, or an instinctual philosophy. Democracy kicked it up in Whitman and Dickinson, our great sovereign poets. In Gertrude Stein democracy kicked it up like a ball. Wallace Stevens's work is all about an aesthetic, a playful, sovereignty.

Donne got to it first, and not just as prince of wits and Copernicus of poets, living "eminent, in a degree / Beyond our lofty'st flights," in the words of Henry King, Donne's executor, but, as Jonathan Post has said, as "a kind of Hieronimo or Hamlet of verse," cagier than thou—in which, as Post adds, he gave himself over to unique acts of "poetic self-ravishment," to spunky I-assertions, and a "fuller range of attitudes and expressions than previous amatory verse had acknowledged."[1] He got to it despite his frequent and understandable servility to the English court. Got to it, in part, precisely by begging a pattern from worldly kings. Renaissance means that the *imagination* can set you up; it has that power. So it was in Shakespeare; and the Donne of the *Songs and Sonnets* is like a corner of Shakespeare's own sovereign realm, where a room that could be copied out of Vermeer is complete with a mapped globe and a bed covered with a king's furs and an astrologer's gown, and the sound of one man talking, brilliantly.

In Donne, sovereignty has two forms: a soul's amorous identification with another soul, and imagination's play. And the greater of the two is imagination. Ecstasy is the subject, imagination the form.

With his hotdoggery, Donne wrote on the cusp between the idea of the subject as, by definition, *subjected,* subordinate to an external authority (king, priest, God, law), and the sovereign experience of a radiant *surplus* of being. His poems for patrons are inescapably subservient. His songs and sonnets—love's tootlings and organ preludes—are sovereign.

Sovereign in being witty, poetic, erotic, ecstatic, rhythmic, and combative—that is, in being roused, in feeling stronger than death ("the sovereign is he who *is*," wrote Georges Bataille, "as if death were not")[2]—Donne is a marvel of surplus energy. When it's healthy, poetry is nothing but sovereignty. Like eroticism and love it anticipates the disappearance of the subject (in both senses) in the wilds of wonder. It's not an *ahem*. "Why shall I polite it," wrote Stein. "Pilot it." Again: "Do breathe when you can."

"The subject," Bataille says, "is the being *as he appears to himself from within*" (237, Bataille's emphasis). The *sovereign* subject is one who momentarily feels himself into limitlessness, that miracle. The songs exist to be the verbal formulas and equivalents of such moments. Royalty objectifies it for *others;* Donne preferred it direct, in eroticism, in laughter, in amorous identification, and in poetry. He gravitated to fictions of his own preeminence or, more generously and infinitely, of a preeminence à deux. He would be not a subordinate subject of a king but a miracle of feeling in which the limits of objects, as also of single subjects, have been discarded like hampering clothes. The forensic task was to convince the lover that physical eroticism was not, as even royalty tended to be, a miring down. The proof of sovereign emotion lay in the tone, whether it was mockingly playful or movingly "sincere." Modulating the example of the court, it was a tone of either sovereign worldly or sovereign sacred play, indifferent to all small market measures. Donne's "metaphysical" distinction lay in turning even high thought into a many-keyed instrument, introducing into what are usually purely solemn considerations a playful impulse that temporarily proved stronger in him than the anxieties of having to get on in the world.

In what follows I will reflect further on sovereignty and play—on sovereign play—in Donne's *Songs and Sonnets,* but with particular emphasis on the sovereign playfulness of his metaphors, those keys, those toys, those devices that can be set on an altar of the imagination like a precious icon and then, in the next stanza, be cast aside, often for the sake of another metaphor. Such is play. Such is sovereignty.

"THE FLEA"

For really the imagination is a game of (a) resemblance, (b) invention (whether of an adjective, a character, or a scene), and (c) fertility—hence its necessary and essential fickleness and restlessness. The concepts of consistency, steadfastness, and fidelity play no part in it, which is why tyrannical regimes distrust and persecute it. The imagination has at its best an incomparable precision, but its law is energy, which is, as Blake said, eternal delight; and in its economy nothing is saved, nothing is sacred, except *inspired play.*

Much as Plato himself distrusted poets, he yet said that "life must be lived as play, playing certain games, making sacrifices, singing and dancing, and then a man will be able to propitiate the gods."[3] Earlier Heraclitus had gone further: the universe itself, he said, is Zeus's divine game. All the more reason, if so, for a poem to be sportive. In any case play, as Johan Huizinga argued in *Homo Ludens,* is the only free activity in the universe—the only thing not servile with necessity.

In *Songs and Sonnets* Donne is, in Plato's sense, sacred and pagan; in Huizinga's sense he is free and spontaneous. One knows this from the sovereignty of his tone even more than from the pyrotechnics of his intellect. A mind of sheet-metal sheen, strength, flexibility, and bright and snappy ripple is needed in the midst of competing systems and solutions, none without its appeal. For Donne such pluralism was less a predicament than an opportunity. In his love poetry, if not in his religious verse, he wasn't after the right answer. He could enjoy the luxury of believing that there was no longer a right answer; he could play. But even if there had been an "answer," would he have been after it? He chose, he delighted to be able, to exercise his own sovereignty. To be sovereign is never to scratch one's head and give up on a quandary, except in play. Sovereignty says, This is my chance to move, make noise, flash light, like a waterfall or a thundercloud. Am I driven to the wall by exigencies of thought? Listen to my tone and find out.

Donne's famous flea is thus not merely his art's mascot but its microcosm, with respect both to his metaphysics (Donne's theme of the magical union of two lovers, a feat the flea effects instinctively) and to his catch-me method. The flea mirrors both Eros and poem—is both connective and kinetic, pinchy and jumpy, like Donne's wit.

Donne's most imposing concern is with the space love creates—at once a hub and an everywhere, and the one earthly exception to time. For the speaker in "The Flea," the lovers in their synecdochic transposition, as commingled drops of blood in the flea's "living walls of jet," have entered a "temple." The imagination has the sovereign prerogative to arrange the lighting as suits, and when it comes to fictions, love is the more imperious the more it is full of its own delight. Apart from rooms, love, in Donne, is happiest with maps, compasses, and pillows, and it is associated with things that expand without breaking (a drawing compass, beaten gold). It is least safe with the "rags" of time—minutes, hope, seasons, growth, climax.

Yet Donne's romance with inner space figured as outer space can't hide his infernal, his imaginative, his self-delighting restlessness. Donne is himself part flea. His whole happiness may appear to be a morrowless, marrowed good morrow, but his practice is always to alight, bite, ingest, and move on. Don't move, never change, he says to Love, while, like a manic worker in clay, he dances about it, slapping shaping prodding.

Donne of course loves to triumph with his intellect (it's such a sovereign sensation) in compressed space and over obstacles his mind itself loves to generate, partly, again, out of a luxurious Renaissance hesitation among competing systems but very largely and sportively and exhibitionistically because he delights in testing his wit. Outwardly he's the hero of love, but behind that mask a jester of mental sleights, winks, cunning surprises, and happy thrusts looks out, awaiting his due applause.

Donne's virile and playful assurance is a wonder. As a talker he's a gamester. The woman in "The Flea" is on to the speaker's game and up for it. Purpling her nail, she thinks she has him; she victoriously announces that neither she nor he is any "the weaker" now that the flea is dead; what it took from them (and *married* within itself) was hardly their sexual natures. Of course, he has his watch-me-top-that comeback:

Cruel and sudden, hast thou since
Purpled thy nail, in blood of innocence?
In what could this flea guilty be,
Except in that drop which it sucked from thee?
Yet thou triumph'st, and say'st that thou
Find'st not thyself, nor me the weaker now;
    'Tis true, then learn how false fears be;
    Just so much honour, when thou yield'st to me,
    Will waste, as this flea's death took life from thee.[4]

Agilely changing the equation between the flea and their lives ("Oh stay, three lives in one flea spare") to the flea and *her honor*, the speaker proves no less forensic than erotic, a mental athlete no less than a would-be seducer. Which role is really in the service of the other? In each, in any case, he's all con moto. *Pace* T. S. Eliot, he can't be read solemnly. Catch me, catch a flea.

Pace William Empson, too, for all his greater deftness as a reader of Donne. Empson ambiguously agrees with Clay Hunt that Donne's miraculous poem "The Canonization" isn't successful (mutters from Hunt about cleverness).[5] "The Canonization"! Not successful!

Empson was surely right to ply Donne away from the tight, sober clutches of Ramist rhetoric (to which Rosemond Tuve had consigned him in her book *Elizabethan and Metaphysical Imagery*). But I think he hit the wrong note when he said, all the same, that the "mystical doctrine" of the "great love-poems . . . was always a tight-rope walk, a challenge to skill and courage" (93). It was more a dance, I would say, with a very few exceptions, chiefly "The Ecstasy." "Mystical doctrine"? There is no doctrine in "The Canonization." If a speaker tells you that his love is the very pattern of unworldly love, and that he will someday be prayed to as the very saint of love, the more easily because the poem he speaks in and "builds" will serve as a well-wrought urn for his ashes, does he really mean for you to believe him? Donne's megalomania as a lover is sport—sovereign, often comic, sport.

This speaker is a pert and pretty piece of theater, nothing more. After all, he begins, famously, with the fine outburst, one that, not least through its colloquial force, carries to the back of the auditorium, "For God's sake hold your tongue, and let me love." Then, lest you didn't get the humor of that piece of bravura, he immediately adds, "Or chide my palsy, or my gout, / My five grey hairs." He means to be *royally* entertaining, and is.

If he's serious, as well, it's largely in stanza 3, the hotbed of the illusion of a "doctrine":

> Call us what you will, we are made such by love;
>   Call her one, me another fly,
> We are tapers too, and at our own cost die,
>   And we in us find the eagle and the dove;
>   The phoenix riddle hath more wit
>   By us; we two being one, are it.
> So, to one neutral thing both sexes fit.
>   We die and rise the same, and prove
>   Mysterious by this love.

Before testing this passage for doctrine, a few words about what Donne's "mystical doctrine" is supposed to be. The one idea that, even for Donne, has compelling gravity (at least for a given moment—it's not really an obsessive theme even in the *Songs and Sonnets*) is the "new soul," the "abler soul," as it's called in "The Ecstasy," which love magically mixes together, spontaneously, without an alembic, out of the mixed souls of two lovers. Sealed by a golden sovereignty, the theme is indeed John Donne's; it attaches to no other name. Donne owns it by right both of the beauty with which he imbues it and of his sacred regard for it. If the poets of his age were far more theme- or genre-bound than poets are today, now that all the walls are down, he yet found in the innermost chamber of the love poem (if, again, only sporadically) a holiness of identification that exalted the genre, making it essentially about the marriage of two souls. Two equals (if not always: witness "Air and Angels"). Two sovereigns.

Effectively as a conception of love, of sensuality, as the bone marrow of what was nonetheless primarily a union of two souls, it was something new in the world—not, as with the troubadours, "a longing of affect for the absolute meaning that shies away" (as Julia Kristeva put it in *Tales of Love*),[6] nor Aquinas's intellectual love, either, nor Bernard of Clairvaux's "spontaneous affinity," God sanctioned (Kristeva, 155), but, instead, an affect complete in itself, a total qualitative transmutation of being, a summa—neither voracious with self nor tyrannically ideal. On the other hand, what *is* an amorous and passionate love if not a "miraculous" co-identification? Out goes time; inward, into each other, go the two identities. Identificatory love is a psychoanalytical commonplace. Donne's exalted religious vocabulary of union in the midst of his radiated body heat and witty animadversions is the novelty—the kind that, in retrospect, seems a natural, inevitable flowering of the Renaissance.

But "doctrine"? Rather, a canvas painted over in sometimes the same, sometimes varying, hues. For instance, "Our two souls therefore, *which are one*," and four lines later in the same poem, "A Valediction: Forbidding Mourning," "*If they be two*, they are two so / As stiff twin compasses are two" (my italics). Not even an "or" to oil the change. Nothing is (or means to be) settled. Rather, a feeling is being interpreted. In this respect Donne is already modern.

Again, what is love? Donne's answer: a moth burning in a flame. No, a taper burning itself out. Rather, an eagle in unimaginable union with a dove. Or say a phoenix dying in flames and rising the same. Really one neutral thing. Check, check, check, check, and check. A wobbly dance, then, among possibilities, among the serially emphasized components of a complexity. As interpreted. As put forward with a fertile exuberance.

"The Canonization" defines both love and poetry by metaphor, without regard for logical consistency. Moth *and* Phoenix? Contradiction. Sonnets are love's "pretty rooms" *and* lover's "well wrought urns"? Reader, be indulgent. Again, the sonnets are hymns yet *also* the products of love's war against all that would shatter identity: the words "You . . . / Who did the whole world's soul extract, and drove, / Into the glasses of your eyes, / So made such mirrors, and such spies" fill love with a certain clamoring rage. Still, the glasses (mirrors *and* spyglasses, a typical complexification, all the more so if one adds Carey's guess that the glasses are alchemical vessels) don't shatter—a wonder if not a contradiction. These and the other metaphors and propositions enter one after the other, clash, ravish, are put out in the trash, are preserved in urns, in fertile, fertile, fertile abundance and turnover and oversupply, in utmost serious intensity, and in intractable quasi-doctrinal *play.*

Really, what Donne shows is that it doesn't matter how love is defined or even what it says. What matters is that it is expansively metaphoric. It throws out a net and captures resemblance. It's an activity, a direction, a presumption of eternity, not a doctrine. If in one sense it's a safe alienation from the world, a "hermitage" (still *another* metaphor), it's also an activity, a radiance, a tropism. And so is the poem; in its metaphoric activity, it's the right hand of love.

SOVEREIGNTY IN A LITTLE ROOM

The light that I've set out on my cabin porch has turned the undersides of the nearest cedars the whitey green of cabbage leaves. A new light on an object, or a subject, tugs at its market value.

Just so one little room, if flooded with love, can be an everywhere.

Again, love, for Donne, overmasters space. Love is the great awakener, the alchemist who turns the base matter of one state—time, or gender, or alienation—into the gold of another—space, or neutrality, or belonging. (It is somehow the same space whether it be the isolated "hermitage" or the world-displacing, if also world-colonizing, expansiveness of love.) Because it is transposed, like metaphor, identification infinitizes: love is "metaphysics." The meaning of metaphysics is that if two entities appear similar, they are the same, *one* in an ideal being whose presence is safe from both the extensivity of space and the deferrals of time.

Nothing so brings this home as the flooding over of love in a little room: "For love, all love of other sights controls, / And makes one little room, an everywhere." Here, the words *love, all love* almost separate out from the syntax in monumental, eternal completeness. And *one* rises like a swifter fish to seize the stress ahead of *lit-*, which, rhetorically, is smaller fry. *One* is indeed the sovereign miracle.

The self is made into a soul through the amatory act of unification: projection ("My face in thine eye") and introjection ("thine in mine appears") resulting in repetition ("And true plain hearts do in the faces rest"). Otherwise, dull privation and lean emptiness (as in "A Nocturnal upon St. Lucy's Day"). In *The Rest Is Silence,* Robert Watson, quoting Arthur Marotti on Donne's pain at "being a sociopolitical nonentity," empties Donne's "fragile egoism" like a box of rustling tissue after tissue.[7] Only love could draw from such nothingness a quintessence, a gift, giving and given to. The vowel in "thine eye, thine . . . mine," steadied by the gratified hum, repeats and groups as intimately as two gazes, four eyes.

"The Good Morrow" ends by displacing its space-fond, cartographic metaphor—"two . . . hemispheres / Without sharp north, without declining west"—with language drawn from alchemy:

Whatever dies, was not mixed equally;
If our two loves be one, or, thou and I
Love so alike, that none do slacken, none can die.

Balance, as in the grammatical repetition of "none do slacken, none can die," is all. Balance is the soul's proof against change, its sovereignty.

To repeat: in Donne sovereignty has two forms: co-identification and imagination's (but also intellect's) play. Effectively these are "one." Love is an act of the imagination, just as the poetic imagination, which is mainly metaphor (witness good morrows and everywheres and hemispheres and mixings), is an act of love, of mating, in the medium of linguistic signs. Co-identification is the link between love and metaphor. Kristeva, putting metaphor entirely on Eros's writing table, says that "the figure of speech is amatory" and that the lover is the subject of the metaphor: "The undeniable referential effect of [the metaphorical] process, which stems from the referent having been made ambiguous, should not conceal its subjective basis. The signifying unit (the 'sign') opens up and reveals its components: drives and sensory elements . . . —while the subject itself, in a state of loving transference, flares up from sensation to idealization."[8]

A little room, light, exclusions, others to feel superior to (in Donne, love is full of itself in both senses of the expression), the sovereign sentiment of largesse and noblesse oblige, and the no less sovereign exercise of command—these come together as effortlessly as they do winsomely in "The Sun Rising," a poem Donne didn't so much write as let write itself, write Donne. From the sleepy grumble of the opening, "Busy old fool, unruly sun," and the knocking protest of line two, "Why dost thou thus" (the expressive sputter of those three last variously similar words!), to the offense-tracing precision of "Through windows, *and* through curtains call on us" (my italics), to the whir of the little wheels of seasonal motion in the alliteration and humming nasals and purring *uh*s of "Must to thy motions lovers' seasons run," to the no less saucy counterpointed opening of the increasingly spiky "Saucy pedantic wretch," and indeed through all the remaining lines, the poem is theatrical and rhetorical perfection. It feels real.

Here time is scorned as an assortment of "rags" ("hours, days, months"), whereas love dresses (or undresses) the speaker as a king and makes of his beloved a gemmed and spicy "state," indeed "all states," the sovereign earth itself—all the world "contracted" (a nonalienated counterpart to the extracted world's soul in the bitter-postured "The Canonization"). The lover-king has grown so inwardly big that he could "eclipse" the sun's beams "with a wink." Similarly, his lover's eyes could blind the sun's. Love is more powerful than time. It colonizes space. It is all riches.

Love, moreover, rearranges ontology. The factual proves theatrical, a simulacrum; conversely, the figure proves genuine and substantive. "Princes do but play us": the speaker, playing at being all kings ("all here in one bed"), has the cheek (comedic, sublime) to charge them with playing *him*. Love plays out of its overflowing fullness. Love is real; the rest is pretend. Love is an awakening; the rest is dream (as in "The Good Morrow"). Wake up, grow up, grow titanic, get rich: fall in love.

Sovereign, again, is the love in "The Anniversary" that makes us kings even "Here upon earth, . . . and none but we / Can be such kings, nor of such subjects be; / Who is so safe as we?" Hear the ringringring of the *e*s (including the one in "kings"), balanced by the guttural comfort of the *uh*s, in "be such kings . . . none . . . we . . . be such kings . . . of such sub- . . . be." The music of a tingling-but-grounded sovereignty.

Enough of the truth of affect beams through such arrogant plays of fancy to make the reader feel, roughly four hundred years after their first swaggering arrival, complicit with, warmed by, ready to cheer, their glad-hearted self-satisfaction.

Which means that Donne has let us know what they react to: time, our passing, our unimportance.

What was of moment a few hours ago, in the scene of my writing, were the peach-and-pink clouds that, graying rapidly underneath in the dusk coming up out of nowhere, out of everything, sailed behind the green-black tops of the furthest fir trees. Valediction. Donne is the master of this moment, of the hour of departure. Why was he drawn to it?

He loved, he traveled, he parted only to return—but, more than that, he was all but preoccupied with the fragile, elemental fabric of reality. He was nothing, for all his skepticism, if not alchemical at heart. What is elemented and mixed-in-a-certain-way can be remixed, demixed, de-elemented, by even the fatal indiscretion of a tear. Donne's imagination could thrill to that catastrophic sublime—witness "A Valediction: Of Weeping." Donne was by no means set on the Automatic of Reassurance—as witness, again, "A Nocturnal upon St. Lucy's Day."

A complication arises in the genre of the valediction that would *forbid* mourning, for language itself resembles absence, elegy, loss. Of course, at the end of a century of language interrogation (under klieg lights), it's easy to overstress poetry's confinement within language that is always already solipsism or to find *b* and *y* and *e* and the rest (to echo a line of Michael Palmer's) "all speaking in the dark with their hands." But, in this case it's John Donne who initiates the worry: sonnets are not only pretty rooms but well-wrought urns. There, it is said. Language's magic is faulty. Donne had a pre-"language-game" suspicion of letters' "dark eclipses" (to take a phrase from "A Valediction: Of the Book"). Epistolary letters, not the alphabet kind. But, really, they're the twisted sheets of the same bed.

To Donne, inscriptions and their cousins—impressions, reflections, drawings—are at once the originals' extensions and absences. His mind plays—and I stress "plays"—back and forth between the two ideas, as if between megalomania and melancholy. Great is the miracle of being as original *in the copy* as in the original. And Donne has a fondness for this miracle. Thus a name scratched on a window, if it's a lover's name, and looked at by a lover, is as good as the same lover's being present, in large part, and internalized in the beloved as the name is embedded in the glass, even though all but the skeleton-name of the lover's body be somewhere else—sojourning in France, or on a warship, burning, and awaiting re-union with the three souls of the soul (rational, vital, and sentient) in a resurrection:

Then, as all my souls be
Emparadised in you, (in whom alone
I understand, and grow and see,)
The rafters of my body, bone
Being still with you, the muscle, sinew, and vein,
Which tile this house, will come again.
("A Valediction: Of my Name in the Window")

Love is a treasury of multiplication, of copresence: "Here you see me,"
the same speaker says of his incised name, "and I am you." Two meton-
ymies—his name, her reflection—to one transparent being fit:

'Tis much that glass should be
As all confessing, and through-shine as I,
'Tis more, that it shows thee to thee,
And clear reflects thee to thine eye.
But all such rules, love's magic can undo,
Here you see me, and I am you.

In this case, representations both incorporate and intermingle the origi-
nals: I am you. So says love's colonizing ontology, in playful, sportive,
wishful, but fundamentally hopeless terms.

"Hopeless" because representations' ontological transfers can make the
originals, now copy-originals, more vulnerable to destruction. The
speaker's ontological faith soon wavers—he runs through less magical
possibilities for his scritched-in name. "A Valediction: Of Weeping"
pushes the fragility of such a union-through-representation to the limit:

Let me pour forth
My tears before thy face, whilst I stay here,
For thy face coins them, and thy stamp they bear,
And by this mintage they are something worth,
For thus they be
Pregnant of thee;
Fruits of much grief they are, emblems of more,
When a tear falls, that thou falls which it bore,
So thou and I are nothing then, when on a divers shore.

Just as love encloses two beings in one swelling affect, so her face, in this
poem, rounds in his rounded tears—and nothing except want of en-
couragement keeps us from imaging his face in her tears, and his face in

her face in his tears, and so on, in a regressive series of murderous pregnancies. Emergency! How dangerous, this lover's trick of transferred identities! A mere impression thus plays havoc with ontology. Donne writes at the exact point of an imaginary physics where lives can be swept, because wept, away. No wonder he counters the flooding meter of the closing heptameter and the implications of *divers* with the protesting, singular *shore!* (Unique to the poem, the stanza form is a graph of letting go then thinking better of it, as it gives way to and pulls back from long lines. "Let me pour forth" is a brilliant, terrible beginning—its near rhyme of "pour forth," naked in its accents and incrementally breathy and unprotected by grammatical completion, is simply left gaping. And the "or" sound—a teardrop from the maiden name of Donne's wife, More, which is also mirrored entire in the poem, as others have noted—returns in *more, bore,* and *shore* at the end of the last three lines. The *r,* which appears elsewhere, also adds its gravelly atom, its sound of a vowel being ground away into worthlessness.)

Here a reflection that consists of a synecdoche (a face) is at the same time nothing less than the lover's entire and original physical being: "When a tear falls, that thou falls which it bore." In a further complication the metaphors (of minting, of pregnancy) scribble over these versions still another understanding of the tears, in figurative shorings-up of their perishability. The stamped coin seeks to coincide with the three-dimensional tear and its rounded reflected face. Love and metaphor alike flout the physical law that two or more things cannot occupy the same space at the same time. But what a crowd, sometimes, when they do. And how volatile the mixture.

Donne's feeling for condensed confusions of kind is the strongest thing about him, the necessary antidote to the scattering brightness of his mind. What I stress here is that his play with impressions (whether those of love, on tears, in windows, in mirrors, on the page) are already, at one or another pitch, evidence of separation or loss, whatever their imaginary quotient of increase.

The traveling foot of the celebrated figure of the compass in "A Valediction: Forbidding Mourning" not only draws a circle, a commonplace geometrical pattern that bears the emblematic meaning of constancy (being, as it is, homogeneous, without angular deviation, and so referred at every point back to the equidistant center), but depicts a circumference that is never, at any point, closer to its center. It's like "walking in a circle," the outline of a dark eclipse.

She—and the fixed point is of course a she (here gender makes a reentry)—is (again of course?) not aligned with inscription. The traveling foot has, as it were, briefcase, paper, pen; the fixed foot has only a stay-at-home reliability and a preoccupation with the other foot's absence, as it leans after it and hearkens (quite as if the wandering foot were indeed a speaking or writing being). Writing (like drawing) is, as such, a wandering, a crosser of distances; listening is only a leaning. The poem both forbids mourning and is, as writing, an instance of it, a circle forever distant from its invisible center. Inscription is mourning in its backfire, cross-fire phase. It assumes an absence.

THE PATHOS OF SYNECDOCHE ON THIS SIDE OF METAPHOR

Not every transfer is a happy, expansive one. The "bracelet of bright hair about the bone" in "The Relic" is famously moving not least because it figures a physical mating at once literal *and* memorial: posterotic, post-vital, posteverything except a final disintegration (*that* loss, *that* death).

The bracelet clings about the bone as if for dear life. Love is the ornament of the always-already dying flesh: it will adorn, if there is nothing else, the very bone, if there is even so much as that. The sexual imagery of encirclement is just a phantasmal echo of intercourse—on reflection, shudderingly grotesque. The *b*s in "bracelet . . . bright . . . about . . . bone" (almost evenly spread out, as they are) form a sympathetic chain. They become seriously bare and biting only with the grim phrase "about the bone," in contrast to their softening assimilation to the *r* in the positive description of a *bright bracelet*.

In all, the description has the pathos of an incomplete, an uncompletable, metaphor. Juxtaposition, not transposition. Naturalism, not miracle. Fidelity, not fusion. Synecdoche, not metaphor. Dead matter, not passionate flesh.

But none I think do there embrace.

METAPHOR AS TWINNING

Where metaphor enfolds, simile bridges—it's a gesture toward resemblance, not an enforcement of it, and so less magical, less sovereign. The comparison of lovers to a drawing compass begins as a simile—"two, . . . / As stiff twin compasses are two"—but then pushes simile aside for metaphor: "Thy soul the fixed foot, makes no show / To move, but doth, if th'other do." The effect is the more imperial in that punctuation doesn't make "the fixed foot" an appositive. It is true that, in the rhetorical draft created by the preceding simile, "thy soul *as* the fixed foot" is a legitimate inference. But as we read on, even the spectral *as* disappears. The lovers *are* the compass, the compass *is* the lovers—without remainder. Take a knife to the lines, and still you can't separate these components. If the author himself does it for you in the final stanza with "Such wilt thou be to me, who must / Like th' other foot, obliquely run," the concessionary mechanism of the word *like,* a too-flimsy spring, pops out again (as after "Like gold to airy thinness beat"), and a sovereign identification closes the poem: "Thy firmness makes my circle just."

Donne's lovers all but conduct their lives in figures: synecdoches, metonymies, similes, metaphors. Reality is such as to facilitate a "vicissitudinary transmutation," in Donne's sumptuous Latinate mouthful: "Ayre condensed becomes water, . . . And Ayre rarified becomes fire,"[9] and a fact condensed becomes a metaphor, and a fact rarefied becomes a metonymy, or a synecdoche, or a simile.

The compass image of a twinning (the two legs kept relative to one another by the "joint" of the pivot) is doubled by the comparison itself, another twinning—tenor and vehicle being the legs of a single figure. In metaphor the tenor is the fixed foot, and the vehicle travels. I illustrate *x* by reaching over here for *y;* my reach is an airy expansion, a wandering, an adventure. Metaphor exists for the sake of freer imaginative movement, which means a more kinetic life for *x,* as also for *y.* Why are we here? To move. Love agrees: "Love . . . / Always is to joy inclin'd, / Lawless wing'd & unconfin'd, / And breaks all chains from every mind" (Blake). So metaphor is as "natural" a figure for the theme of twinned souls as the compass itself is for metaphor and, of course, love.

Sensing much or all of this, and strategically staging the metaphor, in any case, as a pattern for remaining composed despite a parting, Donne conducts his lesson-by-metaphor with an almost perfect sobriety, a crystalline technical control. Emulating Aristotelian scientificity, he performs a homely demonstration—disarming, soothing—of a sacred mystery. The compass metaphor is antisentimental and antisublime; its mind is pure geometry. The much-labored Renaissance theme of constancy is thus almost comically, almost absurdly, defamiliarized, but with so charming an aptness, all told, that the sublime enters in, sideways, as astonishment. Classically cool, the comparison has all its wits, all Donne's wits, about it. Refusing to get drunk, it lays an engineering finger to its brow.

All the same, looked at closely, the metaphor behaves willfully; it gets its own way. Like a compass with a loose pivot, it opens up overfreely, escapes logic's perfect control. Consider: when one foot of the compass "obliquely runs," it may stop at a certain point and draw a circle; but a traveling man, if he doesn't circle the whole earth, is more likely simply to return, obliquely. Emblematically apt and pat, and very pretty to imagine, but fanciful as "narrative," the figure comes in as an excess, a deviation, a bonus. Here the imagination seems to say, "Let *figure*—whether geometrical or rhetorical—have its day. Love, after all, is itself a happy surplus." (Arnold Stein notes of the Elizabethan concept of wit "the breadth and depth of its tolerance of the imaginative, in its willingness to entertain fictions as an expression of the joyous energy of the serious mind."[10] One might more truly say the energy of the joyous mind.) The compass thus rebels against its utilitarian role. It behaves for a moment, then goes whee in a circle. The circle, of course, justifies itself instantly, with emblematic aplomb. How readily it fools us! The imaginative act of transmuting souls into compass feet—which is irrational to begin with, like a joke, an intoxicated confusion of kind—so relishes its momentum that it goes on past its initial idea and is for a moment positively atwirl.

Even so, "A Valediction: Forbidding Mourning" is, in its entirety, unforced and exquisitely felt, kindness itself in tone. It's free of Donne's occasional busyness—of persuasion, bedazzlement, combat, effort to core or score. Although seven of the nine stanzas develop independent comparisons, the poem floats its figures like skiffs on which the poem itself floats. They are the lightest, most gracious things in the world.

LOVE AS METAPHORICS, METAPHOR AS AMOROUSNESS

In the first of the two climactic comparisons in "A Valediction: Forbidding Mourning," a love is being beaten:

> Our two souls therefore, which are one,
> Though I must go, endure not yet
> A breach, but an expansion,
> Like gold to airy thinness beat.

If the image of a beating isn't mourning, it's at least a suppressed cry of anguish, masochism muffled by the insensate condition of the gold. One could fancy that "breach" is kept from blasting the love by the "reach" and "each" it encloses like circuit breakers. Of course, the *jouissance* of a pounding, as well as the experience of a vanishing luster, is softened by the departure's association with the metal sacred to alchemy. (Of help, too, are the stabilizing hums in "expansion" and "thinness" and the bridging continuity over the invisible "breach" line between metrical units of both "airy" and "thinness," two in a row, running.) Where does gold, so perfect, so ductile, go when it goes away from itself? You can guess. You must make yourself as the golden stone, says the fifteenth-century *Book of the Holy Triplicity*, if you want to enter the pure heaven. In fact, or so notes the physicist David Deutsch in *The Fabric of Reality*, gold you can stick your hand through is no longer gold. When the atoms "are sufficiently far apart it becomes misleading to think of them as forming a continuous sheet."[11] The chemical "proof" of Donne's figure—the novelty of using science to validate metaphysics—is actually carried into realms of fantasy. The figure is gorgeously extravagant. Amorous. An act of faith.

Love spends metaphor like a spider's rappelling filament from its own same-as-other bowels. Again, "the literary experience," as Kristeva puts it, "stands revealed as an essentially amorous experience, unstabilizing the same through its identification with the other."[12] Donne's speaker at once expands and thins himself as "subject" by projecting his experience in terms of, onto the image of, and effectively into the "substance" of another element, until the physical malleability of the gold upstages the infinite expansiveness of the soul of love. The figure creates a tertium quid that's constrained by neither of its two constituents but is, instead, a glowing, indefinite back-and-forth movement between them, a vibration. Its miracle is that it exists, dazzlingly, nowhere but in the movement of transference. This is what makes it amatory. Love and metaphor alike are motions. From same into same-and-other, along a golden and diffuse path called idealization. "Metaphor as damaging the Single meaning, as symptom of its toppling over into infinity, is . . . the very discourse of love."[13] The stakes of metaphor, like those of love, lie in surpassing finitude without leaving a single atom of one's condition in this world, just as the beaten gold becomes invisible without ceasing to be a material thing.

Nothing so assures us that the speaker is in love as the inspired one-yet-two of the meaning of his simile, its final undecidability (as concrete image, as metaphysics). Simile and metaphor are ecstasies of destabilization. *Being like* is neither *being* nor *nonbeing; it's being in play,* stereoscopic ontology.

AIRINESS

Airiness is again a physical crux in the curious, dazzling, not altogether trustworthy and satisfactory poem "Air and Angels." If you take the ideal of the feminine and call it an angel, and the physical at its purest and call it air, and condense the angel-she into body-air, what do you have? The inferiority of women's love to men's, says the poem at the end, suddenly replacing the swan with an ugly duckling.

At first, the ideal, invisibly inhabiting space, knocks on the air but is not admitted:

> Twice or thrice had I loved thee,
> Before I knew thy face or name;
> So in a voice, so in a shapeless flame,
> Angels affect us oft, and worshipped be;
>   Still when, to where thou wert, I came,
> Some lovely glorious nothing I did see.

In this ravishing half of the first stanza—quick, excited, supple with its changing line lengths—angels are desire's presumed, required, and elusive othernesses. Metaphor or metaphysics? Perhaps Donne, giddy with the juggled theories of the times, could hardly tell. The play between the two possibilities is infinite and undecided. The game is to ride the back of the metaphor toward the wonder of metaphysics; to have it all, thrill and safety net, at once. The great moment in the lines is, of course, the par-adoxical—disappointed, ecstatic—report, "Some lovely glorious nothing I did see." (The way "Some" throws itself on the three strong stresses that start off the next three words, "lovely glorious nothing," where the *o* of *lovely* returns, infatuate, in *nothing* is utterly winning.) To see so little yet see so much. Something glorious; some nothing. The writing quivers at the loveliest edge of miracle.

Love is the soul's "child" (second metaphor) and, like its parent, needs a body. Materialized, however, the angel overbalances even the speaker's remarkable capacity for admiration: "I saw, I had love's pinnace [this almost says penis, and penis is almost apropos] overfraught":

> Every thy hair for love to work upon
> Is much too much, some fitter must be sought;
>   For, nor in nothing, nor in things
> Extreme, and scatt'ring bright, can love inhere.

So the speaker needs something less dazzling to focus and stabilize his love. What could that be? The answer is her love for him, and not because it resembles his but because it is a lesser thing than either her body or his love. Unbedazzling. Prose to his poetry:

> So thy love may be my love's sphere;
>   Just such disparity
> As is 'twixt air and angels' purity,
> 'Twixt women's love, and men's will ever be.

Effectively, then, the speaker reverses the arrangement: he is as the angel, and she as the air an angel wears in order to be visible. His love gives her a body, which is like overbright air; and, in an asymmetrical exchange, her love gives his love "body," which is steadying because like ordinary air. Whatever the "nothing" of her starting point, she thus ends up identified with body. And he would have her so: "what thou wert . . . I bid love ask," he says, asking it of a love already more his than hers. In all, the slithery scheme of propositions proceeds as follows: (1) she is without body, a veritable angel; (2) her body (brought about by his love) is like an angel dressed in air; (3) his love is like an angel that dresses her soul in air, making it a body; (4) her love, by contrast, is not an angel, but a lesser item than either her body or his love.

The conclusion is, then, a burst of recovered sovereignty. Until he found its amatory point of poise, the speaker was too puzzled, too "overfraught," to be self-enjoying. But, a solution found, he's not only reassured but self-congratulatory. Does a poem that begins as the most exquisite of meditations on the presence/absence of ideality in love really end, then, as a male boast? Is this any way to woo? Is the woman expected to laugh and say, *Touché?* Or perhaps respond with the wit of a combative Shakespearean heroine? If Donne had wanted the poem to be a piece of cleverness at women's expense, why didn't he remember to make it playful at the start, instead of heart-stoppingly beautiful? And why are the final lines, if playful at all, so callous seeming, so mocking a coup? Donne, one had thought, was a wit, not a brute.

Even allowing for the usual buzzing-fly factor of ambiguity, the final lines strike me as primarily not a jeu d'esprit but a pitiless exercise in cynical lucidity. Although the angel metaphor first seems to posit the woman as a soul, the end of the poem effectively cancels out the soul in her. Let us turn at this point to Donne's queasily slithering questionings in problem 7 of *Paradoxes and Problems,* which is entitled "Why Hath the Common Opinion Afforded Women Souls?"; with its now-conspicuous omission of a *Not* before *Afforded,* it never once considers the answer: because, like men, they have them. What a dizzying round of speculations, instead, none of them generous or even fair: for instance, "do we, in that easiness and prodigality wherein we daily lose our own souls, allow souls to we care not whom, and so labour to persuade ourselves that since a woman hath a soul, a soul is no great matter? Or do we but lend them souls?"[14] Dissonant as this piece of male entertainment is with the sweet meeting and mingling of souls in, say, "The Ecstasy," it is nonetheless of a piece with the final insult to women in "Air and Angels." Donne's poem exposes the ego mechanics of masculine idealizations of women, but its lucidity isn't aimed against itself.

HOW ARE EYES LIKE BUTTONS?

What we see in "Air and Angels," as in so many of the songs and sonnets, is the negotiation in Donne between two forms of *jouissance,* phallic and feminine. The *jouissance* of mystics, Lacan says, is feminine: turned toward infinity and the inexpressible. Donne the mystic needs, so the man in him urges, the balance and ballast of phallic *jouissance* as well, the *jouissance* linked with the body and with time (the penis rises and falls). The two Donnes often meet together and reason within the precincts of the poem. The negotiations require all his insight, cleverness, and rhetoric. Donne's speakers want a good lay but with nothing less than a brightness that condenses from the metaphysical air.

I've taken the metaphor of "negotiation," of course, from "The Ecstasy." Here the feminine or mystic Donne is in beautiful ascendance. The description of the ecstasy of the mingling of two souls into an abler one is sustained with extraordinary brilliance, an amazing mingling in itself of analytical description and exquisite evocation of feeling. But to this the phallic boy, if remaining super cool, adds his honeyed quota of argument and persuasion. He's even more exhibitionist than usual, indulging, as he does, the fancy that some passer-by may hear his "dialogue of one"— speech, after all, is the speaker's present potency—and "mark" (see) their ecstasy and their lovemaking, should he succeed in persuading the lady to enter into it. He might almost be addressing the imaginary listener, man to man. But in fact his immediate forensic focus remains the lady.

The poem is not least interesting for the tricky ambiguity of its many comparisons, which moved T. S. Eliot to pick quarrels with them. The figures are largely in the hands of the phallic youth, even as the mystic discourses loftily. They complicate the surface argument. Caught as they are in a teacherish poem, they seem uncertain of their right to play. Yet of course they do. Figures always manage to get in some play.

Donne first delineates and celebrates a mutual gaze that "sees" in the other the unutterable ideal. Subject and object become as elevated as they are confused, lost in an amatory no-space and no-time. But already at the beginning of the poem, a pagan, sensual strain introduces a note of unsatisfied physicality.

The two lovers are seated on a flowery bank, as by a riverside. "Our hands were firmly cemented," says the speaker,

> With a fast balm, which thence did spring,
> Our eye-beams twisted, and did thread
>   Our eyes, upon one double string;
>
> So to' intergraft our hands, as yet
>   Was all the means to make us one,
> And pictures in our eyes to get
>   Was all our propagation.

Impatience can be detected in the expression "as yet" ("as yet / Was all the means") and even in the begrudging use of *all* ("all the means"), as in "that's all there was." But the metaphors, too, are giveaways. John Carey traces "cemented" to Paracelsus and the alchemical process by which solids penetrate one another at high temperatures. But the lack of penetration is really the speaker's complaint: this "cement" is a tendentious hyperbole for plain sweat, and "balm," like "cement," tells of a frustrated desire for a glued-together sweetness along the whole length of the body. ("As souls unbodied, bodies unclothed must be, / To taste whole joys," Donne writes in "To His Mistress Going to Bed.") Eliot says of the next quatrain that "the blemish . . . is first, that the figure of the hands as cemented is not left to itself, but is rubbed over by the more complicated image of grafting," but this is perhaps to miss the point: the violent sexual "cut" of an engrafting is precisely what hasn't been attained "as yet."[15] The second figure seeks to surpass, if not to rub out, the first. The situation is this: Donne is overlaying on the description of a spiritual ecstasy a grumble about its exclusion, as yet, of a sensational ecstasy.

As for the braided eye-beams, so physically uncomfortable an image to imagine the eyes entering into, they anticipate the caught-together, painful pleasure of sexual intercourse. The eye, said a theory of the time, puts out beams for contact. But to be strung together in this optical-material fashion, with eye-buttons that don't connect up directly with a hole in the beloved, is to be strung along, to be martyred for love. "The threading of the eyes like buttons on a double thread," Eliot elaborates, "not only fails to render the sense of losing oneself in an ecstasy of gazing into the eyes of a loved person, it actually aggravates the difficulty of finding out what it is all about." But Donne's unsightly image (deliberately so, no doubt, given that Donne was all smoothness when he chose to be) betrays the speaker's unease with being synecdoched into a gaze; it is psychologically revelatory. The amatory trance keeps the libido on a tight (a too tight?) rein. The politics of Donne's metaphor is sexual and disgruntled. There's something textbookish about Donne's presentation of the ecstasy—as theory, illustration, ideal—and the body "naturally" lobbies against it. Its protest, heard in the figures, is instructive in a different way.

The other thematically sensitive comparison comes in a later stanza, where the subject is still the "new," the "abler" soul mixed from the already "mixed souls" of the two lovers. But the incomplete articulation of the comparison (an unconscious maneuver?) leaves it transmissible to the body as well:

A single violet transplant,
    The strength, the colour, and the size,
(All which before was poor, and scant,)
    Redoubles still, and multiplies.

When love, with one another so
    Interinanimates two souls,
That abler soul, which thence doth flow,
    Defects of loneliness controls.

Here, then, is the quietest of replantings of the literal, frankly pagan violet in stanza one:

Where, like a pillow on a bed,
    A pregnant bank swelled up, to rest
The violet's reclining head,
    Sat we two, one another's best.

The transfer is two-edged: on the one hand, the violet is uprooted and turned into a figure in the service of elucidating a soul-passion; on the other, this only shows that the flower—which is, after all, the sexual organ of the plant—is still on the speaker's mind, despite the sway of his soul-trance. The pagan setting of the poem would sooner be taken up by the soul than altogether forgotten. No, it will not be forgotten.

In this poem Donne's speaker would both be above nature and sitting on its bank. Its pregnant bank. Eliot, again, may have missed the point. He called the opening imagery one of the most hideous mixed figures of speech in the language. To compare a

> bank to a pillow (it is surely superfluous to add "on a bed" since a pillow may be presumed to have much the same shape wherever it be disposed) does neither dignify nor elucidate. . . . Having already learned that the bank was shaped like a pillow, we do not require to be told that it was pregnant, unless an earthquake was preparing, which was not the case.

"May be presumed," "does neither dignify nor elucidate," "we do not require to be told"—stuffy phrases. What we are "required" to see is really that the pillow is the local, topping mound on an already swollen bank; that however sexy it may look in itself, a pillow is sexier still on a bed; and that such a swelling may speak of the great order of organic fertility. "Pillow . . . bed," "pregnant bank"—the writing is alliteratively kissy with the sexuality Eliot's temperament wished to deny.

It is even dangerously seductive, what with its image-coils and licks of the syllabic tongue (for instance, the long *i* in "Reclining" that pulls the *i* in "violet" toward its deep-throat hum). This poet could talk the clothes off of almost anyone—never mind that he said he sang "not, Siren-like, to tempt" but was "harsh." Here nature's line is—naturally—a swell, a curve, a wave or rise and fall. By contrast, the ecstasy is a horizontal negotiation in mid-air ("Our souls, / . . . hung 'twixt her, and me"; "Our eye-beams . . . did thread / Our eyes"), even as the lovers' bodies lie like effigies on a tomb, in a flat-line death pose:

And whilst our souls negotiate there,
    We like sepulchral statues lay;
All day, the same our postures were,
    And we said nothing, all the day.

To dwell for a moment on these lines: what do the souls, which are later said to mean and speak the same and to be one "abler soul," have to negotiate? It must be the unstated topic of what their union stands to gain or lose by including the sexual body. (Latent here, perhaps, is the period cliché of the woman who has to be talked out of her regard for virtue.) Meanwhile the writing mutters against the delay. I find the last two syllables of "sepulchral" hard to enunciate. *Pul-* doesn't pull itself into *-chral.* The sound dies before *chral* all but crawls out of the hiatus. Almost the word doesn't want to be got through (any more than one wants to enter the real thing). The *ls* encourage a pronunciation that half buries the vowel. The internal rhyme, centered in the awkward *ul* sound, fails of harmony. The fuller sound of the following *all* brings us back, so to speak, into the daylight. But the inverted word order in "All day, the same our postures were" comments on the unnaturalness of this still-postured state.

Then, too, ambivalence reigns in the difference between "All day" and "all the day." The latter, shaking off the spondaic drone of "All day," breathing more freely in its article, and concluding a natural word order, is a winning resolution to the uneasiness of an emptied chronos conveyed by "All day."

There's no such alienation from natural time, from swells, circles, and arcs, in stanza one, where nature seems to say, "Lovers, do you see? Let the violet be your example. Go to bed in my immediate rhythms." The syntax folds, tucks, includes. It makes a pillowing parenthetical space for "like a pillow on a bed," then climaxes the bank's swelling with a caesura ("swelled up, to rest"), a moment-after comma, cut-breathed like the "swel'd" of the original edition. Then "Sat," coming as it does in an emphatic position, makes to plant and green the lovers on the bank. Here the inverted word order ("Sat we two") produces an all but erotic jolt.

The implications of the violet's early placement are finally developed when the speaker argues for the body's erotic and orgasmic inclusion in the soul's union:

> But O alas, so long, so far
>   Our bodies why do we forbear?
> They are ours, though they are not we, we are
>   The intelligences, they the sphere.
>
> We owe them thanks, because they thus,
>   Did us, to us, at first convey,
> Yielded their forces, sense, to us,
>   Nor are dross to us, but allay.

His tone is patronizing—"We owe them thanks"!—but at least and at last he makes a pitch. Does he acknowledge, though, the temporal problem of the body? He doesn't explain how the body's inevitable experience of anticlimax can keep from dragging the ecstasy back into time. Not that he posits an unending ecstasy. But midway through the poem he changes from past to present tense, as if to defend the ecstasy from passing.

Physical love is not altogether acknowledged as the violet that dies. Further, it is reduced, even as it is elevated, to serving as a textbook illustration of a love generous enough to include the body. Enter a stranger to the margins of the scene, so as to give the occasion the significance of an instruction. But if "one such as we," does he really need to read in the "book" of their sexual intercourse that the "body" is Love's book, disclosing "Love's mysteries"? Is voyeurism a necessary complement to love-making, a securing of its lessons? Rather, the sexual act, in being observed and read as a teaching, is preserved from its mere physical transiency, its character of ending in itself, like the violets that blow.

In all, though utterly remarkable, "The Ecstasy" isn't Donne at his sovereign best. Didacticism is never sovereign. The poem doesn't detach itself from a spiritual accounting of cost.

WHAT DONNE EXEMPLIFIES

Donne claimed for himself more of the free space of imaginative and emotional joy and play than almost any other poet has done. It helped that the age presented a potpourri of amorous possibilities. Donne's marital eroticism rises and shines between the darkness of Greek love and of modern love (Freud's, Duras's), two variants of the same bitterness. (In the Greek poets, Anne Carson notes, love exposes "a self not known before and now disclosed by the lack of it—by pain, by a hole, bitterly.")[16] For a blessed moment in the seventeenth century it was possible to think of love not as a melting threat but as the dearest form of sovereignty. Deftly, Donne turned the Renaissance hesitation between the Ovidian treasury of antiquity and the legacies of Platonic and Christian metaphysics, not to mention alchemy, which may date back to Egypt, into an opportunity to flit, parry, and braid—to dance among alternatives. Above all he celebrates the capacity for a sovereign joy, free of the destructiveness that Lacan detects in the wilder reaches of *jouissance*. If it was left to Donne's contemporary, Descartes—as Karl Lowith has said—to free "the man who knows about himself from the authority of the ecclesiastical bond,"[17] Donne so freed and knew himself in the *Songs and Sonnets*.

Donne is the poet as the athlete—almost the clown—of erotic wit. In his work soul and body hang in the balance. Love stands breathless, waiting to know how much it can include, what its makeup will be. But, really, it has a deep assurance of its own, and this is what frees the poems to play. Not everything depends on the naked heart thinking solemnly. Aesthetics is freedom or it is nothing.

Donne the negotiator. The mediator. Surrounding and between. Agile. The power broker. Unbroken. Not anguished. Not modern. Sportive, rather. Dazzlingly competent. In charge.

Distanced from us.

Immediate.

Superior.

NOTES

1. Jonathan F. S. Post, *English Lyric Poetry: The Early Seventeenth Century* (London: Routledge, 1999), 2.

2. Georges Bataille, *The Accursed Share* (New York: Zone Books, 1991), 3: 222.

3. Quoted in Johan Huizinga, *Homo Ludens: A Study in the Play Element in Culture* (1938; repr., Boston: Beacon Press, 1950), 19.

4. All quotations from Donne's poetry are from *John Donne: Selections,* ed. John Carey (New York: Oxford University Press, 1990).

5. William Empson, *Essays on Renaissance Literature,* ed. John Haffenden (Cambridge: Cambridge University Press, 1993), 1:92.

6. Julia Kristeva, *Tales of Love,* trans. Leon S. Roudiez (New York: Columbia University Press, 1987), 282.

7. Robert N. Watson, *The Rest Is Silence: Death as Annihilation in the English Renaissance* (Berkeley: University of California Press, 1994), 159.

8. Kristeva, *Tales of Love,* 91, 275.

9. Quoted in John Carey, *John Donne: Life, Mind, and Art* (New York: Oxford University Press, 1980), 174.

10. Arnold Stein, *John Donne's Lyrics: The Eloquence of Action* (Minneapolis: University of Minnesota Press, 1962), 98.

11. David Deutsch, *The Fabric of Reality: The Science of Parallel Universes—and Its Implications* (New York: Allen Lane/Penguin Press, 1997), 35.

12. Kristeva, *Tales of Love,* 279.

13. Ibid., 336.

14. Carey, *Selections,* 141.

15. T. S. Eliot, *The Varieties of Metaphysical Poetry,* ed. Ronald Schuchard

(New York: Harcourt, 1993). For this and the following quotations from Eliot on "The Ecstasy," see 109–10.

16. Anne Carson, *Eros: The Bittersweet* (Princeton: Princeton University Press, 1986), 66.

17. Karl Lowith, *Nietzsche's Philosophy of the Eternal Recurrence of the Same*, trans. J. Harvey Lomax (Berkeley: University of California Press, 1997), 138.

SIX

Anomaly, Conundrum, Thy-Will-Be-Done

On the Poetry of George Herbert

CARL PHILLIPS

But I am lost in flesh, whose sugared lies
  Still mock me, and grow bold:
Sure thou didst put a mind there, if I could
  Find where it lies.

"DULLNESS" (21–24)

To have my aim, and yet to be
Further from it than when I bent my bow.

"THE CROSS" (25–26)

HE SEEMED TO ME, AT FIRST, SUBVERSIVE. *I was younger then. Of George
Herbert, what I knew was he'd been a priest. Of devotion, what I imagined
was: how difficult can it be? Only cross belief with enough discipline—
  Also honesty—love—somewhere, figuring . . .
  About the flesh, I understood as much as about ambition: truly, nothing at
all.*

The Temple, comprising essentially all of Herbert's poems, seems increas-
ingly a private record, even as the prose work *The Country Parson* was
intended—for himself as much as for others—to be a publicly available
instructional work: "a complete pastoral," as Herbert puts it in his note

to the reader.[1] In the prose we are told that the parson "condescends to human frailties both in himself and others" (chap. 27) and that

> the parson, having studied and mastered all his lusts and affections within, and the whole army of temptations without, hath ever so many sermons ready penned, as he hath victories. And it fares in this as it doth in physic: he that hath been sick of a consumption, and knows what recovered him, is a physician so far as he meets with the same disease and temper; and can much better and particularly do it, than he that is generally learned, and was never sick. (chap. 33)

Thus, the more objective stance of the purposefully didactic prose. It is in the poetry, however, that we see the frailty of the pastor—of, finally, any individual—laid bare, that we see him engaged in the very wrestling from which he will emerge experienced (not just "generally learned") and will consequently give to the poems themselves a degree of earnestness that I find in the work of no other seventeenth-century poet.

What becomes clear in the prose is that Herbert believes that the pastor should have suffered bouts of affliction but that he is not to advertise such moments; rather, the fact of the pastor's private experience, to the extent that it is evident at all, will be most obvious in the quality of the guidance and wisdom he is able to extend to his parishioners. That is, there is a distinction in the prose work between Herbert's era and our own, in which the exposure of our public figures' private flaws would seem to endear us all the more to them. By the above logic the poems of *The Temple*—in showing the would-be devoted sometimes wrestling with, sometimes all but yielding to, and sometimes admitting to *having* yielded to temptation, and in capturing the same speaker unrepentantly railing against God or, presumably as blasphemous, inquiring into and challenging the fairness of God's ways—read as a private record. This record suggests in its overall design less an author who has in mind the best way to please and thereby win a readership than one intrigued by the irregular, unpredictable shifts of heart and mind that are what it is to be human. As with the best of the lasting writers (just now Dickinson and Hopkins come to mind), what takes its origin in personal experience becomes a touchstone for human experience more generally. And it is in this regard that I tend to agree with Anthony Hecht and others who have described Herbert as a confessional poet. He *is*—both in what approximates the liturgical sense of that word (the Reformation having made confession technically unavailable for Protestants) and in the sense that was celebrated as a seemingly new literary movement three centuries later. Herbert's poems seem written *toward* a need to understand, for *himself,* the ways of God and how they figured into his own life; they are an honest and, to a large extent, self-interested inquiry into questions whose answers did not entirely accord with personal experience. In the course, however, of exploring these questions, their answers, and the further questions that the answers raise, Herbert produces the poetry that is not only revelatory of individual struggle but remains, as well, powerfully relevant to human experience today.

Why affliction?—Why, inevitably, our suffering? These are questions Herbert asks repeatedly in *The Temple,* even as he—characteristically—knows that the answers are not so far from hand; the problem, rather, is in their being at best fickle comforters.

Looking at *The Church,* the central part of *The Temple* (and ignoring the two book-ending parts, each a single poem—"The Church-Porch" and "The Church Militant," respectively [which, as Louis Martz has pointed out, "seem rather imposed on either side than organically related to the whole," xxv]), it is worth noting that Herbert opens the main portion with "The Altar," then immediately follows it with "The Sacrifice," a poem (not coincidentally, the longest of Herbert's poems, at 252 lines) that details the event that makes the altar so significant to Christian thought, that is, Christ's crucifixion. The next eight poems all meditate on both the crucifixion and what man's response should be to it:

> Then for thy passion—I will do for that—
>   Alas, my God, I know not what.
>   (*"The Thanksgiving," 49–50*)

> I have considered it, and find
> There is no dealing with thy mighty passion:
> For though I die for thee, I am behind.
>   (*"The Reprisal," 1–3*)

> O my chief good,
> How shall I measure out thy blood?

How shall I count what thee befell,
  And each grief tell?
            ("*Good Friday*," *1–4*)

Clearly, Herbert means to suggest that it is imperative we remember the passion of Christ adequately; we are duty bound to respond, inasmuch as it is by the death of Christ for humanity that humanity has access to salvation. But how to respond? One way is by seeing Christ as a model for imitation; this includes approximating, as much as we can, the very affliction that Christ suffered. In so doing we more worthily enjoy the resurrection that Christ won for us:

                With thee
            Let me combine
        And feel this day thy victory:
        For, if I imp my wing on thine,
    Affliction shall advance the flight in me.
                ("*Easter-wings*," *16–20*)

Another justification for affliction is related to why sin is necessary, a fact that emerges when we look at two poems that appear one after the other and, as a pair, present an important aspect of Herbert's thought. First, the poems:

Mattens

    I cannot ope mine eyes,
  But thou art ready there to catch
  My morning-soul and sacrifice:
Then we must needs for that day make a match.

    My God, what is a heart?
  Silver, or gold, or precious stone,
  Or star, or rainbow, or a part
Of all these things, or all of them in one?

    My God, what is a heart,
  That thou shouldst it so eye, and woo,
  Pouring upon it all thy art,
As if that thou hadst nothing else to do?

    Indeed man's whole estate
  Amounts (and richly) to serve thee:
  He did not heav'n and earth create,
Yet studies them, not him by whom they be.

Teach me thy love to know;
That this new light, which now I see,
May both the work and workman show:
Then by a sun-beam I will climb to thee.

Sin (II)
O that I could a sin once see!
We paint the devil foul, yet he
Hath some good in him, all agree.
Sin is flat opposite to th' Almighty, seeing
It wants the good of *virtue,* and of *being.*

But God more care of us hath had:
If apparitions make us sad,
By sight of sin we should grow mad.
Yet as in sleep we see foul death, and live:
So devils are our sins in perspective.

In "Mattens" Herbert says that despite the many blessings provided by God (as celebrated in stanzas 1–3), man chooses—or has, as an empirical creature, no other choice—to study not the invisible creator but his more immediately knowable, because visible, creations. Having said that, Herbert goes on to ask that God himself be made as visible as his creation— "May both the work and workman show"—and that the visible be further rendered into something tangible—"Then by a sun-beam I will climb to thee"—an unlikely event and one that, given the earlier stanzas of the poem, Herbert already knows to be inappropriate to wish for. Where, after all, is faith?

Equally unseeable, says the next poem, is sin, which Herbert would also have be made visible, until reaching the conclusion that "devils are our sins in perspective." Even as devils offer a perspective by which to understand sin, so does the poem on sin offer a perspective on the subject matter of "Mattens," namely, God's blessings. This is why sin is necessary and—to return to the original discussion—it is an explanation for the existence of affliction in our lives: how better, Herbert would ask, to understand salvation (by which we are to be released from affliction) than by affliction itself, affliction being a modified version of salvation's opposite, damnation? And again, sin provides the perspective by which to know, via our own affliction, the greater affliction of Christ ("like stones [sins] make / His blood's sweet current much more loud to be," Herbert says in "Church-lock and Key," 11–12).

Thus, the rationale. But reasoning notwithstanding, there remain for Herbert two difficulties with affliction. One is that affliction is ultimately inadequate when it comes to knowing Christ's affliction in its entirety. For not least of the distinctions between Christ and natural humanity is that it is via sin that persons are subject to affliction (beginning with Original Sin); Christ suffers in a state of sinlessness. As Herbert puts it, "I am behind," by which I take him to mean that human beings, in their efforts to imitate Christ, are at an insurmountable disadvantage from the start; all of those efforts, therefore, will necessarily fall short.

The second problem with affliction is less sophisticated but no less true: namely, affliction doesn't feel good.

In "The Windows" Herbert describes humanity as "a brittle crazy glass" (2)—by "crazy," meaning cracked, flawed. We are also told, however, in "Repentance," that "Fractures well cured make us more strong" (36). In light of what Herbert says about affliction, sin, and their places in our lives, it seems reasonable to understand by this glass metaphor that sins— and the afflictions we suffer as a consequence of sin—can be ultimately good for us. If we are bettered by sin—made "more strong"—can't there be made an argument for indulging in sin, the more thoroughly to know the blessings of God? How can it be that we are made better by the very sins that we are instructed to rail against? Is it true that we are so bettered, or is this the only recourse, when it comes to thinking about the matter—given that, for the Herbertian Christian, sin is as inevitable as our yielding to it, as is our consequent suffering for having yielded? Not the least aspect of Herbert that wins for him my allegiance and trust—and makes him a distinctly earnest poet among his contemporaries whose work too often can seem mere flourish—is his silence in the wake of these questions.

How often it is that Herbert's poems will on one level argue—and persuasively—against the very arguments they no less persuasively put forward on a more immediate level. The poem "Justice (I)" can be seen, in terms of its form and rhyme, as a balance or set of scales, in which the weights are God and humanity:

Justice (I)

    I cannot skill of these thy ways.
Lord, thou didst make me, yet thou woundest me;
Lord, thou dost wound me, yet thou dost relieve me:
Lord, thou relievest, yet I die by thee:
Lord, thou dost kill me, yet thou dost reprieve me.
    But when I mark my life and praise,
    Thy justice me most fitly pays:
For, I do praise thee, yet I praise thee not:
My prayers mean thee, yet my prayers stray:
I would do well, yet sin the hand hath got:
My soul doth love thee, yet it loves delay.
    I cannot skill of these my ways.

An inability to understand God in line 1 is by line 12 replaced with the confession (admission?) that the speaker does not understand his *own* ways; the implication is that the correct gesture, on our part, is not to attempt to understand God, not to question God's ways, but to consider what—in asking that God justify himself—is being said about our own inadequacies, about our presumption and arrogance. The notion that God is finally superior to—and not answerable to—our understanding is conveyed in the respective rhyme schemes of the two longer-lined "quatrains" that serve as internal frame for the poem. In lines 2–5, which address God's response to the speaker, the rhyme scheme is *a-a-a-a*, the single rhyme suggestive of solidity, that which is unwavering, fixed—as consolidated in its tonal position as in its strength. Lines 8–11, which examine the speaker's responses to God, display a *b-c-b-c* rhyme scheme. If the earlier quatrain gains its strength from its sustaining a single note, as it were, then the second quatrain is arguably more suggestive of wavering, of straying, of suffering a weakness because of a lack of comparative unity of sound. In short, the poem can be said to argue—on the level both of content and of the rhymes by which that content is conveyed—that human beings are inferior to God and are shown to be all the more so by their reluctance to acknowledge their subordination to God.

However, can't we also say that a rhyme scheme of *a-a-a-a* is finally monotonous, redundant, unimaginative, oppressive in its lack of tonal variation and, accordingly, sophistication? By this logic, isn't a *b-c-b-c* scheme more melodic, more advanced because more varied?

If the poem is a scale, then, who tips it? God or humanity?

"Justice (I)" is one of many Herbert poems whose ambiguity deepens with each reading. There are, as well, many poems that deliberately do not progress forward—that is, they begin in a moment of despair or of confusion and end in a similar moment. Or perhaps it is more accurate to say that these poems have as their trajectory the trajectory of prayer, which is unidirectional and upward (a "reversèd thunder," "Prayer [I]," 6)—any return, in the form of answer (as, again, with prayer) happens in response to, which is to say *outside of,* the poem. What is being withheld is the easy resolution that a less reflective or more arrogant poet would be quick to offer. In not resolving the questions that arise, Herbert gains more authority, inasmuch as he seems to say the most honest thing to be said about the conundrum of God and humanity—in short, that conundrum is the fact: God punishes and rewards, as human beings both win and fall from grace; and the line between reward and punishment, between plummet and ascent, is decidedly blurred. This is everywhere apparent in *The Temple,* whose poems move with relentless accuracy to the irregular strophe of the human spirit, which is to say, to the rhythm of all our human strengths and weaknesses. In *The Country Parson* Herbert speaks of "a double state of a Christian even in this life, the one military, the other peaceable. The military is, when we are assaulted with temptations either within or from without. The peaceable is, when the Devil for a time leaves us, as he did our Saviour, and the angels minister to us their own food, even joy, and peace, and comfort in the Holy Ghost" (chap. 34).

That is the prose statement of a dilemma, not a resolution to it. *The Temple* is the poetic enactment of that dilemma. To read the poems is often to wade more deeply into dilemma; to meditate, in turn, on those dilemmas is in a sense to experience a kind of affliction in the form of seeing clearly our fallen condition. Yet haven't we seen in the poems that all affliction brings with it instruction? Conversely, no instruction without affliction—

Governing movement of *The Temple:* strophic, decidedly and inevitably, in keeping with the emotional, psychological, and intellectual shifts of an individual trying to bring into equilibrium the unknowable nature of God and the nature of humankind, which is finally predictable. An impossible task—for if the distinguishing trait of humanity is intellectual curiosity, it is also that very trait that must lead us routinely counter to God (see Genesis; and, after that, history itself). It is no coincidence that strophe and antistrophe define the choruses that are standard in Greek tragedy, those plays in which what aspect of human nature isn't in some way thrown into light?

Herbert, of course, no stranger to the classics.

To every great poet there is a particular arrogance whose nature is twofold: it permits the poet to write with the conviction of one who believes he or she is in possession of the truth; nevertheless, it does not blind the writer to his or her own potential failings. The latter quality produces the earnestness that, in turn, distinguishes the merely bombastic from the credibly authoritative.

If questioning the ways of God is one of the items with which Herbert openly wrestles throughout *The Temple*, another is writerly ambition. As with the two poets mentioned earlier—Hopkins and Dickinson—Herbert seems (quite reasonably) aware of his gift; the problem is, What to do with it? How to temper it to best serve God and not oneself? How to fashion the perfect offering and then avoid a dangerous pride in one's own achievement? How to be a virtuoso of form and metrics yet seem less to be flaunting than appropriately harnessing that talent?

The question of the artist's responsibility is raised early in *The Temple*, shortly after it has been established that as human beings we are responsible for following the model of Christ in his suffering—a resolution that was no sooner reached than it confronted the question of *how* to approximate such a model, given our human disadvantages. Similarly, in "The Temper (I)" Herbert both announces that the artist (by which he means, of course, his own case, that of the Christian artist) is responsible for praising God and proceeds to ask how such praise should be put forward—again, given the spiritual instability that attends being human:

> How should I praise thee, Lord! how should my rhymes
>   Gladly engrave thy love in steel,

If what my soul doth feel sometimes,
    My soul might ever feel!

                (1–4)

Yet take thy way; for sure thy way is best:
    Stretch or contract me, thy poor debtor:
    This is but tuning of my breast,
        To make the music better.

                (21–24)

The two stanzas argue for, at the very least, a parallel between spiritual and artistic devotion; for Herbert it seems clear that the two are in fact not parallel but one and the same. The well-tuned breast (that is, the spiritually responsible one) will inevitably produce the music (literal music but also music as metaphor for a fitting devotion) appropriate to God. But even as the two types of devotion are akin, they inherit the same difficulty, namely, a human instability. Again, the action to take is clearly stated—in "Jordan (I)," in "The Quiddity," but most pleasingly and economically, both, in "Jordan (II)":

When first my lines of heav'nly joys made mention,
Such was their lustre, they did so excel,
That I sought out quaint words, and trim invention;
My thoughts began to burnish, sprout, and swell,
Curling with metaphors a plain intention,
Decking the sense, as if it were to sell.

Thousands of notions in my brain did run,
Off'ring their service, if I were not sped:
I often blotted what I had begun;
This was not quick enough, and that was dead.
Nothing could seem too rich to clothe the sun,
Much less those joys which trample on his head.

As flames do work and wind, when they ascend,
So did I weave myself into the sense.
But while I bustled, I might hear a friend
Whisper, *How wide is all this long pretence!*
There is in love a sweetness ready penned:
Copy out only that, and save expense.

(The friend, incidentally, is usually identified as Christ; see Martz, 457.) Simplicity, it would seem, is crucial—an honesty of line and of sentiment analogous to an uncomplicated honesty with respect to God (that is, a simplicity of spirit). This last is the point that "Confession" so persuasively makes, arguing against an intricacy of heart, in favor of an openness that will protect us from sins:

> Only an open breast
> Doth shut them out, so that they cannot enter;
> Or, if they enter, cannot rest,
> But quickly seek some new adventure.
> Smooth open hearts no fast'ning have; but fiction
> Doth give a hold and handle to affliction.
>
> *(19–24)*

Yet, as with the inevitably complicated human soul, how is Herbert to adopt a plainness of style when he is so expert at poetic craft? And in light of the question that he raises in "Providence"—"But who hath praise enough? nay, who hath any?" (141)—mustn't the artist also avoid being accused of stinting on his craft? The line is, again, as blurred as the line between certain vices, the ones "whose natures, at least in the beginning, are dark and obscure: as covetousness and gluttony" (*The Country Parson,* chap. 26). Add to all of this that, like human beings, words are themselves at a disadvantage that necessitates their being ever inadequate to the responsibilities demanded of them, inasmuch as words "Doth vanish like a flaring thing, / And in the ear, not conscience ring" ("The Windows," 14–15). Finally, there is the fact that

> None can express thy works, but he that knows them:
> And none can know thy works, which are so many,
> And so complete, but only he that owes them.
>
> *("Providence," 142–44)*

—*owes* meaning "owns" in Herbert's time, with the sole owner being God himself.

What is a man of words—and especially of Herbert's facility with them—to do? Just as we have uncovered ways to justify sin, it is possible to argue that a commitment to conveying praise worthy of God justifies an inventiveness of form; that is, the artist is (or should be) engaged in a constant search for the most perfect form in which to cast his offering. My sense is that this was no mere justification for Herbert—he was earnest in his desire to put forward his best, for God. I also find it hard to imagine, though, that Herbert took no pride in such elaborately structured and clever poems as "A Wreath," whose end words, framing the poem four times over, turn out to form an actual wreath on the page, whose center—formed precisely where the two center lines of the poem make a pivot of enjambment—is the phrase "to thee / To thee," appropriate to a poem that concerns the offering of praise. Here is the poem in its entirety:

A wreathèd garland of deservèd praise,
Of praise deservèd, unto thee I give,
I give to thee, who knowest all my ways,
My crooked winding ways, wherein I live,
Wherein I die, not live: for life is straight,
Straight as a line, and ever tends to thee,
To thee, who art more far above deceit,
Than deceit seems above simplicity.
Give me simplicity, that I may live,
So live and like, that I may know thy ways,
Know them and practise them: then shall I give
For this poor wreath, give thee a crown of praise.

A similar sense of satisfaction must have been part of Herbert's reaction to what he had been able to accomplish with but only two rhymes—and only the same four words with which to generate them—throughout his "Clasping of Hands," the first stanza of which follows:

Lord, thou art mine, and I am thine,
If mine I am: and thine much more,
Than I or ought, or can be mine.
Yet to be thine, doth me restore;
So that again I now am mine,
And with advantage mine the more,
Since this being mine, brings with it thine,
And thou with me dost thee restore.
    If I without thee would be mine,
    I neither should be mine nor thine.

And consider the first couple of stanzas of "Paradise," which enact in end words the poem's subjects—that humanity is ever enclosed within Christ, who is in turn contained within God (as the word with which the first line of each tercet ends proves to enclose two other words), and that a person's blessings lie in being refined gradually, pared away at by the knife of God:

> I bless thee, Lord, because I GROW
> Among thy trees, which in a ROW
> To thee both fruit and order OW.

> What open force, or hidden CHARM
> Can blast my fruit, or bring me HARM,
> While the inclosure is thine ARM?

As with many a question in Herbert—in this case how to temper an ambition to serve God as expertly as possible with an ambition, as an artist, to surpass what one has done before or is capable of doing in future—this question elicits from the poet a silence as humble as it is honest. It is honest because Herbert understands that the demands of art and of piety—inasmuch as these are tempered, necessarily, by human nature—will often be in a conflict that to reconcile would at best be artistry, but never art. Even as to try to reconcile the ways of God is the stuff of science or logic, or perhaps philosophy. None of these is faith.

—

Poems like those just mentioned, in particular like "Paradise" or like Herbert's translation/version "Coloss. 3.3 Our life is hid with Christ in God," find pleasure as much in the play of typography as of word:

> *My* words and thought do both express this notion,
> That *Life* hath with the sun a double motion.
> The first *Is* straight, and our diurnal friend,
> The other *Hid* and doth obliquely bend.
> One life is wrapped *In* flesh, and tends to earth:
> The other winds towards *Him,* whose happy birth
> Taught me to live here so, *That* still one eye
> Should aim and shoot at that which *Is* on high:
> Quitting with daily labour all *My* pleasure,
> To gain at harvest an eternal *Treasure.*

This is play, indeed, but not *mere* play. Part of the message in Herbert's work is the message that is the title of the poem just cited. The human desire may be to have everything made visible; this is not only evident in

"Mattens" and "Sin (II)," but I note, too, how the poems that immediately follow those two poems in *The Temple* are almost all, for several pages, poems whose center is a concrete, tangible aspect of the church: "Church-monuments," "Church-lock and Key," "The Church-floor," "The Windows"—as if in response to an urge for a more concrete understanding of God. But the fact, Herbert suggests, is that the ways of God are abstract and ungraspable. This would seem to explain why those very concrete-in-subject poems are immediately followed by the poems "Trinity Sunday," "Content," "Humility," "Frailty," "Constancy," "Affliction (III)"; it also, to return to the poems of wordplay, suggests that much of what Herbert intends in those poems is a reminder about the elusive, the hidden meanings of God—some more attainable than others. In "Coloss. 3.3 Our life is hid with Christ in God" a clear message lies italicized within the plain-face type; the poem itself is thus a concrete means of speaking about the abstract and hidden. (If it does not unveil the ways of God entirely, it gives us a way to approximate such a discovery, on the level of words—a pleasure smaller than but analogous to the reward of knowing God more entirely after death.) So, again, there's an ambiguity. A poem for which the poet could be accused of self-indulgence—brandishing with less than appropriate pride his knack for crossing wit and intellect—can also serve as evidence of the poet's commitment to speaking earnestly of his God. This is related to our earlier discussion of "Justice (I)," whose message continues to show new sides of itself with each rereading. Is it arrogance or humility at work there, and is the message blasphemous or devout?

For me, whether he does it through wordplay, through metrical dexterity, or through a gift for argument that recalls how dangerously close is rhetoric to sophistry, Herbert suggests that there is nothing merely superficial, nothing absolutely clear when it comes to God, the soul, the body's restiveness, temptation, and how to reconcile them all. There are always other layers—which is why devotion requires vigilance, patience, both—as there is eventually always a ne plus ultra: this is where acceptance is required—faith, presumably, about which Herbert says, "Faith needs no staff of flesh, but stoutly can / To heav'n alone both go, and lead" ("Divinity," 27–28).

I have said that the constant inventing of new forms and rhyme schemes can be understood as mimetic of the devoted's tireless searching for the vessel most fit to present to God—a God whose desires, like his methods, are unpredictable, ever elusive. But I also see the poems as physical enactments, on the page, of the body's restlessness, as much in the face of temptation as before the facelessness of God. Without reading the words of the poems, only looking at them in terms of their shifting lines and morphing shapes on the page, they return to me again and again the same questions: what is the body's proper conduct? What of the soul?

—

As with poets, so too with poems: some remain more interesting than others. Much has, of course, to do with the reader: if I continue to prefer Dante's Hell to his Paradise—what, then? Likewise, with the poems of Herbert. In poems such as "Business," with its patience-straining trochaics and its decidedly pat ending—"Who in heart not ever kneels, / Neither sin nor Saviour feels"—do I resist easy conclusion? What is it about a metrical regularity that (here anyway) is off-putting? I have a similar ambivalence about a poem like "Vanity (I)," whose argument follows a rather conventional tripartite structure, each part presenting an allegory, essentially the same one (the individual—whether as "fleet astronomer," "nimble diver," or "subtle chymick"—seeks to know everything), which is then countered by a final stanza whose question—"what hath not man sought out and found, / But his dear God?"—is predictable enough. "Constancy," "Sunday," "Avarice"—I'm aware that the poems that appeal to me less are in general also those that take as subjects sins to guard against, or holy days, or religious duty. (A notable exception is "Prayer [I]," in part because it includes—surprisingly, at first—sin as a component of prayer and in part because it moves associatively from image to image, each increasingly more vague, the final definition of prayer being only, and abstractly, "something understood." That is, it pretends to no simple answer.) What these particular poems lack is an agony that would imply a speaker who has survived experience, which would in turn produce the earnestness that characterizes most of Herbert's poems. They also tend to be delivered in third person—that is, they lack the *I* whose intimacy will render a genuine agony even more so.

Another way of looking at the less satisfying poems—recalling what Herbert says in *The Country Parson* about the two sides to every Christian, "the one military, the other peaceable"—is that these poems issue from the peaceable side of Herbert. And peace somehow never seems quite to warrant long attention from us, compared to strife—or in saying so do I speak more of my own than of the world's tendency?

Or perhaps the poems are meant to seem somewhat predictable, routine—the effect perhaps not coincidentally suggests the child or the not especially committed adults who in church can be found repeating from memory the psalms and hymns whose words they may know but whose meaning they have never stopped to consider. Are the poems intended as a kind of example-in-negative of "correct" behavior? Yet Herbert remarks with disapproval how "many say the catechism by rote, as parrots, without ever piercing into the sense of it" (*The Country Parson,* chap. 21). Is it again, then, myself? . . . Most often these poems seem Herbert's way of reminding us that we cannot yield entirely to affliction, that even attending to our souls out of duty if not always out of commitment is an effort in the right direction, that is, in the opposite direction from sin.

Whatever the reasoning, what prevents these poems from seeming, in the end, aberrations of naivete is their *placement* within *The Temple.* If we encounter one of the potentially naive or sermon-like poems, we are never very far away from a poem that offers a speaker questioning the very sentiments that have been earlier expressed. As a result the poems that lack agony read, to me, like a self all but rehearsing, going through the rote motions of what it knows to be "right," even as we can sense the self's lack of conviction; that is, the effect is of a self understanding instinctively that there's a big difference between religious expectation and what is possible given human limitation. For example, "The Pearl. Math. 13.45" speaks of a balance that has finally been achieved, a correct acceptance of the relationship between God and humanity:

> My stuff is flesh, not brass; my senses live,
> And grumble oft, that they have more in me
> Than he that curbs them, being but one to five:
> > Yet I love thee.
> > *(27–30)*

But it is immediately followed by "Affliction (IV)," which opens on a note of wrenched outcry:

> Broken in pieces all asunder,
> > Lord, hunt me not,
> > A thing forgot,
> Once a poor creature, now a wonder,
> > A wonder tortured in the space
> > Betwixt this world and that of grace.
> > *(1–6)*

The placement of the two poems has its implicit argument: any sense of balance, any temper ("the due or proportionate mixture of elements or qualities," says the *OED*) must needs be temporary. It will always be the case that "I cannot skill of these thy ways" ("Justice [I]"), that our inability will be but one aspect of our affliction, and that all respite from affliction throws affliction into relief only—it does not end it.

———

Considering how, save for a single line, all thirteen of its stanzas examine the same point in the same way—human beings are foolish, their hands foul, their eyes blind to God's greatness, therefore entirely unworthy even to serve God, never mind the receiving of blessings—the poem "Misery" should be among the poems that I find less appealing, more dogmatic and too indifferent to a very real, human agony. Why is this not the case?

For a long time it seemed to me to have to do with how the third person, in which seventy-seven of the lines are cast, is abandoned for the first person, in the poem's last line:

> But sin hath fooled him. Now he is
> A lump of flesh, without a foot or wing
>   To raise him to a glimpse of bliss:
> A sick tossed vessel, dashing on each thing;
>   Nay, his own shelf:
>   My God, I mean myself.
>
>   *(73–78)*

By means of a simple shift in point of view, Herbert—with an honesty that is the more devastating for seeming to have been accidentally stumbled into—implicates himself in the very behavior that he has spent all this time denouncing.

That is part of it, yes. But also I think the poem succeeds by what I shall call its mathematics. As a poet I place great value on a poem's title and on its last line and on the relationship between the two. Given how Herbert suggests in the poem that the misery of the title refers to the miserable condition of man, and given how he also includes himself as an example at the poem's end, I have sometimes seen all of the poem's lines between the title and the last line as an equals sign. One level of the poem's mathematics is misery = myself.

Punctuation is another of a poem's aspects with which I am always concerned; it creates the silences, in the form of variously timed pauses, in which at least half of a poem's meaning, I am convinced, resides. The last line of "Misery" reads, "My God, I mean myself." I read the line two ways: "My God" is meant as apostrophe; that is, God is the addressee of the remark that follows—"I mean myself." But also, in the pause that the comma inserts, a temporal space is opened up, and inside it there is time to wonder if Herbert could possibly also have in mind the comma as equals sign. That is, another translation of the line is "by 'my God' I mean 'myself.'" In that sense the line suggests a boldness or arrogance that we have, after all, seen in plenty of Herbert's poems, those in which the poet cries out in Job-like fashion against the inexplicable ways of God, demanding that those ways be justified.

More math: misery = my God = myself. I mean by this an equivalence in terms of ideas rather than of "merely" numerical play, although it is worth noting that *misery* and *myself* are each seven letters long—as is the phrase "my God," if we include the space between those two words; and why not, given the weight that seems particularly to attach both to Herbert's punctuation and his use of pause within a given line? In either context the equation reinforces the theme that we have seen in poems of typographical play, namely, that there is an inextricable relationship between God, humanity, and suffering—we have only to pare away one to find another enclosed, in an impossibly circular fashion: impossible, because the circle never changes (it being the nature of a circle to remain unbroken), yet its coordinates are in constant shift.

⌒

[Last night]
 Favorite poet?
  George Herbert.
 Favorite poem by?
  "Artillery."
 Best line in?
  "Then we are shooters both. . . ."
 Favorite line:
  "Shun not my arrows, and behold my breast."

Of "Artillery," this mostly: that it is one of many Herbert poems that present human life as an ongoing process of bargaining (even when, as here, the speaker knows there is no real bargaining—"no articling with thee"—to more than speak of) between God and human beings. Most often the bargain is unidirectional; that is, Herbert puts his terms forward in a poem, and the poem ends. In these instances the poem resembles— no, it *is*—prayer, when it isn't psalm, which is praise sent in one direction. Both figure here:

Artillery

As I one ev'ning sat before my cell,
Me thoughts a star did shoot into my lap.
I rose, and shook my clothes, as knowing well,
That from small fires comes oft no small mishap.
    When suddenly I heard one say,
    Do as thou usest, disobey,
    Expel good motions from thy breast
Which have the face of fire, but end in rest.

I, who had heard of music in the spheres,
But not of speech in stars, began to muse:
But turning to my God, whose ministers
The stars and all things are; If I refuse,
    Dread Lord, said I, so oft my good;
    Then I refuse not ev'n with blood
    To wash away my stubborn thought:
For I will do or suffer what I ought.

But I have also stars and shooters too,
Born where thy servants both artilleries use.
My tears and prayers night and day do woo,
And work up to thee; yet thou dost refuse.
    Not but I am (I must say still)
    Much more obliged to do thy will,
    Than thou to grant mine: but because
Thy promise now hath ev'n set thee thy laws.

Then we are shooters both, and thou dost deign
To enter combat with us, and contest
With thine own clay. But I would parley fain:
Shun not my arrows, and behold my breast.

Yet if thou shunnest, I am thine:
I must be so, if I am mine.
There is no articling with thee:
I am but finite, yet thine infinitely.

Just as bargaining involves two, so does prayer—even in those cases like "Artillery," in which (unlike, say, "The Collar," "Jordan (II)," or "Dialogue," among others) God himself does not respond with counterterms. In fact, it seems that God is most present for Herbert in those poems (the majority) in which God is not actually a "character" or speaker. If anything, there is a heightened intimacy—the intimacy of two in one corner of the same very large room: one is speaking, one listening. . . .

And in the poems in which God does appear—in word or as dramatis persona or via messenger (again, "Artillery")—it is never in the word, the representation, or the messenger that I detect the truer presence of divinity. It's elsewhere, in that part of the poem that Stanley Kunitz calls a poem's "wilderness"[2]—he means, I think, the necessary part of a poem that eludes analysis because it has to and that makes its presence known to our sometimes-too-rational selves only by its very resistance to those selves. That resistance is of course not visible, but it is palpable; to feel it, though, the flesh alone is for once as helpless as—

as I think Herbert would say it always will be—

⁓

"*But I have also stars and shooters too. . . .*"
Yet what can it mean, but folly, to place confidence in the weapons available to us if we know the weapons themselves to be inferior—if they have intentionally been made so—if the maker is also our opponent—
"*We are shooters both—*"
Yes, except one of the two parties—and that party not our own—holds finally all power; what point, then, in shooting at all—to pass the time that will pass anyway—any event—without us?
"*Thy promise now hath ev'n set thee thy laws*"
By promise, default, oversight, pity—how is it victory, if secured thus? Conversely, what is victory to the one who can only find defeat, each time, a stranger?
"*I am but finite, yet thine infinitely*"
All victory, then, as meaningless—and ours finally—and not our own. As for defeat: that it is ultimately not possible—just immediately so.

Anomaly, conundrum, *thy-will-be-done:* all three, says Herbert, whom I find not so often embracing as standing braced, human, frightened, cock-sure, and full of questions before—what, exactly? That which he cannot understand?

If Herbert would know the mystery that is God, he is also just as baffled by and at the same time in awe of the mystery of himself—sometimes more so. After all, the invisible and unsubstantial must by definition elude us, at least in terms of the eyes, of the hand. But how much more frustrating not to be able to understand what—being flesh—requires relatively little to know?

There are mirrors; or you could touch me.
Here, where you see I touch my very self.

―

The particular beauty of "The Pulley" has to do with the impurity of the comfort it offers.

The Pulley
     When God at first made man,
Having a glass of blessings standing by;
Let us (said he) pour on him all we can:
Let the world's riches, which dispersèd lie,
          Contract into a span.

     So strength first made a way;
Then beauty flowed, then wisdom, honour, pleasure:
When almost all was out, God made a stay,
Perceiving that alone of all his treasure
          Rest in the bottom lay.

     For if I should (said he)
Bestow this jewel also on my creature,
He would adore my gifts instead of me,
And rest in Nature, not the God of Nature:
          So both should losers be.

     Yet let him keep the rest,
But keep them with repining restlessness:
Let him be rich and weary, that at least,

> If goodness lead him not, yet weariness
>   May toss him to my breast.

It is difficult to know how to feel about the news that our restlessness is essentially God given. On one hand, there's a comfort in knowing that the restlessness that makes us stray sometimes from God is of his own making—we are refreshingly blameless. But there's a perverseness, isn't there, to such a God? How else to understand a deliberate withholding of blessings? What does it mean about God and about man if any bond between the two can only be achieved through stratagem?

Yet, perverse or not, the God of "The Collar" endures thirty-two lines of man's restlessness, lines of outcry against God, which God then counters with a single word, "*Child!*" In which word I hear admonishment, welcome, fear, intimacy, the tone of what forgives as much from pity as from respect. . . .

I have said how Herbert withholds easy solution. The way, in the poems, God does? Or perhaps Herbert searches earnestly enough but does not find, in the end, easy solution—in which way, he recalls our best selves. . . .

I once described my own poems as "advance bulletins from the interior," by which I meant that over time they delivered to me a meaning other than—more troublingly personal than—the meaning I had more consciously intended or at least thought I'd intended. To the extent that the poems have some relevance to their readers, I am grateful. That they also deliver their own confessions—for they do not seem my own entirely— makes me aware of the ways in which poetry can correctly be called dangerous. This is why to write requires great care on so many levels. It also requires, incongruously, a certain appetite for risk. One proceeds with honesty. At risk, always, is the truth itself.

I mention this because how I view my own poetry, how I approach the reading and writing of it, cannot help having something to do with how I respond to and come away from Herbert's work. Don't we, necessarily, see the world and everything in it (literature included, of course) through the lens of our selves, each self responsively shaped according to the world's actions on it? As far as I know we step free of the world no more easily than we relinquish the lens through which we see it—by death alone. Necessarily, in this life, I *am* that self.

For what I would, that do I not; but what I hate, that do I.
ROMANS 8:15

Herbert persuades by the very thing with which his poems are so fre-
quently ill at ease: his flawed self. It is not so much that he admits to flaw
(as much is said in the prose) but that he brings flaw into view as instruc-
tive example (one definition, incidentally, for confession)—an instruction
intended, I believe, primarily for himself. He persuades by openness, even
in those poems in which high artifice figures—if anything, the elaborate-
ness of form often throwing the directness of personal cry into greater
relief.

If there is an overall message by the end of *The Temple,* it seems to
emerge not from intellectual or literary engagement but from a life that
has with no little difficulty come through to the farther end of hardship
of body and soul—much to its own surprise:

> O my only light,
> It cannot be
> That I am he
> On whom thy tempests fell all night.
> *("The Flower," 39–42)*

Lines like "The fineness which a hymn or psalm affords, / Is, when the
soul unto the lines accords" ("A True Hymn," 9–10) speak in part to the
need for something as seemingly obvious as committed feeling—in poetry
it's otherwise all form and function. And in part, the lines address the
hymn—in the form of correct behavior—that we are told we should strive
to make by calibrating our souls to the lines drawn out for them by God.

What is not said is that any of this is without its difficulty. It is mostly
strife, which in "The Banquet" we are instructed to love, although how
to do so is never stated in practical terms. My sense by the end is that we
essentially learn to live with what will, anyway, be there—be it God, strife,
our human frailties.

In the final poem of *The Temple* (again, I omit "The Church Militant")
the soul is "guilty of dust and sin," but it is nevertheless encouraged by
Love (God, I have always assumed) to "sit down . . . and taste my meat":

Love (III)

Love bade me welcome: yet my soul drew back,
       Guilty of dust and sin.
But quick-eyed Love, observing me grow slack
       From my first entrance in,
Drew nearer to me, sweetly questioning,
       If I lacked anything.

A guest, I answered, worthy to be here:
       Love said, You shall be he.
I the unkind, ungrateful? Ah my dear,
       I cannot look on thee.
Love took my hand, and smiling did reply,
       Who made the eyes but I?

Truth Lord, but I have marred them: let my shame
       Go where it doth deserve.
And know you not, says Love, who bore the blame?
       My dear, then I will serve.
You must sit down, says Love, and taste my meat:
       So I did sit and eat.

Absolution?
Salvation?
Or, having admitted to his share of the blame, God's peace-offering?
Or consolation, but too late?

As in so many places in Herbert, and what brings me back again and
again to the poems: a silence, one that I don't want so much anymore to
penetrate or (related, I begin to suspect) that I don't need to, no. Increas-
ingly, may it be enough, to hear it.

NOTES

1. Poems and prose are cited from *George Herbert and Henry Vaughan,* ed.
Louis L. Martz (Oxford: Oxford University Press, 1986).
2. Quoted in Selden Rodman, "Tongues of Fallen Angels," in *Interviews and
Encounters with Stanley Kunitz,* ed. Stanley Moss (Riverdale-upon-Hudson,
N.Y.: Sheep Meadow Press, 1993), 24.

SEVEN

Milton in the Modern

The Invention of Personality

WILLIAM LOGAN

WHAT IF WE KNEW, to its determining hour, when Milton wrote each of his sonnets? He can't have meant, in the ripeness or rottenness of their conception, for them to appear together, the way they do as specimen days in some collections. Yet he published them together himself, gaggled like geese in both 1645 and 1673, omitting only those the mercurial temper of politics rendered inopportune. Gathered together, yet rendered apart— Milton's two dozen sonnets vary within and without, divided from each other and from the tradition. The sonnets are a peculiar instance, a peculiarly conflicted instance, where tradition proposes and the artist disposes, where the poet's inheritance permits his deviation from tradition, and *only* the inheritance permits such deviation. Milton's sonnets represent one of the first moments—perhaps *the* first moment—when a poet writing in English took his form for granted, when the poet's respect for the rules required him to break the rules. Where the innocence of form was lost, the moment of Eliot's *dissociation of sensibility* began. If we believed in such things, that would be the beginning of the modern.

The sonnet is an old form in English but older elsewhere, first picked up by poets who showed their taste by what they collected in travels to the Continent, whether objets d'art or the trifle of a language, some affectation or affection of manner, a trivial poetic form. It would be impossible to recreate the sonnet-mad decade of the 1590s, when young men abandoned themselves to sonneteering, without reference to tulipomania or the South Sea Bubble in the centuries that followed; but even wars may seem fancies or crazes, however much they cloak themselves in belief.

Ben Jonson, in his witty, probably drink-fueled conversations with Drummond of Hawthornden in 1619 (some of the only table talk of Elizabethan playwrights to survive), claimed the sonnet was no better than Procrustes' bed—*where some who were too short were racked, others too long cut short.*[1] The boyish poets of the 1590s were trying to impress each other as much as their lovers. In a way difficult to imagine a very few years later, they became addicted to a poetic form. Poetic forms may seem difficult to poets for whom rhyme and meter are not common currency, but writing sonnets can be as hard to stop as swallowing laudanum or drinking absinthe.

Sonnets can never be as hardened in the reading as the writing; but they show how easy it is to wear out a form, to make writer or reader sick through overexposure. (It is one reason to think Shakespeare wrote his over a shorter rather than longer period—they burn with intensities of months or years, not decades.) By the turn of the century the craze was over: when Shakespeare's sonnets were published in 1609, they must have seemed stale memories of the vanished Elizabethan Age. New king, new courtiers; many in the old court had died or been executed before Elizabeth's death (Burghley and Essex, for example). The *Sonnets* did not arouse much comment when finally published (some say because the book was too personal, more than sonnet sentiment allowed) and apparently did not reach a second edition. The sale was small compared to *Venus and Adonis,* which had inflamed young Elizabethans only sixteen years before and was still in print. By 1640, when Shakespeare's sonnets were reprinted, they were so old-fashioned the new publisher did not hesitate to change the sexes willy-nilly, making the fair youth a fairer lady.

Milton was spurred to sonnets twice in his life, or rather in two periods: as a proud and headstrong university student of the late 1620s, a boy who had absorbed Petrarch and Della Casa, Tasso and Bembo; and as the older, grittier, battle-scarred pamphleteer. The surviving sonnets are numbered 1–19 in the edition of 1673, which also includes an unnumbered sonnet with a tail ("On the New Forcers of Conscience"), but not a few left in manuscript—three to heroes of the Civil War and one, on blindness, that preens with mention of Milton's defense of liberty. Their published order, though roughly chronological, has allowed scholars to disagree about exact composition. (These notes on Milton have been written on the backs of

Parker, the biographer; Smart and Honigmann, who edited the sonnets; Carey and Leonard, who edited editions of the poems. I've used Carey's text but have followed one reading in the Trinity manuscript.)[2]

The seven sonnets of Milton's Cambridge days are a vision of nightingales and shepherdesses, pastoral romance out of college handbooks. The first and last are in English—Sonnet 1 begins, unpromisingly, "O nightingale, that on yon bloomy spray" (*bloomy spray*, indeed!). It is in fact the first English sonnet on the nightingale. The five sonnets between have been cast in Italian, an occasionally clumsy Italian a romantic college boy might invent. In his biography, W. R. Parker makes a pretty tale of them, a plaintive love story that may have fact filtered into it; but if Milton were as tongue-tied as the tale suggests, his beloved could easily have been fantasy. The convention- and cliché-ridden lines have had life squeezed out of them; what could have been more tempting, for a boy schooling himself on Italian sonnets, than to dream up a *bella donna* as his object of desire? (Milton was mulish, admitted to "honest haughtiness,"[3] and for unspecified offenses had been sent down his first year—perhaps he was unworldly about women. Other undergrads called him "the Lady of Christ's College," and it wasn't flattering.)[4]

If the girl did exist, if the sonnets aren't a farrago of fitting lies, her name was probably Emilia and she might have been a singer of talent. A suitor's pair of sonnets (2 and 3), wooing her in flowery, formal terms, are interrupted by a canzone, complaining that Milton's friends have been teasing him for writing in Italian (rather than speaking up in English, as Parker has it)—the canzone is in Italian, too. The sonnet that follows (4), to his close friend Charles Diodati, confesses the poet's mortifying shock at falling in love. The closing sonnets (5 and 6) return to address the young woman in conventional if hothouse metaphors, with flashes of lightning, an adamant heart. Much of Sonnet 5 is taken up describing a sigh. Only when writing to Diodati (whose father was Italian—Milton could have met an Italian girl in the family circle) does something of the erotic leak in.

The poet has fallen in love, not with a sonnet's ideal sweetheart of gold hair and rose cheeks (*Nè treccie d'oro, nè guancia vermiglia*) but with a girl with black lashes. In no other way does Milton betray any notion that a poet might break the rules (though scholars are impressed by his tortured syntax, which a reader must assume is not mere clumsiness). In no other way has he learned a thing from Shakespeare, whose *Sonnets* might have been difficult to find twenty years after publication. To read Milton, you'd think sonnet writing had fallen into mere bookishness after Shakespeare's plumes of rhetoric. The poet who in *Lycidas* took pastoral elegy by the throat hasn't been born.

The final sonnet of Milton's youth (7), probably dated late in 1632 (possibly a year earlier), probably some months after he left Cambridge (he had taken his M.A. in July), is by a writer more confident in his soiled phrasings if still content in the purity of convention—in the Trinity manuscript, a draft letter encloses the sonnet as "some of my nightward thoughts . . . made up in a Petrarchian stanza."[5]

> How soon hath time the subtle thief of youth,
>   Stol'n on his wing my three and twentieth year!
>   My hasting days fly on with full career,
>   But my late spring no bud or blossom sheweth.
> Perhaps my semblance might deceive the truth.

The language never again measures up to the opening metaphor's sharp practice. *Subtle* was a subtle word (Milton may have known the Latin originally meant "finely woven"); and perhaps the main sense here is, as the *OED* suggests, crafty or cunning in a treacherous way. But Milton used it in other ways: shadowing the meaning are "not easily grasped"; "skillful, clever"; and "characterized by penetration, acumen." Milton later wrote in *Areopagitica* of a "Nation not slow and dull, but . . . acute to invent, suttle."

Many boys feel their youth vanishing without accomplishment (to feel old at twenty-three is no feat); and this feeling would have been keener when many boys died young (think of the pressure Shakespeare brought on his "lovely boy" to hurry up and have children), when plague could ravage a college town, as Cambridge was ravaged in 1626 and 1630. Yet this boy had already written *L'Allegro* and *Il Penseroso*. (Milton was a little proud of looking boyish—at forty he looked thirty, he noted in *Defensio Secunda*.)[6] His termite-ridden Petrarchan sonnets had blossomed into these twinned poems in a form quite un-English, poems drenched in Shakespearean reading, not just *A Midsummer Night's Dream* and *Romeo and Juliet* but minor plays besides. Two years earlier Milton had written the epitaph "On Shakespeare," published among the prefatory poems in the Second Folio (1632). Milton must have had access to the First Folio; perhaps he received a gratis copy of the Second (the bookseller lived just down the street from Milton's London home). In 1640 the epitaph reappeared in *Poems: Written by Wil. Shake-speare, Gent.,* the book that brought the sonnets back into print.

One can imagine a smitten youth, impatient in feeling but imperfect in Italian (or a youth imagining what it was to be smitten), composing the Emilia sonnets to impress a girl who knew the language, knew it when Milton's friends did not (this is Parker's fairy tale); but even if she existed, the girl might have been allegorical by the time she made her way into verse. Similarly, a young man who had expected to be ordained at twenty-three, who disliked theological students at Cambridge (*There is really hardly anyone among us . . . who, almost completely unskilled and unlearned in Philology and Philosophy alike, does not flutter off to Theology unfledged, . . . learning barely enough for sticking together a short harangue*),[7] might feel the harrying of time, especially when practicing the verses to which his ambition was increasingly, if privately, devoted.

The sonnet is a form particularly permeable to a brief suit of inspiration and is sufficiently tangled to provide resistance to making the barren lines bear. For later poets it has been the empty vessel kept at hand, into which inspiration might be poured. Its brevity forces the poet to attenuate his thinking and concentrate his energies: the divagations permitted by blank verse, even encouraged by it, are subject to different laws of passion. When inspiration is hot, a poet may not want to muse over what form seems suitable—to think with formal calculation would be to lose the steaming immediacy, which is why icier and more formulary passions look so much worse in the sonnet. Milton's Italian sonnets are those of a cold fish—even emotions hot in the feeling can be frosty on the page, unless art intervenes.

The sonnet thrives on hot blood—it is Italian after all. That is bad argument but not, not necessarily, an untrue observation. Such notions of intrinsic character are absurd, yet they bring the opposing case into antagonistic relief: that form has no character *whatsoever* and in *no* way responds to certain types of inspiration. Such a case, neatly in the negative, has flaws as telling as its responsibilities. We know from the successes of a form—in the villanelle, say—that it acts on some designs, some meanings, more willingly than others. With its recuperations and choral returns, its brevity, it is difficult for the villanelle to answer to narrative, which is why narrative can be a tour de force (Elizabeth Bishop's "One Art" is a triumph over form as much as a triumph of form). The rhyme scheme of Shakespeare's sonnet was formally most responsive to three examples and a moralizing turn (a turn so often immorally tacked on it could have been detached and used elsewhere—it's not surprising, only embarrassing, that Sonnets 36 and 96 have the same closing couplet). The breaches of form's decorum, its tacitly elicited phrasing, are therefore often its victories.

After this, youth really did fly on. There was a long hiatus of withdrawal and private study, and only after the outbreak of war a decade later did Milton return to sonnets. In 1642 he was living in London, in Aldersgate Street. He had spent a year on the Continent, visiting the exiled Grotius in Paris, the nearly blind Galileo in Florence. *Comus* and *Lycidas* had reached print. Charles Diodati had died. Having abandoned thoughts of the priesthood, Milton had become something of a pamphlet polemicist on the Reformation. In the spring of 1642 he had mysteriously married one Mary Powell—disappearing into the country, *home he returns a Married-man, that went out a Batchelor.*[8] Some weeks later she returned just as mysteriously to her parents. By August the Civil War had begun.

The comedy of potted history was not comedy to those living in London when the Parliamentarian army retreated that October, leaving the roads open to the troops of Charles I. In the panic Milton wrote a sonnet and tacked it to his door (or so his amanuensis was led to believe). It began:

> Captain or colonel, or knight in arms,
>   Whose chance on these defenceless doors may seize,
>   If ever deed of honour did thee please,
>   Guard them, and him within protect from harms,
> He can requite thee, for he knows the charms
>   That call fame on such gentle acts as these,
>   And he can spread thy name o'er lands and seas.

This is a curious and unpromising act of extortion. Sweating soldiers would probably not stop to read a sonnet before smashing in the door—this, like his somewhat lead-footed verses on the death of the carter Thomas Hobson, may be one of the rare poems to promise Milton had a sense of humor (though a very dark sense). Only a poet with no hope of success would say, "Lift not thy spear against the muses' bower." *Spear?* The Cavaliers have become Alexander's Macedonians.

Although very droll, this incident does hint at stoic courage or a withering high-mindedness in the face of danger. What matters is that Milton was—at least in jest—willing to offer his poetic talents, in whorish fashion, to prevent the pillage of his household. (The poem is as donnish as its distant legatee, Auden's "'The Truest Poetry Is the Most Feigning.'")

No one took him up on the offer because, possibly short of ammunition, faced with quickly mustered militia, the royalist army retreated. To Milton's friends the joke might have seemed gallows humor, the sort wits approve; but it strikes an odd note, included beside love sonnets in his first book of poems, published in 1645. The war had been over for just half a year, less or not at all when the book was arranged—such a poem is either wicked ("Here's what I was prepared to do, at a low point") or triumphal ("How far we have come from the dark days"). This sonnet marks out its ground to one day, one hour, in a mood where pride stiffened the purpose of panic; and Milton thought that mood worth preserving. It is from the strangeness of that moment, that failure to follow the conventions of sonnet writing, that we gain access to character: the form of the sonnet has been opened to alien matter.

Poems of Mr. John Milton was almost ignored. As Parker points out, the first edition was still being sold fifteen years later. However often Milton's occasions of sonnet writing accorded with occasions of temper (or, more commonly, of moods variant to those that could be channeled into religious verse), they oddly respect his oddities of character. Few poets want to appear only in one guise, but poets like to repeat their successes—applause is the spur to repetition. The sonnet gave Milton an out; it was a form at first too trivial for serious art (yet not so trivial it couldn't later be used to serious purpose). Although Tasso had addressed heroic figures in it, although—on rare occasion—the Elizabethans had cheated it of the clichés of love, Milton gave the sonnet up to personality, and so gave it personality. He could make grim jokes or smooth lies (10, "To the Lady Margaret Ley," is unctuous compliment), or he could write encomia for older friends (13, "To Mr. H. Lawes, on his Airs"); but not until the sonnet turned various did personality intervene. That is, the form of variety came before inventions in the verse line.

> Harry whose tuneful and well-measured song
>   First taught our English music how to span
>   Words with just note and accent, not to scan
>   With Midas' ears, committing short and long.

The sonnet for composer Henry Lawes prefaced his *Choice Psalms* (1648)—the Civil War did not rupture the friendship between royalist musician and republican poet (the poet's own brother fought for the royalists). Milton's personality lounges across that chummy "Harry" (it marks its distance from Sonnet 4—which began with a friend's *last* name—and its closeness to the familiarity of Falstaff). Invention (Lawes's ability to set the music as if the words mattered) had become idiom. Here you begin to sense how lightly, by 1646, Milton was able to address the sonnet; and in three violent sonnets the same year (or nearly the same year) the depth of that personality is judged.

Milton was proud of his writing, and prickly. His divorce tracts had given him notoriety. (What do you do when your adolescent bride leaves you? If you're Milton, you not only think of divorce, but you start to write pamphlets about it. The poet was thirty-three, the bride seventeen and a royalist—perhaps differences more important to her.) In three sonnets he attacked those who attacked him, the Presbyterians once his allies.

> I did but prompt the age to quit their clogs
>> By the known rules of ancient liberty,
>> When straight a barbarous noise environs me
> Of owls and cuckoos, asses, apes and dogs.

This is the beginning of Sonnet 12, "On the Detraction which followed upon my Writing Certain Treatises," a formal title formally at odds with the witty virulence that follows. More than half a century early, these lines take on the savagery of Pope. They fall to a bitter ending:

> For who loves that, must first be wise and good;
>> But from that mark how far they rove we see
> For all this waste of wealth, and loss of blood.

By *that* Milton means *liberty*—freedom from the religious shackles of marriage to an incompatible temperament (though after three years his wife returned and bore children), freedom from prior censorship (*Areopagitica*), and freedom from the stiffened conventions of the verse line. In this sonnet there is a slightly dishonest bewilderment ("I did but prompt . . ."), as if Milton couldn't quite understand why his views provoked hostility. Vituperation has its uses: it turns the prey into predator. In his next two sonnets (I am following John Carey's chronology) Milton breaks with all the settled understandings of idiom his early sonnets had acquiesced to.

Milton's *sonetto caudato*, "On the New Forcers of Conscience under the Long Parliament," had its genesis in battles among Protestant sects for the right of dissent. Beneath arguments for heterodoxy its lines declare themselves for heterodoxy of style, for release from the censorship of poetic idiom.

> Dare ye for this adjure the civil sword
>   To force our consciences that Christ set free,
>   And ride us with a classic hierarchy
>   Taught ye by mere A. S. and Rutherford?
> Men whose life, learning, faith and pure intent
>   Would have been held in high esteem with Paul
>   Must now be named and printed heretics
> By shallow Edwards and Scotch What-d'ye-call.

Scotch What-d'ye-call! He might mean Robert Baillie, but whoever he meant, it is comically demeaning to forget his name and injury as well as insult to rhyme on the forgetfulness. The colloquial use of names (or nonnames) and the angry straitening toward prose syntax almost break the sonnet form as well as sonnet diction. The last of the three sonnets must be quoted entire.

> *Sonnet 11*
> A book was writ of late called *Tetrachordon;*
>   And woven close, both matter, form and style;
>   The subject new: it walked the town awhile,
>   Numbering good intellects; now seldom pored on.
> Cries the stall-reader, Bless us! what a word on
>   A title-page is this! And some in file
>   Stand spelling false, while one might walk to Mile-
> End Green. Why is it harder sirs than Gordon,
> Colkitto, or Macdonnel, or Galasp?
>   Those rugged names to our like mouths grow sleek
>   That would have made Quintilian stare and gasp.
> Thy age, like ours, O soul of Sir John Cheke,
>   Hated not learning worse than toad or asp;
>   When thou taught'st Cambridge, and King Edward Greek.

There is much to admire here, beginning with the subject: the author's pride-pricked reaction (Parker called it "amused contempt")[9] to the spurning of his book, "now seldom pored on"—notice, given that the etymology of *subtle* was "woven close," what might be a quiet compliment to himself. The book is a man, as good as a man, sauntering about town—

a book about town! (Horace described his book of epistles as a strolling whore.) There's gaiety within the bitterness.

The portrait of bookstall reader, not someone who's going to *buy* the book, is cruelly deft, and unusual—it reeks of the street, of close observation, where Shakespeare's vignettes, when he has them, seem fancies. Consider how neatly the comic rhymes (*Tetrachordon/pored on/word on/ Gordon*) toy with violence of feeling—as if without comedy the violence could scarcely be expressed. Yet some of the comedy is directed back at the author for having titled a pamphlet so. Only Milton could write such a book with such a preposterous title and then write so idiomatically about having written it. In the Trinity manuscript the line stands, "I writ a book . . . ," which might have been even better; but the revision makes up in acidic detachment what it loses in flat admission.

Then the remarkable lines: ". . . while one might walk to Mile- / End Green. Why is it harder sirs than Gordon, / Colkitto, or Macdonnel, or Galasp?" That enjambment on the hyphen must have been shocking—it had been done only rarely in English verse (there are classical examples in Catullus, Horace, Sappho). As John Hollander notes in *Vision and Resonance,* it was used in poems modeled on Greek meters. Milton, in smuggling the device into English pentameter, may have been borrowing from Ben Jonson, whose Pindaric ode "To the Immortal Memory and Friendship of That Noble Pair, Sir Lucius Cary and Sir H. Morison" has a witty enjambment on "twi- / Lights, the Dioscuri." Jonson would have known classical examples (and this is a classical allusion); but in "A Fit of Rhyme against Rhyme" he blames rhyme for "jointing syllabes," meaning disjointing them.

Milton's line break is even more disturbing in the Trinity manuscript, without initial capitals: *Mile- / end Greene.* It promises that none of the proprieties is safe any longer—not thoughts on divorce, not the trimness of verses or the chasteness of words bound within lines (indeed, *Mile-* has been divorced from *End* rather cuttingly). It's no less confident in its misbehavior than Robert Lowell's enjambment, when breaking the bonds of his pentameter, of "the duck / -'s web- / foot" some three centuries later.

If Scottish names made familiar by civil war are hard, they are not so hard they can't be turned to verse, and they are made harder by "spelling false" (though Milton also means "misinterpreting")—even as Milton, perhaps haplessly, has done, Coll Keitache becoming Colkitto; Gillespie, Galasp; Macdonald now Macdonnel. These three sonnets are among the most thrilling in the rise of colloquial idiom in English verse (if it hadn't been blasphemous, Milton might have thought he'd harrowed hell). What is important in the progress of diction is not what sounded natural in a period but what survived that sounded natural to a later period. (As in many things, accident sometimes overwhelms design.) Until Wordsworth, whose much more conscious attempt to reproduce the "real language of men" was only partly successful, no one advanced the cause of plain speech any further—not even Rochester and Swift, whose satires stood on the outskirts of the permissible and so licensed the impermissible. Milton's layered ironies, his comic turns in tragic proportion, his cross-bow-fired syntax, the language of the street—these secured the sensibility of the modern. After this almost anything could fall into verse.

Milton suffered the conflict between languages perhaps more severely than any major English poet, suffered the conflict, as Shakespeare did not, of whether to write in English at all. *Paradise Lost* might have been an even better poem in Latin, but the tension in Milton between his native tongue and his natural scholarship perhaps meant that in English he did not always have to make his lines learnèd. The tensions of personality were of course not the invention of Milton alone: there are passages in Jonson (his epigrams love the roil of the streets), as well as Donne and Herbert, and further back in Wyatt, where the personality of diction seems distinctly modern; but for different reasons, accidents of taste and access, none proved as influential. Just as we owe pentameter in English more to Wyatt and Surrey than to Chaucer, we owe what we owe in diction to Milton's example. We might therefore blame Milton for both the grand style and the ripening of the vernacular.

Milton has often been denounced for the Latinate contortions of *Paradise Lost,* for the grand style that seems all too grand; but this was conscious choice, not unconscious debility. The sonnets show how complexly comfortable, how coiled with the dramas of meaning, his plain syntax could be. Even roused to the fury of his polemics, Milton was a chillier character than Shakespeare—Milton's lines shiver with a rectitude deeper than metrical practice. Most of the sonnets were composed while his eyes were still of use (after *Lycidas,* in 1637, every occasional verse he wrote in English was a sonnet). A double handful, which include the most vivid, were not. A self-knitted form is not really any more difficult to compose blindfolded, or blind, than blank verse: the rhymes keep internal order and do not require, though they may permit, the cunning enjambments Milton gave to blank verse. In *Lycidas* we get emotion cloaked in pastoral. In the sonnets, at best, we get the emotion unmediated, with frightening directness.

Although after he was totally blind (in about 1652), composition had to cede something of improvisation to memory, the coolness is an aspect of character—his distance and even grandeur were not just a conscious harkening to classical models in a time riven with civil violence, but an imposition, a usurpation, a welcoming of the moral modalities of rhetoric. Milton often sounds as if he's delivering a set speech by Timon or Leontes, and he sounds as if he will never leave the stage.

Memory can be tricked, or tricked out—it isn't all that hard to compose and recall twenty or thirty lines at a pitch, not as hard as modern poets believe, not having been schooled in memorization or the concealed lath of meter. Most poets, in our century without memory, have no occasion to memorize; feats of recall, whether a matter of course or a course of desperation, seem more impressive. Anyone who has acted knows memory can improve, can hear over what it has multiply heard. Aural memories rise up unseen, as olfactory ones do; eidetic memory, the inward form of seeing, of insight (consider blindfolded grandmasters able to play chess exhibitions over twenty boards), need not have more than an intuition of hearing. It would be interesting to know whether the brilliant enjambments of *Paradise Lost* show how visual Milton's verbal memory became— that only a man who could cast his eye on a mental page would have come so frequently to the cunning reversals that tease or torment the eye at line break, that *Paradise Lost* was composed by someone who could see his composition like a printer, not just recollect it by ear. Or, rather, that he could hear the meaning suspended, line by line, enjambment by enjambment, *the sense variously drawn out.* (That he trusted his ear perhaps too much is revealed in his spellings—his hearings—of the Scottish names in Sonnet 11.)

Milton's great sonnets were all written after he was blind. Despite their intensity of *visual* language, they have nothing like the freedom with verbal idiom found in the sonnets written soon after the end of the Civil War—he has all but become his grand style and will shortly become only his grand style (*Paradise Regained* may seem less grand than *Paradise Lost,* but the style is grand compared to anyone else's). The sonnets share, however, far greater confidence in the use of personality—they are among the most reflective and personal verses of the seventeenth century or the century after.

The three sonnets that confirm the genius of the form are too well known to quote, 15 ("On the late Massacre in Piedmont"), 16 ("When I consider how my light is spent . . ."), and 19 ("Methought I saw my late espoused saint . . ."). They do not take the risks of idiom that have made their confidences possible, but they exist in confidence that idiom can repair the distances of personality, that the poem can become the fluent medium of expression in the words of the day (Sonnet 15 is like a newspaper headline, before there *were* newspaper headlines). That Milton chose to heighten the language, to leave it in the dressier realm of literary expression used in *Paradise Lost,* does not mean he had forgotten his gains or deepened his losses. Sonnet 16 closes with a line stoic in its disappointment and stern in its resolve ("They also serve who only stand and wait")—a line justly famous but not often praised for modern simplicity.

The end of Sonnet 19, the vision of his dead second wife, shows Milton had not spurned his discoveries, only that he could choose his effects. The sonnet begins thick with Greek mythology and biblical reference; but the vision slowly clears, unveiling the woman with a veil, at least in the diction, which reaches its climax at its simplest and most moving:

> Her face was veiled, yet to my fancied sight,
> Love, sweetness, goodness in her person shined
> So clear, as in no face with more delight.
> But O as to embrace me she inclined
> I waked, she fled, and day brought back my night.

The metaphor is not just metaphorical—the poem ends in the terrible isolation of the blind, a blindness that shivers with guilt if not self-pity. Here, in the last simplicity of diction, is the personality stripped bare, without defense against whatever vision chooses to embrace it. It recalls the best and most intimate of Sir Thomas Wyatt's poems, "They flee from me. . . ."

We know, to the day or nearly the day, when Milton wrote some of his sonnets; and this helps define the limitations, as well as the lassitudes (or luxuriances), of his relation to form. Milton didn't have to write them as sonnets: he chose the form more than it chose him—no one would say, looking at his Italian sonnets, that he came naturally to it. For that matter, looking at what were probably Shakespeare's amateur efforts, Sonnets 1–19, one wouldn't say that of Shakespeare, either. In their early work both poets are rigid with formal proprieties, with a due (and past-due) sense of occasion—they have written out presentations, not passions (whether this means later passions were true or just better constructed is moot). The passions perhaps came for Shakespeare when he knew the sonnets had been warmed to, even if unsuccessful in warming his "sweet boy" to marriage bed or the fathering of children; yet, however beautiful Shakespeare's sonnets are, they rarely seem personal *to him.* However distressingly personal the sonnets become, until we penetrate the diction, they never seem the poems of a man who has just revealed something it unnerves him to reveal.

Unlike Shakespeare's, Milton's sonnets, his later sonnets, seem drawn to real events, to momentary changes in a disrupted life (a life in some ways so regulated only disruption would have been worth poetry). The trivial and occasional nature of the sonnet (which Milton turned from love plaint to news bulletin, private musing, heroic address, invitation to a walk), which could be serious but need not be sullen, permitted a greater and less restricted range. Milton could be personal in the sonnet in a way he rarely risked elsewhere. If we care to know the hour of Milton's composition, it is because each poem is so *much* the invention of a distinct moment. The sonnets are often called occasional, as if to dismiss them; but in this, this too, they are cruelly modern. A poem called to account by a particular day, a naked homely event (rather than some distillation of the general) breaches the conventions between us. We feel the pastness of the past more keenly when poetry is aligned not with fiction but with history.

Perhaps I have gone too far, suggesting that in poetry the modern notion of personality first becomes accessible in Milton's everyday language, but only if the impress of personality does not lie in our own use of that language. To write in form now, with ears alienated by nearly a century of free verse, is to look back to any earlier period—any period later than Shakespeare's, at least—with a longing toward a past that did not suffer our own dissociation of sensibility, that had a less conscious and less embarrassed relation to its forms but a notion of how the vernacular might triumph within form. I use Eliot's phrase advisedly, with avarice rather than irony, knowing its faults but with respect for its sometimes unappreciated virtues. Any period is likely to feel its ruptures from the past more than its binding ligatures: we are always in the material condition of the Fall, though our notions of Paradise change. For Eliot, in 1921, it was the atonement—or at-one-ment—that poets like Donne achieved without reflection. The metaphor of the mirror is arch as well as brutal—we have long since rendered demonic any creature without reflection.

Any poet who chooses public statement on public matters will write as the ghost of Milton: Robert Lowell haunts my examples here. He began with the poetic diction Milton settled into at the end: Lowell started as epic and ended as personality, and this was considered an advance. The personal is not frightening to our age: we have accepted, as the highest condition of modern poetry, sensibilities of extremity, whether in the avant-garde or in the disrupted psychologies of confessional poetry. We are playing out a myth of the artist that is our inverted romance of sensibility. Lowell's unrhymed sonnets, which it is unfashionable to consider among the best of his work, have an immediacy of response lacking in the studied concerns of *Life Studies.* He found the sonnet a form that allowed him to say anything, and though he wrote hundreds to Milton's two dozen, though none approaches the artistry of Milton's finest, they are the modern inheritance of that invention of personality for which Milton is responsible.

If Milton speaks to the condition of our verse, it is partly as an artist who did not fit, who began to write after most of a century that had shattered a religious concord and was soon to violate a political dispensation. A poet of the 1640s might look back with longing to another time. That Milton was Protestant and republican rather than Catholic and monarchist doesn't make much difference to the condition: both sides longed for stability. That was the point of winning. Personality has to be acquired in each age; but to the romantics, our immediate ancestors, it was Milton's sonnets that spoke immediately and most distinctly. Had Milton chosen to press his discoveries further, had he cast *Paradise Lost* in the idiom the sonnets had begun to invent, how different literary history might have been. It is with mocking, perhaps Miltonic justice that among memories of Robert Lowell in the mental hospital lies one pertinent vision: Lowell reading aloud a revised version of *Lycidas.* The visitor does not record how long it took to realize that Lowell believed he *was* John Milton.[10]

NOTES

1. R. F. Patterson, ed., *Ben Jonson's Conversations with William Drummond of Hawthornden* (London: Blackie and Son, 1923), 6.

2. See William Riley Parker, *Milton: A Biography,* 2d ed., 2 vols. (Oxford: Clarendon Press, 1996); J. S. Smart, ed., *The Sonnets of Milton* (Glasgow: Maclehose, Jackson, 1921); E. A. J. Honigmann, ed., *Milton's Sonnets* (London: Macmillan, 1966); John Carey, ed., *John Milton: Complete Shorter Poems,* 2d ed. (Harlow, England: Longman, 1997); John Leonard, ed., *John Milton: The Complete Poems* (Harmondsworth, England: Penguin, 1998).

3. Parker, *Milton,* 1:43.

4. Ibid., 1:43, 2:739n52; Don M. Wolfe, ed., *Complete Prose Works of John Milton,* 8 vols. (New Haven: Yale University Press, 1953–82), 1:283n62.

5. Milton to a Friend, 1633, in Wolfe, *Prose Works,* 1:320.

6. Ibid., 4:583.

7. Milton to Alexander Gill, July 2, 1628, ibid., 1:314.

8. Helen Darbishire, ed., *The Early Lives of Milton* (London: Constable, 1932), 63.

9. Parker, *Milton,* 1:300.

10. Stanley Kunitz, "The Sense of a Life," in *Robert Lowell: Interviews and Memoirs,* ed. Jeffrey Meyers (Ann Arbor: University of Michigan Press, 1988), 234 [repr. from *New York Times Book Review,* October 16, 1977].

EIGHT

Finding Anne Bradstreet

————

EAVAN BOLAND

I

THIS IS A PIECE ABOUT ANNE BRADSTREET. But there is another subject
here as well. Its nature? For want of an exact definition, it is subject matter
itself: that bridge of whispers and sighs over which one poet has to travel
to reach another, out of which is formed the text and context of a pre-
decessor. That journey into the past—not just Anne Bradstreet's but my
own—is the substance of this essay.

I have always been fascinated by the way poets of one time construct
the poets of a previous one. It can be an invisible act, arranged so that
none of the awkwardly placed struts are visible. But the discussion of
invisibility is not my intention. I am interested in the actual process of
reconstruction, in the clear and unclear motives with which a poet from
the present goes to find one from the past. I am interested, therefore, in
the actions and choices that have the power to turn a canon into some-
thing less authoritarian and more enduring: from a set text into a living
tradition. The sometimes elusive, yet utterly crucial, difference between
a canon and a tradition is also part of this piece. So in that sense I want
the plaster work to show and the background noise to be heard.

All of this seems worth saying at the beginning because I found Anne
Bradstreet first in a revealing context. Not in her own words: not in the
quick, fluent, and eventually radical cadences that mark her style. My

first discovery of her had an ominous irony about it, so I will begin with that.

American poetry was hard to find in Dublin when I was a young poet. It was the mid-sixties. The names of American poets and their poems were not just unavailable in the bookshops: they were unavailable in the air. Part of that was simply enclosure. In the previous decades Ireland had come through an intense, inward adventure of its own. Its own poetry, its own poets, its domestic sense of having beaten the odds in both a historic and aesthetic sense were the dominant tropes of its literary self-perception. In that sense the Irish poetry world stood on what Arnold eloquently called "burning ground." Everyone shared in it. Everyone stood on it. It was an exciting literary culture, precisely because it was so enclosed. In a newspaper article Patrick Kavanagh made a vivid distinction between literary provincialism and parochialism. Parochialism, he wrote, was that blind conviction of being at the center of things, of knowing no other place: it was the summer crossroads where he first made up ballads on football. It was the city that talked about itself endlessly: Joyce's city, with its draped curtains, glittering coastline, and malicious jokes. Provincialism, however, was the hankering for an elsewhere, an anxious measuring of the local against some other, distant standard. In that sense Dublin was—in the best sense—parochial.

A few things got through: a random sampling of the excitements of elsewhere. One of these was *Homage to Mistress Bradstreet* by John Berryman. Published in 1953 in the *Partisan Review*—and then as a volume in 1956—it was a tour de force, a cunning mixture of eulogy and elegy. Its language and syntax, its odd and vehement music had packed its energies in Yeats's proverbial ice and salt and readied them to cross the Atlantic. Over the next decade the poem made its way into the conversations of young Irish poets. Some of this was because of Berryman himself. He came to Dublin in the mid-sixties, made friends, made enemies, caused a certain amount of mayhem, and briefly entered a poetic way of life that thrived on all three.

I remember struggling with *Homage to Mistress Bradstreet*. It was not easy to read for any student or young poet who was used to the Irish poem. It bore no resemblance to anything else. It was a rough, sinuous evocation of a snowy New England I had never seen, a Puritan rubric I had never heard of, a historical reinvention I knew next to nothing about. As a piece of information it was a lot less clear than *Lycidas* and a lot less transparent than *Adonais*. It was also stubbornly mannered, hard to follow, given to cross-jumps of tone and point of view. I was twenty years old and a bad-tempered parochial in Kavanagh's definition, and I was not at all sure I wanted to persevere with it.

Yet my first information about Anne Bradstreet came from that poem. "Born 1612 Anne Dudley, married at 16 Simon Bradstreet, a Cambridge man, steward to the Countess of Warwick & protégé of her father Thomas Dudley, secretary to the Earl of Lincoln. Crossed in the *Arbella*, 1630, under Governor Winthrop."[1] But none of those practical details arrested me. The woman, the poet, was not yet visible. What disturbed and struck me were those fifty-seven stanzas. I didn't give them up. I continued to read. I floundered around in the richly divided identities of the piece. Part ode. Part dialogue. Part harangue. Part séance. And then the poet's voice, usurping the very identity he is seeking out.

(2)
Outside the New World winters in grand dark
white air lashing high thro' the virgin stands
foxes down foxholes sigh,
surely the English heart quails, stunned.
I doubt if Simon than this blast, that sea,
spares from his rigour for your poetry
more. We are on each other's hands
who care. Both of our worlds unhanded us. Lie stark,

(3)
thy eyes look to me mild. Out of maize & air
your body's made, and moves. I summon, see,
from the centuries it.
I think you won't stay. How do we
linger, diminished, in our lovers' air,
implausibly visible, to whom, a year,
years, over interims; or not;
to a long stranger; or not; shimmer and disappear.[2]

These stanzas by Berryman prove the point: using the materials of a different moment, he boldly and obstinately constructs a poet and a past. By the time the poem concludes, he has forced his way into the presence of Anne Bradstreet: that young woman who sailed from England at the age of eighteen, who found the Massachusetts winters harsher than those in Lincolnshire, who bore American children, who wrote love poems to her husband, who resolved her quest for style in a radical, domestic polemic. The problem is that by the time the poem is over, we know how the Massachusetts winter drifts down through a broken syntax, how a scalding faith may once have sounded, how musical those names and salutations were. We can even guess about John Berryman's need for a past, a place, a source. But what do we know about her?

2

Anne Dudley was born in 1612, in Northamptonshire, in an England that had been nine years without its imperious queen and would, in another four, lose William Shakespeare and the raffish ethos of the Tudor world. Post-Elizabethan England. Already sewing the wind of the Civil War that was less than thirty years away. Already feeling the pinch and reproach of real-life Malvolios.

Her father was Thomas Dudley, at first clerk to Judge Nicolls in Northamptonshire and then steward of the earl of Lincoln's estate in Sempringham. These were not great people, but they lived in the shadow and peace of greatness. Her father would have known about fine wines and treasured books and the weighty ermines of the court. He would have talked to the ambitious builders and covetous architects of the period. Although he himself had never been to university he had been tutored by a graduate, so he was able to give his daughter some knowledge of Greek and Latin and French.

It is hardly possible to imagine that England. It was a paradox, a contradiction, a place marching toward regicide and fratricide yet still in sight of the glories and upheavals of the Elizabethan Age. Although Anne Dudley must have heard reminiscences, within the shelter of the earl of Lincoln's estates, of the Armada, of the queen, of ships returning with silks and spices and new tastes and stolen riches, her reality was darker. When the Massachusetts Bay Company was formed in 1628, she was sixteen years old. Her father and her new husband, Simon Bradstreet, were founding members. The nonconformist protest was intensifying, and rage at the taxes and restrictions of Charles I was suddenly the text for action. The old England, with its grace, pride, and remembrance, was now a life-threatening fiction.

In 1630 these founding members began their "errand into the wilderness," as Samuel Danforth called it.[3] The *Arbella* set sail from Southampton. Three months later John Winthrop wrote that "there came a smell off the shore like the smell of a garden."[4] They were safe. They landed at Massachusetts. For Puritanism it was a new context. For America a new history. For Anne Bradstreet a new story. Or half of one. As she steps onto the shore of New England, she disappears. The young woman who loved England is lost in America. "I . . . came into this country, where I found a new world and new manners, at which my heart rose."[5]

Anne Bradstreet is that rare thing: a poet who is inseparable from history. The proportions are not usually so equal and compelling. She can be located in the same way as a place name on a map, and we can judge the distance more accurately because of that. After all, it was history that swept her up, out of the graceful houses and prospects of Lincolnshire and into a three-month sea voyage. History that brought her to the shores of Massachusetts. History that included her in the rigorous self-definition of the Puritans. History that almost demoted her to a figure in the background of a turbulent time.

But when she encountered the New World, she was met not so much by history as by daily routine and hardship. The first winter was cruel and hungry. Food was scarce. "Clams, and muscles [*sic*], and ground-nuts and acorns"[6] must have seemed a poor diet after the feasts of Lincolnshire. Even her father wrote the bleak truth back to England: "There is not a house where is not one dead, and some houses many."[7] But her life at that moment was set in a mold of survival and compliance, both. First the hard winters, the forced adaptation. Then it was swift and relentless shifting: from Salem to Charlestown, to Cambridge, to Ipswich, and finally to Andover. With each move, each unquestioning pursuit of her husband and father, each trekking after Dudley and Simon Bradstreet, she wrote herself deeper into that difficult history.

The mid-thirties found the Dudleys and Bradstreets living in Ipswich, with a parcel of land, some more prosperity, a gradual easing of conditions. Now twenty-four years old, with two children, Anne Bradstreet had partially recovered from the lameness she had suffered during her eighteenth year. She was raising her children, absorbing her landscape, writing in earnest. And there I leave her for the moment so as to widen the story of which she is a part.

3

The mysterious life and achievement of Anne Bradstreet—her occasionally surprising and quick-moving poems, her fresh and intense outlook—is a story I will keep circling around here. No one approach is completely satisfactory. History, culture, political change are all part of it. But not all of it. Some of her truth may have less to do with history than with social anachronism. Because Anne Bradstreet is a founding American poet, it is easy to forget that she was also a dying star in the context of European poetry: a poet writing against a background of adamant faith from a country deeply troubled by the usurpation of religion by politics. A poet of the coteries, when the wider community was becoming fashionable. A poet whose inner and outer life remained powerfully undivided, when the subtle divisions between them—from which romanticism would eventually emerge—was beginning to evolve in England.

It is ironic that had Anne Bradstreet stayed in England, her ecosystem would have been radically different. In a country with an incipient Civil War, a poisoned and politicized religious system, and, after that, an approaching Restoration, where women would be considered bait for princes rather than poets in their own right, how would she have fared? Any consideration of Anne Bradstreet's work has to take this into account: she left a poetic tradition in which she would almost certainly have remained anonymous and founded another in which she is visible, anomalous, and crucial.

4

How do I see Anne Bradstreet? The answer is not simple. To start with, there is no figure in Irish poetry like her. To read of her travels and her pieties, to consider the male power that surrounded her and to which she deferred, and finally to hear her plain-spoken and resistant voice convince me of some out-of-the-way poetic truths. Here is one of them:

When we speak of the way a poet constructs the poets of another age—which is a good deal of my subject—certain things get missed. When I was a young poet, it was an article of faith that modernism was the watershed, the event that changed every poet's view of the recent and distant past. If I wasn't persuaded then, I am even less convinced now.

No, the real watershed—the place where poets divide—is in the version of those centuries—the sixteenth, seventeenth, and eighteenth—which are talismanic possessions for the young poet. Not just in poetry. After all, in those centuries galaxies were found and poetic forms rediscovered; faiths were changed and diseases named. Those are the centuries that divide or attach poets.

Those are the last continents of time where the hinterland of poetry lay as a gleaming, shining distance, still to be named and changed. Just to see that hinterland, just to lay claim to those possessions, is for the young poet often the first unforgettable sensing of the freedom and the grandeur of the art.

But my version of those centuries is the Irish, not the British or American one. There is a world of difference. As Anne Bradstreet was seeking the New World, Ireland was losing the old one. As the Massachusetts Bay Colony was testing its ideas of grace, Ireland was sinking deeper into its knowledge of abandonment. As Simon Bradstreet was touching the light of manifest destiny, the Gaelic order, the bards and the unlucky princes of Ireland were preparing to learn the opposite. And what Anne Bradstreet took with her into her poetry, into the New World—that upward roll of Elizabethan music—is the very cadence that poisoned the wells for the Irish poets.

So when I picture her, this figure from the time and language that dispossessed my own, how can I see her clearly? I am not John Berryman, imagining her on the deck of the *Arbella,* founding his tradition, guaranteeing his music, fearing her elusiveness—"I think you won't stay."[8] Unlike Berryman, my syntax was guaranteed by another group of poets.

But the truth is, I do see her. And somehow the fact that I do, despite not counting her century into my inheritance, seems to prove my point: that the reconstruction of the past, the reconstruction of poet by poet, is willful, inventive, compulsive. The truth is, I cannot afford not to see Anne Bradstreet. She lays her claim across every boundary, in spite of every distance. What's more, she tests my own powers of reconstruction. Pock-marked, slightly lame, outspoken and astonishing in her ability to survive the odds, she comes before me.

5

Anne Bradstreet was thirty-eight when her poetry was published. Not in her native Massachusetts, not even in America, but in an England she would never see again. Her brother-in-law arranged it. He returned to England in 1650, bringing a manuscript of her poems with him and arranging for its publication as *The Tenth Muse, Lately Sprung Up in America.* It would appear to be a strange route to publication but only if seen through modern eyes. Publication for contemporary poets has been a single and sometimes superstitious act: the first book, then the second. But I suspect that in Puritan Massachusetts, as once in eighteenth-century Ireland, the line between what was broadcast and published and locally known and communally written was not at all as clear as it became later: that there was a rich, blurred run of colors at the edge of private authorship and public faith.

The Tenth Muse was published through the efforts of her brother-in-law, the Reverend John Woodbridge, who wrote a winning and eloquent "Epistle to the Reader" at the start of the book. It is Anne Bradstreet's only publication in her lifetime. Not until she had been dead six years did a second, amended edition of *The Tenth Muse* come out. A third followed in 1758. This is a leisurely publication schedule by any standards, and not until 1867 did John Harvard Ellis produce a scholarly and complete text of this book, with more authoritative inclusions.

In his "Epistle to the Reader" Woodbridge is quick to disclaim any poetic vanity on the part of his sister-in-law. He remarks that he has "presumed to bring to publick view what she [Bradstreet] resolved should in such manner never see the sun."[9] Despite this, the poems are only partially successful. A heavy Spenserian shadow hangs over them, as if her girlhood ghost were haunting the paneled rooms of Sempringham. They pay elaborate and conventional tribute to the old heroes and graces of her past: Philip Sidney; her father, Thomas Dudley. The public tone often falters; the language rarely shines. Only *In Honour of That High and Mighty Princess Queen Elizabeth of Happy Memory* cracks open to suggest strength and craft. Despite a clumsy percussion, despite the rhymes swerving and chasing the sentiments around the page, there is a vigor of nostalgia, something haunting and striking about this memory of a powerful woman, written by a woman just learning her own power:

> Who was so good, so just, so learn'd, so wise,
> From all the kings on earth she won the prize.
> Nor say I more than duly is her due,
> Millions will testify that this is true.
> She hath wiped off th' aspersion of her sex,
> That women wisdom lack to play the rex.
> Spain's monarch, says not so, nor yet his host;
> She taught them better manners, to their cost.[10]

There is no mystery about *The Tenth Muse*. It is the oddly confident, sometimes accomplished work of a well-born woman. The mystery comes later. After 1653, in the years following the death of her father, Anne Bradstreet's poems changed. The subjects closed in. Her feelings, her children, the life of her home, the spirit of her marriage—these, rather than elegies for lost courtiers, became her themes. The music shifted: the volume was turned down; the voice became at once more private and more intense. A quick-walking cadence accompanied the neighborly, definite voice in which she now told her story. These were cadences that came from the New England moment in which she lived. At last the complicated England of her youth was receding.

To My Dear and Loving Husband
If ever two were one, then surely we.
If ever man were loved by wife, then thee;
If ever wife was happy in a man,
Compare with me, ye women, if you can.
I prize thy love more than whole mines of gold
Or all the riches that the East doth hold.
My love is such that rivers cannot quench,
Nor ought but love from thee, give recompense.
Thy love is such I can no way repay,
The heavens reward thee manifold, I pray.
Then while we live, in love let's so persevere
That when we live no more, we may live ever.
(225)

Or this, from the last year of her life:

In Reference to Her Children, 23 June 1659
I had eight birds hatched in one nest,
Four cocks there were, and hens the rest.
I nursed them up with pain and care,
Nor cost, nor labour did I spare,
Till at the last they felt their wing,
Mounted the trees, and learned to sing;
Chief of the brood then took his flight
To regions far and left me quite.
My mournful chirps I after send,
Till he return, or I do end:
Leave not thy nest, thy dam and sire,
Fly back and sing amidst this choir.
(232–34)

Where does this voice come from? On the surface, it seems to be earned and made by a woman caught in an unusually rich and powerful dialogue with an authoritarian tradition. Whatever name is given to that authority—maleness, Puritanism, doctrine—the dialogue is sweetened by a strange irony. It appears that the Puritan world can offer a woman poet more permission for domestic and ordinary detail than the Elizabethan one ever did. This is not to diminish the authorship. It is Anne Bradstreet's unique achievement that she could burrow into the cracks, discover the air of history, and find a breathing space to be Puritan, poet, and woman:

> I washed thy face, but more defects I saw,
> And rubbing off a spot still made a flaw.
> I stretched thy joints to make thee even feet,
> Yet still thou run'st more hobbling than is meet;
> In better dress to trim thee was my mind,
> But nought save homespun cloth i' th' house I find.
>   ("The Author to Her Book," 221)

As Adrienne Rich wrote of her: "The web of her sensibility stretches almost invisibly within the framework of Puritan literary convention; its texture is essentially both Puritan and feminine."[11] And the Puritan spirit is more easily reconciled, it seems, within the domestic parameter, with the willful, personal intention of the earthly artist, envious of being remembered. "You once desired me," she writes to her son in 1664, "to leave something for you in writing that you might look upon, when you should see me no more."[12]

In the final years of the 1660s, when a lavish court has been reinstated in the country of her birth, Anne Bradstreet—only a few years from her death in 1672—is a world away from power and costume. She has become the author of a bold, personal narrative, mourning her grandchildren, stripping out the rhythms she once learned as ornament, making them serve true feeling:

> I knew she was but as a withering flower,
> That's here today, perhaps gone in an hour;
> Like as a bubble, or the brittle glass,
> Or like a shadow turning as it was.
>   ("In Memory of My Dear Grandchild Anne Bradstreet," 236)

But where did she get the permission for this? Did she really find the sustenance in a Puritan world for what looks remarkably like private and willful expression? The answer (or answers) to that question puts the most strain on the second subject of this piece: the relation between the past and present of poetry. Between the dead and living poet.

6

Anne Bradstreet not only lived in another time; she continues to dwell in a past that I could never hope to find. Strong-willed, displaced, she appears and disappears in front of me. The pock-marked young English girl, scarred by a mystery illness, becomes an American woman poet in the midst of a drama of fervor and faith, becomes the wife and daughter of powerful men, becomes mother of a powerful son to whom she confided her language and purpose.

I wish I could see her clearly. I wish I could see the pen she wrote with. I wish I could reach back to those first hurt conversations in the Massachusetts colony, to her struggles with grace and her conflict with obedience. I wish I could see her in the house in Ipswich, with her children around her. "Nor cost, nor labour did I spare."[13]

The fact is, I can't. And to overlook this simple realization may well corrupt that contact between poet and poet that I began by considering. Poets of the present may invent the poets of the past all too easily, may wrench them from the disciplines and decisions of the world they lived in with such care and pain and disfigure them in a more convenient present.

The example of Anne Bradstreet is a sobering, chastening warning to such canon making. I cannot, as I've said, reconstruct her. If the young woman is unavailable, the older one is elusive. But even the poet that she is resists, in some strange way, any easy reevaluation by the present. In this may lie one of the enduring fascinations of her work. So in summary I will try to outline some of that resistance here.

The challenge offered by Anne Bradstreet's work is partly to do with its time and location: its origins in one world and its outcome in another. But there is more to the issue than that. In a real way her work lays bare the possible corruptions of the invention of one poet by another, of the past by the present.

If one poet returned to another with simply the prejudices of a time, it would be awkward but understandable: there might be a risk of simplification but not erasure. But this is never the case. We return as poets to the past lugging the huge wing-beams and magical engines and turbines of our age. We drag them across subtleties and differences and demand that our predecessors learn to fly as we have. Providing, of course, they use our machines to do so.

Consider Anne Bradstreet. She lived in a community and adventure of faith, at a real and figurative distance from a continent where both were fading. She struggled with the very concepts of grace, unreason, and compliance that Europe was preparing to throw over. Her first poems—those in *The Tenth Muse*—were structured, formal, and derivative. Her final ones were sharp and musical and impossible to overlook. She waits to be reconsidered. But how can it be done?

In one sense she is a compelling figure precisely because she stands outside the categories we have prepared for the dialogue between past and present. Our concepts of what constitutes the public and private poem will not do when we approach her. Above all, our postromantic definition of what is the inner life and what the outer in poetry, and who patrols the borders, will not serve in her case. If we use these categories, we will blur the astringent angles of what she achieved. But how to do otherwise?

A quick look shows how. If we return to Anne Bradstreet with our definitions of the public and private poem and notions of nineteenth-century inner life, we will be drawn to a single and deceptive conclusion: the poems in *The Tenth Muse* are more wooden and fixed than Bradstreet's later poems. The later poems are fresh, warm, particular. How tempting it is to use our everyday categories of criticism to argue that her inner mind was freed by the death of her father; that this new freedom compelled her to negotiate the inner world of love and domesticity into a private poetry rather than an official one; that she found a private voice within the public ethos of Puritanism; that, if the truth were told, she is a subversive within the larger structures of the early American experience. These are certainly appealing propositions. But are they true?

It would be convenient if they were. It would make Anne Bradstreet immediately available to the poetic wisdoms of our own time. But I am not sure. As an Irish poet I see a flaw in those divisions between private and public. As a woman poet I see a founding inaccuracy in this blueprint of the inner life. No, to understand her at all requires a break with the norms of psychobiography—far too often employed on poets and especially women poets—and an attempt to track her in the broader context where her works belong.

It is tempting to see the girl who left England in 1628 as young and singular, almost a child bride about to travel from ease to hardship, and to read back from her poetry to catalogue her adjustments and realizations. But this view is incomplete. No individual journey can explain the woman who suddenly, in 1662, could write with spirit, with a compelling contemporary eloquence, about desire in marriage, the death of children, the burning of her house. Another explanation is necessary.

The tense and elaborate world of poetry she left behind must have seemed a faraway dream in the mid-seventeenth century on the salty coasts of New England. But her shedding of that world is not easily measurable today. It would be a mistake to look for it in one act of style or one suppression of rhetoric. It has to be judged, like a quark or quasar, by absences, negations, negative energies, suppositions of space and distance.

The England that Anne Bradstreet left behind had already assigned a place to the poet. And it is clearly identified in those poems in *The Tenth Muse* in which she herself echoes the place-making energies of that canon. The place is not to be found in style. It is a series of angles and distances, a series of inferences by which poets reveal the ground they stand on by the words they choose.

By the time Anne Bradstreet sailed for America, the English poet had in these angles and relations an inner and outer world. Like a child, that poetic world had dissociated itself out of self-protection: it had split apart the better to handle the raw, intimate relation to power that history and society had ordained for the English poet of that time. The outer world was often coded into decorums, ornaments, pieces of rhetoric. The inner world was dark, raw, nihilistic. And this dichotomy reflected the fact that the poet of Elizabethan England, and before that Tudor England, was often an artist of grace and gifts who had learned the hard way—Surrey is an obvious example—that power offered no exemption, that poets must write in the shadow of the gallows, as well as in the light of favor. Above all, they had learned how to arm themselves with the gorgeous pastoral of prothalamion—the rivers, the nymphs, the musical harmonies—the better to infer a world of exclusion and pain.

What happened to Anne Bradstreet? To put it another way, What did not happen to her? She did not learn from the young Milton, the young Marvell. She did not see how ornament might imply disorder. She did not learn that the poet's place is in a split-apart world. In fact, the opposite. She came to enact in her life and her work a world of action, faith, expression, family, and ordinary adventure. And in the process the fissure healed. And suddenly—of course not suddenly—we have a woman in middle life whose children are gone, whose house has burned down, who makes no angles, distances, or perspective among faith, event, and feeling. They are all one. They have all happened. So she generates a poem in which they are indivisible, from a sensibility that is not divided. And she changes the history of poetry.

By this interpretation Anne Bradstreet wrote—in her best and later work—in a community so scalded by change and history that the public and private were fused into one and the same. This is a rare circumstance for poetry. Nevertheless, I suspect her poems were indeed written in the crucible of that fusion: they document a privacy that was public and a public faith that was privately realized. They also presume the most intimate and exacting audience: one anxious to hear and see its own new adventures. If all this is true, then the later shift into the intimacy of poems about her husband, her children, her domestic life is not truly disruptive. The poems are merely continuations of this powerful intimacy between poet and community caught in the same dialogue of faith, duty, reflection. Anne Bradstreet's poems shift and reassemble and shimmer with the hard-won confidence of that complex historical self. They are excitingly innocent of the sense that this is, by some definition of her own past, a smaller life. Most important, by being innocent of these definitions, she questions our own.

It would be wrong to make extravagant claims for Anne Bradstreet. Her work is memorable and strange and moving but also uneven and unrealized in certain parts. Yet it would also be wrong to deny how strongly she challenges our rights over the past. However powerful the relation between poet and poet, it must always yield to a poet like Anne Bradstreet, a poet whose work comes from a world both made and suffered and not at all ready to be erased by our easy assumptions, a poet who makes it clear that any relation with her must be on her terms also.

NOTES

1. John Berryman, *Homage to Mistress Bradstreet and Other Poems* (New York: Noonday Press, 1968), 10.

2. Ibid., 11.

3. Samuel Danforth, "Brief Recognition of New England's Errand into the Wilderness," in *American Sermons: The Pilgrims to Martin Luther King Jr.,* ed. Michael Warner (New York: Library of America, 1999), 151.

4. John Winthrop, "Journal," in *Winthrop Papers,* 5 vols. (Boston: Massachusetts Historical Society, 1929–47), 2:259.

5. *The Works of Anne Bradstreet in Prose and Verse,* ed. John Harvard Ellis (Charlestown, Mass.: A. E. Cutter, 1867), 5.

6. Alexander Young, *Chronicles of the First Planters* (Boston: Little, Brown, 1846), 381.

7. Thomas Dudley, "Letter to Countess of Lincoln," in ibid., 325.

8. "Homage to Mistress Bradstreet" (line 40), in Berryman, *Homage to Mistress Bradstreet.*

9. Quoted in Ellis, *Works,* 84.

10. *The Works of Anne Bradstreet,* ed. Jeannine Hensley, with a foreword by Adrienne Rich (Cambridge, Mass.: Harvard University Press, 1967), 195–98. All verse quotations are from this volume. Subsequent pagination will be indicated parenthetically in the essay proper.

11. Hensley, *Works of Anne Bradstreet,* xix.

12. Quoted in Hensley, *Works of Anne Bradstreet,* 271.

13. From "In Reference to Her Children, 23 June 1659," in Hensley, *Works of Anne Bradstreet,* 232.

NINE

Unordinary Passions

Margaret Cavendish, the Duchess of Newcastle

ALICE FULTON

I'VE BEEN A POET FOR TWENTY-THREE YEARS, and I don't cry easily. I've seen poetry at home in its inky T-shirt and at large in its designer dress. I've done time in poetry boot camp and at the top of Parnassus. I've joined workshops held in funeral parlors and delegations to the People's Republic of China. I've raised consciousness, figuratively, in the presence of famous feminist poets and lost consciousness, literally, in the presence of renowned romantic poets. I've been dressed down by colleagues with thought disorders; I've received an honorary doctorate. I've awoken in the artist colony to find excrement smeared over my bathroom by a rejected fellow. I've overheard three men poets, celebrated for their sensitive verse, describe their vengeful rape fantasy: "You hold her hands behind her back while I fuck her and Blameless shoves his fist up her ass." I've been a poet for twenty-three years, I've seen poetry at home in its sour sneakers, at large in its power suit, and I don't cry easily. So I was surprised to find myself moved to tears while reading a poem by Margaret Cavendish, the duchess of Newcastle.

At one time I might have bought into the fiction of dispassionate criticism. However, it now seems disingenuous to elide the emotional components of evaluation: the hysterical rancor that fuels vitriolic reviews, the critic's crush on beloved works. I've come to think that the deepest engagement is possible only when a reader falls for a poet's work, finding there a home away from home, self away from self. Whereas I once might have mistrusted the slippery slope of this position, I now mistrust appraisals that would lop off the critic's affective life. This is not to dismiss analysis or theory. Statements of feeling (*this poetry is exhausting; this poetry is exhilarating*) that fail to investigate the cause of emotive effects are irresponsible and naive. By exploring the poem's form and content, by locating it within an ongoing struggle of tradition, we might understand how emotion couched in language attains durability. I would like to understand the indelible feeling that traveled across three and a half centuries of belittlement and neglect to break my voice as I read.

———

I recently joined a reading group composed of scientists and humanists. At our last meeting a professor of linguistics admitted to "falling in love with" Margaret Fuller, the nineteenth-century feminist. I was delighted by his choice of words. It is unscholarly to own up to crushes. I was in the grip of one myself, but everyone expects gooey thinking from poets. "I'm in love with Margaret Cavendish, the duchess of Newcastle," I admitted. Margaret Cavendish was all I wanted to talk about really. Every conversation that night put me in mind of her or her work. Like all lovers, I prize the traits that others have despised in her: her gaucheness and original style, her guileless pursuit of fame, her eccentricity. Her goodness. I respect and would defend this duchess for her courage, honesty, intrepidness, intellect, fairness, charm, innocence, and common sense. Her goodness. But if these strengths and felicities of character were not amply evident in her poetry, their presence in her life would hold much less interest for me. Had her poetry proved unworthy, I would not have succumbed to what I'm calling "love."

Margaret Cavendish's poetry deserves emphasis because it has been sacrificed to her legend, and her legend has been founded on the laziness of hearsay and the wickedness of misogyny for 350 years. She has had her defenders, of course. Now that I know her, I am fond of her champions. I think better of Charles Lamb for deeming her "the thrice noble, chaste, and virtuous . . . original-brain'd, generous Margaret Newcastle."[1] And I think less of Samuel Pepys, who disliked her because she was "so unordinary."[2] Her detractors' opinions, when scrutinized, tend to dissolve into gossip. They certainly show little evidence of any comprehensive engagement with her work. Although recent scholarship has been far more responsible than the wholesale bludgeonings meted out by literary history, today's attention seems to gravitate toward her prose and plays. In fact, I could find no serious appraisal of Margaret Cavendish's poems by a critic whose primary field is poetry.

Although poems are included in several of Cavendish's thirteen books, her debut publication, *Poems and Fancies,* devotes itself most fully to verse. All of the poems quoted in this essay are taken from that volume. I've spent a few weeks poring over a reproduction of the 1653 first edition, my progress slowed to the luxurious basking pace of poetry by the book's antiquated typeface: its ambiguous *s* and *f* that blur *wise* to *wife.* Because very few people have read her work, my wish is to guide readers toward some of the stronger poems and to suggest their singular merits. It is possible to read Cavendish's verse for its intriguing representations of seventeenth-century folkways or science. Such an approach has its own value and necessity, but it begs the foundational question of quality: why are these good poems? By what means do they create pleasure and, yes, emotion? How do they exist within the context of their epoch and the broader spectrum of aesthetics?

When considered within the nexus of the seventeenth century, Margaret Cavendish's poems bear some resemblance to those of George Herbert and Richard Crashaw. As this comparison suggests, she wrote two different sorts of verse: one is kin to the simplicity of Herbert; the other shares the grotesque sensibility of Crashaw. The first sort is uncontrived in the best sense of the word; the second is contrived in ways that disturb the reader's sense of proportion and taste. Cavendish is not a religious poet, however, and this fact alone assures that any likeness to Herbert or Crashaw will be full of difference.

Whereas Herbert's simplicity is worshipful and austere, Cavendish's plain style is heretical and rustic. Her work is more roughly spun than his, her diction and phrasing more impulsive and fauve. Ragged syncopation and slant rhymes enliven her surfaces, and details of seventeenth-century manners and customs sweeten the content. Her finest poems, impassioned by an artless eloquence, bespeak an innocence of "craft" in the sense of wiles or manipulation. In *Sociable Letters* (1664) she noted that "some may say that if my Understanding be most of Sheep, and a Grange, it is a Beastly Understanding; My answer is I wish Men were as Harmless as most Beasts are, then surely the World would be more Quiet and Happy than it is."[3] Her imagery often arose from her knowledge of farming, and she also drew on the female spheres of housewifery or, as in the following excerpt, fashion:

I *Language* want, to dresse my *Fancies* in,
The *Haire's* uncurl'd, the *Garments* loose, and thin;
Had they but *Silver Lace* to make them gay,
Would be more courted then in *poore array.*
Or had they *Art,* might make a *better show;*
But *they are plaine,* yet cleanly doe they goe.
The world in *Bravery* doth take delight,
And *glistering Shews* doe more attract the *sight;*
And every one doth honour a rich Hood,
As if the *outside* made the *inside* good.
And every one doth bow, and give the place,
Not for the *Man's sake,* but the *Silver Lace.*
Let me intreat in my poore Bookes behalfe,
That all may not adore the Golden Calf.
Consider pray, *Gold* hath no life therein,
And *Life* in *Nature* is the richest thing.[4]

Her deepest subject is not the human relation to God but to the natural
world. Her poems challenge Hobbes's assertion of humanity's preemi-
nence, especially as revealed in the manipulation of language. "All Crea-
tures may do as much," she wrote,

> but by reason they do it not after the same manner or way as Man, Man
> denies, they can do it at all; which is very hard; for what man knows,
> whether Fish do not Know more of the nature of Water, and ebbing and
> flowing, and the saltness of the Sea? or whether Birds do not know
> more of the nature and degrees of Air, or the cause of Tempests? . . . For,
> though they have not the speech of Man, yet hence doth not follow,
> that they have no Intelligence at all. But the Ignorance of Men concerning
> other Creatures is the cause of despising other Creatures, imagining
> themselves as petty Gods in Nature.[5]

By stressing the materiality of the human state and the mysterious divinity
of the creaturely world, Cavendish posits a radical reversal of grounds:
"And for the *Mind,* which some say is like *Gods,* / I do not find, 'twixt
Man, and *Beast* such odds . . ." ("Of Humility"). The intensity of her
fellow feeling, coupled with her freshness and guilelessness, makes her a
poet of great charm and genuine moral weight.

When evaluating untried poets, T. S. Eliot suggested that we ask not
are they great? but "are they *genuine?*"[6] The word *genuine,* however, has
come to suggest a rhetoric of sincerity that is by no means hard to sim-

ulate. In his essay on "The Metaphysical Poets" Eliot noted that Herbert's simplicity had been "emulated without success by numerous modern poets."[7] The trend continues in contemporary poems that mistake the simplistic for the simple and equate straightforward syntax, modesty of tone, and ordinary language with the genuine. Thus threadbare sentiments and sedentary ethics may be touted as "deeply felt" as long as they are plainly put. Many poets today, perhaps most, strive for such transparency, but the choice is more symptomatic of aesthetics than of ethics or character. The word *genuine,* however, connotes integrity and scruples; it suggests an authenticity of feeling and a depth of purpose that is unrelated to ease of understanding or clarity of surface. In her ambivalent essay on Cavendish, Virginia Woolf allowed that "the vast bulk of the Duchess is leavened by a vein of authentic fire."[8] But how does one assess the "authentic" or "genuine" without slipping into critical fallacies that suppose themselves privy to the poet's unstated motives? I think one can begin by asking what the poet has to gain or lose from the stand she has taken. If a poet risks the ridicule, scorn, abuse, and contempt of her age, I suspect I'm in the presence of "the genuine."

Cavendish was not only the first English woman to write for publication, but she was an ardent feminist whose sense of justice extended, as we will see, to the natural world. That she has been punished for her crimes in favor of humanity is beyond question. In *Margaret the First* biographer Douglas Grant notes that her compassion made her "speak out of turn in a century when cruelty to animals was all too common."[9] Her empathy surely was strengthened by her identification with beasts as mutual sufferers. In 1667 she was conflated with an animal in John Lacy's adaptation of *The Taming of the Shrew.* Cynthia M. Tuerk notes that Lacy's "Sauny the Scott" retains Shakespeare's names for all the characters with the exception of the shrew, whom he christens "Margaret." Tuerk speculates that Lacy transformed "the controversial . . . Duchess of Newcastle" into "the plain speaking, scolding 'Petticoate Devil' who must be tamed into submission through the use of brutality and violence."[10]

Seventeenth-century misogyny was founded, in part, on Plato's conception of woman as an animal possessed of bodily life but bereft of reason and intellect. Cavendish recognized man's assertion of sovereignty as a self-serving belief that condoned the subjugation of nature and, by extension, women. Although her poems do not openly analogize animals to women, her prose and plays frequently present the comparison. In *Orations of Divers Sorts* (1662) she wrote that women "live like Bats or Owls, Labour like Beasts, and Dye like Worms."[11] She worried that women should grow Irrational as Idiots, by the Dejectedness of our Spirits, through the Careless Neglects and Despisements of the Masculine Sex to the Femal, thinking it Impossible we should have either Learning or Understanding, Wit or Judgement, as if we had not Rational Souls as well as Men, and we out of a Custom of Dejectedness think so too, which makes us Quit all Industry towards Profitable Knowledge . . . for we are Kept like Birds in Cages, to Hop up and down. . . . [W]e are Shut out of all Power and Authority. . . . [O]ur Counsels are Despised and Laught at; the best of our Actions are Troden down with Scorn, by the Over-weening conceit, Men have of Themselves, and through a Despisement of Us.[12]

Rather than arguing for woman's superiority to beasts, however, Cavendish argued that man, too, was an animal, and that animals were man's creaturely equals.

Although Cavendish's feminist stand attracted much spite, her empathy for otherness lends authority to her finest poetry. "A Dialogue of Birds," which I will excerpt, humanizes animals by endowing them with voices, emotions, and thought. Rather than the treacle and cuteness portended by such personification, the poem has the dignified purity of the ballads Cavendish loved to sing. Its songlike qualities predict the work of another self-educated "nature" poet, Robert Burns.

Both Cavendish and Burns have a canny eye for country details; both press the vernacular into a tumultuous prosody, and both strike an ingenuous, forthright tone. Yet Cavendish's poems are less playful and bantering than Burns's; their empathy is different in kind, more sober. Burns's "To a Mouse" recounts with winsome specificity that creature's trials before concluding: "Still thou are blest compared wi' me! / The present only toucheth thee." He then invokes memory and anticipation as sources of human suffering unknown to mice. Cavendish would make no such claim. Among beliefs she wished repealed was "That no Beast hath remembrance, numeration, or curiosity" ("The Animal Parliament"). In Burns's poem, moreover, the plowman-speaker informs the mouse of its own hardships. "A Dialogue of Birds," on the other hand, affords animals the agency and eloquence of testimony. The human observer is out of the picture, and this effacement assures that pity for animals does not devolve into self-pity. The matchless poignancy of Cavendish's animal poems can be attributed to the absence of human agendas, as well as the exactitude and freshness of the depiction. Witness, in the opening passage, how the image of the lark torquing its small force skyward is effectively extended to the corkscrew vibrato of its song:

As *I* abroad in *Feilds,* and *Woods* did walke,
I heard the Birds of severall things did talke:
And on the *Boughes* would *Gossip, prate,* and *chat,*
And every one discourse of *this,* and *that.*
I, said the *Larke,* before the *Sun* do rise,
And take my flight up to the *highest Skies:*
There sing some *Notes,* to raise *Appollo's* head,
For feare that *hee* might lye too long a *Bed.*
And as *I* mount, or if descend downe low,
Still do *I* sing, which way so ere *I* go.
Winding my *Body* up, just like a *Scrue,*
So doth my *Voice* wind up a *Trillo* too.
What *Bird,* besides my selfe, both flyes and sings,
Just tune my *Trilloes* keeps to my *flutt'ring Wings.*
    I, said the *Nightingale,* all night do watch,
For feare a *Serpent* should my *young Ones* catch:
To keep back sleep, *I* severall *Tunes* do sing,
Which Tunes so pleasant are, they *Lovers* bring
Into the *Woods;* who listning sit, and mark:
When *I* begin to sing, they cry, *hark, hark.*
Stretching my *Throat,* to raise my *Trilloes* high,
To gaine their praises, makes me almost dye.
    Then comes the *Owle,* which saies, here's such a doe
With your sweet *Voices;* through spight cries *Wit-a-woo.*
    In *Winter,* said the *Robin, I* should dye,
But that *I* in good warm house do flye:
And there do pick up *Crummes,* which make me fat,
But oft am scar'd away with the *Pusse-cat.*
If they molest me not, then *I* grow bold,
And stay so long, whilst *Winter Tales* are told.
Man superstitiously dares not hurt me,
For if *I* am kill'd, or hurt, *ill Luck* shall be.
    The *Sparrow* said, were our *Condition* such,
But *Men* do strive with *Nets* us for to catch:
With *Guns,* and *Bowes* they shoot us from the *Trees,*
And by small *Shot,* we oft our *Lifes* do leese,
Because we pick a *Cherry* here, and there,
When, *God* he knowes, we eate them in great feare.
But *Men* will eat, untill their *Belly* burst,
And *surfets* take: if we eat, we are *curst.*
Yet we by *Nature* are revenged still,
For eating over-much themselves they kill.
And if a *Child* do chance to *cry,* or *brawle,*

They strive to catch us, to please that *Child* withall:
With *Threads* they tye our *legs* almost to crack,
That when we *hop* away, they pull us back:
And when they cry *Fip, Fip,* strait we must come,
And for our paines they'l give us one *small Crum.*
   I wonder, said *Mag-pye,* you grumble so,
Dame Sparrow, we are us'd much worse *I* trow.
For they our *Tongues* do slit, their *words* to learne,
And with the *paine,* our food we dearely earne.
   Why, say the *Finches,* and the *Linnets* all,
Do you so prate *Mag-pie,* and so much baule?
As if no *Birds* besides were wrong'd but you,
When we by *cruell Man* are injur'd to.
For we, to learn their *Tunes,* are kept awake,
That with their *whistling* we no rest can take.
In *darknesse* we are kept, no *Light* must see,
Till we have learnt their *Tunes* most perfectlie.
But *Jack-dawes,* they may dwell their houses nigh,
And build their *Nests* in *Elmes* that do grow high:
And there may *prate,* and flye from place to place;
For why, they think they give their *House a grace.*
   Lord! said the *Partridge, Cock, Puet, Snite,* and *Quaile,*
Pigeons, Larkes, my *Masters,* why d'yee raile?
You're kept from *Winters Cold,* and *Summers heat,*
Are taught new *Tunes,* and have good store of meat.
Having a *Servant* you to wait upon,
To make your *Cages* cleane from *filth,* and *Dung:*
When we *poore Birds* are by the dozens kill'd,
And luxuriously us eate, till they be fill'd:
And of our *Flesh* they make such cruell wast,
That but some of our *Limbes* will please their tast.
In *Wood-cockes thighes* they onely take delight,
And *Partridge wings,* which swift were in their flight.
The smaller *Lark* they eate all at one bite,
But every part is good of *Quaile,* and *Snite.*
The *Murtherous Hawk* they keep, us for to catch,
And learn their *Dogs,* to *crouch,* and *creep,* and *watch:*
Untill they have *sprung* us to *Nets,* and *Toiles,*
And thus *poore Creatures* we are made *Mans* spoiles.
Cruell Nature! to make us *Gentle, Mild:*
They *happy* are, which are more *feirce,* and *wild.*
O would our *flesh* had been like *Carrion, course,*

To eate us onely *Famine* might inforce.
But when they eate us, may they surfets take,
May they be *poore,* when they a *Feast* us make.
The more they eate, the *leaner* may they grow,
Or else so *fat,* they cannot stir, nor go.
   O, said the *Swallow,* let me mourne in *black,*
For, of *Mans cruelty I* do not *lack:*
I am the *Messenger* of *Summer warme,*
Do neither pick their *Fruit,* nor eate their *Corne;*
Yet they will take us, when alive we be,
I shake to tell, *O horrid Cruelty!*
Beate us alive, till we an *Oile* become.
Can there to *Birdes* be a worse *Martyrdome?*
O Man, O Man, if we should serve you so,
You would against us your *great Curses* throw.
But *Nature, shee* is good, do not her blame:
We ought to give her thankes, and not exclaime.
For *Love* is *Natures* chiefest *Law* in *Mind,*
Hate but an *Accident* from *Love* we find.[13]

Over the next two pages the titmouse chides the other birds for neglecting their "Home-Affaires," and heeding this call to domesticity, they set about gathering spilled corn, newly sown seed, ripe cherries, and ant eggs with which to feed their chicks. Their flight home is likened to men returning from market, joined by "a *Troop* of *Neighbors.*" The birds' communal activities—their need to eat, breed, and exchange information—imply their kinship with the human. Embodiment is the leveling factor: we are alike in our ineluctable physicality, and this debt to materiality creates equity. Once in their nests, the birds carol a hymn asking God for a fine tomorrow. The view of the age was that man's immortal soul established his supremacy to nature. In constructing birdsong as prayer, Cavendish suggests that the natural world also communes with God and partakes of divinity by means of unorthodox worship. The poem's closure finds in sleep—with its intimations of mortality—a denominator both common and consoling. In a lovely simile the ebbing of birdsong is compared to a gradual closing of eyes:

At last they *drousie* grew, and heavie were to *sleep,*
And then instead of singing, cried, *Peep, Peep.*
Just as the *Eye,* when *Sense* is locking up,

Is neither open wide, nor yet quite shut:
So doth a *Voice* still by degrees fall downe,
And as a *Shadow*, wast so doth a *Sound*.
Thus went to rest each *Head*, under each *wing*,
For Sleep brings Peace to every living thing.

"John Clare was the nearest thing to the 'natural poet' for whom primi-tivists had been searching ever since the mid-eighteenth century," the *Norton Anthology* asserts.[14] The naif-seekers need not have waited so long: in Margaret Cavendish they could have had their innocent. Yet the un-studied rudeness of her work would not have pleased "the primitivists" in pursuit of a happy savage, painting idyllic naturescapes. Although "A Dialogue of Birds" has something of the sweetness of Clare's verse, Cav-endish generally is a far more disturbing poet. " 'Twas pity that in this Titanic Continent where ⟨brute⟩ Nature is so grand, Genius should be so tame," Emerson remarked of his own day and place.[15] Cavendish's genius was of the untamed variety; her expressiveness, as we shall see, exceeds the rules of decorum and aesthetics. Yet these violations awaken uncanny emotions—from grief to repugnance—and are largely responsible for the force of her poems.

"Nobody, so far as I know, not even an 18th-century minor poet, could imagine any connection between events in the mind of a cricket and those in the mind of a human," Lewis Thomas writes.[16] Robert Burns's "To a Louse," with its comic ruminations on extermination, hardly counts. Fast-forwarding to the nineteenth century, there is John Clare's fanciful por-trayal of "Insects" freed of "labours drudgery." Clare's poem says more about human misery and envy, however, than it does about the "tiney loiterer on the barley's beard." "I will begin to feel better about us," Lewis Thomas concludes, ". . . when we finally start learning about some of the things that are still mystifications. Start with the events in the mind of a cricket, I'd say, and then go on from there."[17] Several of Margaret Cav-endish's poems start in such places—the minds of birds, stags, or hares—and go on to suggest sympathetic connections between animal and human intelligences. Her poems, like John Clare's, are fearlessly anthropomor-phic. But her assignment of human traits illuminates the animals' sen-tience rather than the human psyche.

Within the context of scientific inquiry the dangers of anthropomorphizing are well-rehearsed. In poetics "the pathetic fallacy," a term coined by John Ruskin in 1856, describes the projection of human traits onto the nonhuman. With a nod toward Ruskin the bulk of twentieth-century aesthetics has dismissed the anthropomorphic gesture as inherently sentimental. Postmodern poetry, for its part, doesn't worry about the pathetic fallacy; its concerns are other and elsewhere. But science's fear of the anthropomorphic continues, and that caution begins to seem overdetermined. Perhaps our closeness to animals frightens us into asserting difference. We do tend to subjugate any version of ourselves that is not completely to our liking. There is, moreover, some sleight of mind or doublethink at the heart of the scientific argument. The projection of human traits onto animals is said to distort objectivity: we cannot assume that they are like us. Animal experiments, however, are founded on just that assumption. The similitude that creates the test's value also creates the ethical dilemma. If animals are enough like us to inform us of ourselves, how can we maim and kill them to secure that information? Surely if animals can serve as models for the human, humans can serve as models for the animal. To anthropomorphize is to acknowledge rather than disavow the inflection of human experience on investigations of nonhuman life. Human experience, after all, is the only kind we have.

In "The Hunting of the Stag" (*Poems and Fancies* 113–16) Cavendish uses personification to blur the distinction between human and animal. The poem begins by describing the deer's marvelous physicality: "His *Legs* were *Nervous,* and his *Joynts* were strong." Like Narcissus the stag is given to admiring his reflection in a brook, "Taking such *Pleasure* in his *Stately Crowne,* / His *Pride* forgets that *Dogs* might pull him downe." Although Cavendish no doubt thought of Charles I when composing those lines, the poem does not become an allegory of the death of kings. Just as the absence of moralizing makes John Clare's verse all the more enchanting, the absence of symbolism makes Cavendish's poems more heartfully profound. How tiresome it would be to read the stag as a stand-in for some loftier idea, and how refreshing it is to read him as a deer, expressing his own value or dearness. The poem takes the scenic route, meandering into a fascinating catalogue of trees that does nothing to deepen the tropes or advance the narrative. The stag wanders into a shady wood where ". . . *slender Birch* bowes head to *golden Mines.*" ("*Good* Mines *are found out by the* Birches *bowing,*" a side note ingenuously tells us.) The forest also holds:

Small *Aspen Stalkt* which shakes like *Agues* cold,
That from perpetuall *Motion* never hold.

.   .   .   .

The weeping *Maple,* and the *Poplar* green,
Whose *Cooling Buds* in *Salves* have healing been.

.   .   .   .

And *Juniper,* which gives a pleasant smell,
And many more, which were too long to tell.

The stag's epicurean palate charts his course through *Winter-savoury* and
Cowslips to the ultimate succulence of the farmer's wheat blades. After a
fine feed he is discovered and pursued by the field's owner, his dogs, and
other men who "for sport did come." The stag leaps into a river and tries
to swim invisibly as a fish. "But out alas, his *Hornes* too high do shew."
His proud antlers give him away, and the hunters' watery reflection un-
does his earlier image of noble materiality: "*Feare* cuts his *Breath* off short,
his *Limbs* do shrink, / Like those the *Cramp* doth take, to bottom sink."
The deer struggles until "His *Heart* so heavie grew, with *Griefe,* and *Care,* /
That his small *Feet* his *Body* could not beare." At the end he defiantly
faces the hunters: "But *Fate* his *thread* had spun, so downe did fall, /
Shedding some *Teares* at his own *Funerall.*"

Weeping animals probably make modern readers uneasy. But the un-
varnished closure has its own rude power; its nakedness moves beyond
sentimentality into poignancy. The stag's self-mourning—venial, vulner-
able—is terribly human. The final rhyme contrasts the ritualized grief of
a funeral to the ritualized killing of the hunt. The disproportion—be-
tween the stag's prizing of his life and the men's disdain of it, between
communal formalized mourning and the animal's lonely death—creates
pathos.

Earlier the hunters were compared to boys who "when *Mischiefe* takes
not place, / Is out of *Countenance,* as with *disgrace.*" An endearing trait of
Margaret Cavendish was her tendency to be thrown "out of countenance"
by social occasions. Cavendish's loyal maid, Elizabeth Toppe, described
her in a prefatory letter: "*You were always* Circumspect, *by Nature, not by
Art; . . . your* Ladiship *is naturally bashful, & apt to be out of Countenance,
that your* Ladiship *could not oblige all the* World."[18] But some accounts
suggest "*out of Countenance*" as a euphemism for what could happen to
Cavendish in unsympathetic company. She admitted to being afflicted
with "bashfulness" from childhood. "It hath many times obstructed the
passage of my speech, and perturbed my natural actions, forcing a con-

straintedness, or unusual motions," she wrote.[19] John Evelyn's wife described her conversation as "terminating commonly in nonsense, oaths, and obscenity,"[20] and Dorothy Osborne wrote that Cavendish's friends were at fault to "let her goe abroade."[21] Douglas Grant writes that when "confronted across the room by Mrs. Evelyn, coldly eyeing her from behind the mask of a modest conventional housewife, Margaret's demon seized command, translating her into the affected, grimacing creature whom her guest was later to deride."[22] Sir Walter Scott portrayed her as "an entire raree show . . . a sort of private Bedlam-hospital."[23]

Such testimonies make me wonder whether she might have suffered from Tourette's syndrome, a neurological disorder characterized by sudden, meaningless movements or vocalizations. These tics can include eye blinking; squinting; lip smacking; neck jerking; shoulder shrugging; arm flailing; nail biting; foot stomping; barking; coughing; hissing; humming; stuttering; sudden changes of voice tone, tempo, or volume; the utterance of short meaningless phrases; and, most famously, coprolalia, the compulsion to swear or use socially unacceptable words. The "forbiddenness" of a given expression compels sufferers to say it, against their will. Tics can vanish for long periods; thus Cavendish could have been symptom free when she first attracted the attention of her adoring husband, the dashing marquis of Newcastle.

Tourette's syndrome can induce some spectacularly bizarre behavior, but I wouldn't want such a "diagnosis" to efface a more important—and more evident—explanation for the imaging of Cavendish as literary embarrassment. It seems to me that she serves as a dumping ground for repressed anxieties concerning reputation and authority. Philosopher Robert Paul Wolff writes that the most common reason for acknowledging claims of authority, "taking the whole of human history, is simply the prescriptive force of tradition. The fact that something has always been done in a certain way strikes most men as a perfectly adequate reason for doing it that way again."[24] Despite recurring outré movements, the authoritative mainstream of literary culture, shaped by "the prescriptive force of tradition," emphasizes seemliness, conventionality, and patrilineage. My reading persuades me that fears concerning the transgression of such traditions have been displaced onto Margaret Cavendish. Her views, indeed her entire self-definition, were—and are—culturally incorrect. She championed women's rights; opposed cruelty to animals; argued for religious freedom; dismissed witchcraft, alchemy, and astrology as unfounded superstitions. She also trespassed on the male preserves of writing and science.

Although Cavendish's critics ostensibly thought about her, their own reputations were a large part of the subject. From the start her radically independent style evoked fear of contamination by association. Although she was the first woman invited to visit The Royal Society, the fashionable center of scientific discussion, some members opposed the invitation for fear that her presence would attract mockery. Of Cavendish's book *Nature's Pictures* biographer Kathleen Jones writes: "Although women could identify with the characters in Margaret's tales they hesitated to defend her in case they too were branded as 'ridiculous.' "[25] Through the centuries she has been treated as a contagious site liable to infect writers who ventured a close association. In 1759 Horace Walpole opined that her brain was "diseased with cacoethes scribendi."[26] Those who did venture to write about her used a condescending rhetoric as germ barrier or hid behind a surgical mask of satire.

Virginia Woolf notes that Cavendish became a bogey with which to frighten clever girls. The technique worked all too well. Woolf's several renditions of the duchess are amusing, yet frightened, pieces of writing. Although acknowledging her "wild, generous, untutored intelligence," Woolf compares Cavendish to "some giant cucumber" spreading itself "over all the roses and carnations in the garden" and choking them to death.[27] The genteel flowers snuffed out by this overbearing, phallic vegetable are, I would suggest, such exemplars of acceptable feminine behavior as Katherine Philips, "the Divine Orinda." Philips declared writing "unfit for the sex to which I belong"[28] and became sick with shame after her work was "inadvertently" published. She was, not accidentally, the reigning poetess of Cavendish's moment.

"Margaret's whole attitude to poetry flouted decorum," writes Douglas Grant. "Her real fault in Dorothy Osborne's eyes was an offense against taste."[29] The dismissive appraisals by those who've never read her work, the longevity of gossip, the spread of calumny as good copy, the critical opinions founded on hearsay, the knee-jerk authority of "prescriptive tradition," the ridicule occasioned by bravery—are frightening. Cavendish's role as designated whipping girl of English literature is frightening. The fearful derision and hostility directed at her for three and a half centuries should be retargeted toward the literary culture that created her reception.

Philosopher Mary Midgley offers sobering thoughts on the suasions of false evidence:

Even people who know perfectly well that the so-called *Protocols of the Elders of Zion* were deliberately forged by the Czarist police still find no difficulty in accepting them as evidence. The dark vision is too vivid to be doubted; its force is its warrant. What we see out there is indeed real enough; it is our own viciousness, and it strikes us with quite appropriate terror. And by an unlucky chance, while it remains projected, there is no way to weaken or destroy it. Persecution and punishment of those to whom it is attributed do not soften it at all. . . . Hence the strange insatiability of persecution, the way in which suspicion seems to grow by being fed. . . . The joint repressed aggression of a whole populace makes up a very powerful motive for communal crimes, such as . . . witch-hunts.[30]

—

"I am as fearefull as a Hare . . . only my courage is, I can heare a sad relation, but not without griefe, and chilnesse of spirits," Cavendish wrote.[31] The comparison of herself to a hare suggests the degree of sympathy she felt with hunted prey. Joy Williams writes, "Hunters have a tendency to call large animals by cute names—'bruins' and 'muleys,' 'berryfed blackies' and 'handsome cusses' and 'big guys,' thereby implying a balanced jolly game of mutual satisfaction between hunter and the hunted—*Bam, bam, bam, I get to shoot you and you get to be dead.*"[32] In like fashion the abundantly sane Cavendish was nicknamed "Mad Madge." It was a short journey from being outspoken or "out of countenance" to being declared out of her mind.

"The Hunting of the Hare," reprinted here in full, is the poem that moved me to tears. Of course, emotions are irreproducible results. You could read the poem to your closest companion, as I did, and not be moved as I was. No doubt my entire life prepared me to be stricken at a given point. Not just life, but the intrinsic sinews of DNA before lived experience began. (I wasn't alone in my emotion, though. When I looked at my husband, he was wiping his eyes.)

The Hunting of the Hare
Betwixt two *Ridges* of *Plowd-land,* lay *Wat,*
Pressing his *Body* close to *Earth* lay squat.
His *Nose* upon his two *Fore-feet* close lies,
Glaring obliquely with his *great gray Eyes.*
His *Head* he alwaies sets against the *Wind;*
If turne his *Taile,* his *Haires* blow up behind:
Which *he* too cold will grow, but *he* is wise,

And keeps his *Coat* still downe, so warm *he* lies.
Thus resting all the *day,* till *Sun* doth set,
Then riseth up, his *Reliefe* for to get.
Walking about untill the *Sun* doth rise,
Then back returnes, down in his *Forme he* lyes.
At last, *Poore Wat* was found, as he there lay,
By *Hunts-men,* with their *Dogs* which came that way.
Seeing, gets up, and fast begins to run,
Hoping some waies the *Cruell Dogs* to shun.
But they by *Nature* have so quick a *Sent,*
That by their *Nose* they race, what way *he* went.
And with their deep, wide *Mouths* set forth a *Cry,*
Which answer'd was by *Ecchoes* in the *Skie.*
Then *Wat* was struck with *Terrour,* and with *Feare,*
Thinkes every *Shadow* still the *Dogs* they were.
And running out some distance from the *noise,*
To hide himselfe, his *Thoughts* he new imploies.
Under a *Clod* of *Earth* in *Sand-pit* wide,
Poore *Wat* sat close, hoping himselfe to hide.
There long he had not sat, but strait his *Eares*
The *Winding Hornes,* and crying *Dogs* he heares:
Starting with *Feare,* up leapes, then doth he run,
And with such speed, the *Ground* scarce treades upon.
Into a great thick *Wood* he strait way gets,
Where underneath a *broken Bough* he sits.
At every *Leafe* that with the *wind* did shake,
Did bring such *Terrour,* made his *Heart* to ake.
That *Place* he left, to *Champion Plaines* he went,
Winding about, for to deceive their *Sent.*
And while they *snuffling* were, to find his *Track,*
Poore *Wat,* being weary, his swift pace did slack.
On his two *hinder legs* for ease did sit,
His *Fore-feet* rub'd his *Face* from *Dust,* and *Sweat.*
Licking his *Feet, he* wip'd his *Eares* so cleane,
That none could tell that *Wat* had hunted been.
But casting round about his *faire great Eyes,*
The *Hounds* in full *Careere* he neere him 'spies:
To *Wat* it was so terrible a *Sight,*
Feare gave him *Wings,* and made his *Body* light.
Though weary was before, by running long,
Yet now his *Breath* he never felt more strong.
Like those that *dying* are, think *Health* returnes,
When tis but a *faint Blast,* which *Life* out burnes.

For *Spirits* seek to guard the *Heart* about,
Striving with *Death,* but *Death* doth quench them out.
Thus they so fast came on, with such loud *Cries,*
That *he* no hopes hath left, no *help* espies.
With that the *Winds* did pity *poore Wats* case,
And with their *Breath* the *Sent* blew from the *Place.*
Then every *Nose* is busily imployed,
And every *Nostrill* is set open, wide:
And every *Head* doth seek a severall way,
To find what *Grasse,* or *Track,* the *Sent* on lay.
Thus quick Industry, that is not slack,
Is like to Witchery, brings lost things back.
For though the *Wind* had tied the *Sent* up close,
A *Busie Dog* thrust in his *Snuffling Nose:*
And drew it out, with it did foremost run,
Then *Hornes* blew loud, for th' *rest* to follow on.
The *great slow-Hounds,* their throats did set a *Base,*
The *Fleet swift Hounds,* as *Tenours* next in place;
The little *Beagles* they a *Trebble* sing,
And through the *Aire* their *Voice* a round did ring.
Which made a *Consort,* as they ran along;
If they but *words* could speak, might sing a *Song,*
The *Hornes* kept time, the *Hunters* shout for *Joy,*
And valiant seeme, *poore Wat* for to destroy:
Spurring their *Horses* to a full *Careere,*
Swim Rivers deep, leap Ditches without feare;
Indanger *Life,* and *Limbes,* so fast will ride,
Onely to see how patiently *Wat* died.
For why, the *Dogs* so neere his *Heeles* did get,
That they their sharp *Teeth* in his *Breech* did set.
Then tumbling downe, did fall with *weeping Eyes,*
Gives up his *Ghost,* and thus poore *Wat he* dies.
Men hooping loud, such *Acclamations* make,
As if the *Devill* they did *Prisoner* take.
When they do but a *shiftlesse Creature* kill;
To hunt, there need no *Valiant Souldiers* skill.
But *Man* doth think that *Exercise,* and *Toile,*
To keep their *Health,* is best, which makes most spoile.
Thinking that *Food,* and *Nourishment* so good,
And *Appetite,* that feeds on *Flesh,* and blood.
When they do *Lions, Wolves, Beares, Tigers* see,
To kill poore *Sheep,* strait say, they cruell be.
But for themselves all *Creatures* think too few,

For *Luxury,* with *God* would make them new.
As if that *God* made *Creatures* for *Mans meat,*
To give them *Life,* and *Sense,* for *Man* to eat;
Or else for *Sport,* or *Recreations* sake,
Destroy those *Lives* that *God* saw good to make:
Making their *Stomacks, Graves,* which full they fill
With *Murther'd Bodies,* that in sport they kill.
Yet *Man* doth think himselfe so gentle, mild,
When *he* of *Creatures* is most cruell wild.
And is so *Proud,* thinks onely he shall live,
That *God* a *God*-like *Nature* did him give.
And that all *Creatures* for his sake alone,
Was made for him, to *Tyrannize* upon.[33]

Did I say emotions were irreproducible results? Silly me. On TV last night a relaxation therapist described a test conducted on rabbits. The animals were fed a high-fat diet in order to determine its relation to arteriosclerosis. When the rabbits were "autopsied" (the flimsiest shade of misgiving passed over the therapist's face as he said the word), one group proved to have healthy arteries. This was mystifying because all the animals had received exactly the same food. On investigation a single difference came to light: the healthy rabbits had been cared for by a graduate student who stroked them when she fed them. (At this, a doctor serving as audience smiled benignly: isn't-that-sweet.) Of course, the experiment had to be conducted several times to verify the findings. After a sufficient number of rabbits had been caressed and vivisected, the study concluded that *compassion lowers cholesterol.*

At last a sound argument for loving-kindness. Let's be merciful and lower each other's cholesterol. The experiment also gave a reproducible effect (healthy arteries) stemming from an emotive cause (compassion). *Compassion?* Wouldn't *duplicity, selfishness, coldness, calculation* better describe the experiment's character? The listening doctor's sappy smile made me suspect a connection between sentimentality and synecdoche. To feel selectively, responding with fuzzy feelings to one aspect of an event while repressing any troubling emotions stirred by other aspects is, I submit, sentimental.

❧

Lewis Thomas observed that much of the current environmental concern is based on self-interest rather than concern for nature, "that vast incomprehensible meditative being."[34] Margaret Cavendish consistently took Nature's side. "Dialogue with an Oake" finds a tree arguing with Man, who is about to cut it down. Throughout the poem Man unwittingly testifies to human greed, which he conflates with Man's "divine nature." The poem concludes with an ironic comment on Man's perversity and narcissism: only if the Oake desires the afterlife of harvest, in which it would be transformed into a ship or house, will Man recognize his likeness in the tree and spare it from harvest.

Cavendish wrote a series of dialogues in which two players argue opposing sides of a question.[35] Her gift for seeing the recessive, yin slant of things, the ground rather than the figure, helped her to complicate these polarized conversations. Thus Darknesse tells Earth that the Sun is responsible for night: "I do not part you, he me hither sends / *Whilst* hee rides about, to visit all his *Friends.*" Hate depicts Love as self-serving: "Love loves Ambition, the Mind's hot Fire, / And Worlds would ruine, for to rise up higher." And Ignorance says that Learning "Doth nought but make an Almes-tub of the Braines." Cavendish's penchant for reversals arose not from a contrarian temperament but from her feelings of alterity and the specious arguments used to enforce that position. Notions of what constitutes "natural" behavior always have been invoked as a means of controlling women's lives. Cavendish turned the argument against itself: "It is not only Uncivil and Ignoble, but Unnatural, for Men to Speak against Women and their Liberties."[36] Many of her poems unsettle assumptions of hierarchy. "A Dialogue betwixt Wit, and Beauty" questions superiority founded on skin color:

> Mixt *Rose,* and *Lilly,* why are you so proud,
> Since *Faire* is not in all *Minds* best allow'd?
> *Some* like the *Black,* the *Browne,* as well as *White,*
> In all *Complexions* some *Eyes* take delight.

The dialogues show Cavendish's scientific intelligence, a cast of mind that assumed as little as possible and pressed the given explanations. Her skepticism led her to mistrust superficial perceptions and to critique the evidence of the senses. Using magnetism to exemplify counterintuitive truths, she wrote, "What *Eye* so *cleere* is, yet did ever see / Those *little Hookes,* that in the *Load-stone* bee" ("It is hard to believe, that there are other worlds in this world"). Passion makes us advocates: in the grip of emotion we cling wholeheartedly to one position, and other sides of the argument are lost to us. As if in recognition of this, the dialogues sometimes warp binary thinking by arguing both positions convincingly. Alterity implodes as agency is exchanged between equally convincing speakers. Readers are forced to acknowledge the power of both claims and to establish within the paradox of opposing truths a third, indeterminate space that differs from the fixed positions of dichotomous thinking.

Cavendish objected to standard measures of intelligence, noting that human beings may have "a different Knowledge from Beasts, Birds, Fish, Worms, and the like and yet be no Wiser or Knowing than they; for Different ways in Knowledge make not Knowledge more or less, no more than Different Paths inlarge one compass of Ground."[37] Her passion for equity extended beyond social and humanitarian contexts to notions of the sublime. Paradise was "Equinoctiall" ("Of a Garden"); and "a consecrated place" was one where trees "grew in equall space" ("Of an Oake in a Grove"). One of her loveliest works, "The Motion of Thoughts," uses Euclidean tropes of measurement to describe the light of cognition and the self-referential neural networks that give rise to consciousness. The poem begins with a nature walk that in romantic fashion leads to an epiphany:

> The Motion of Thoughts
> *Moving* along, mine *Eyes* being fixt
> Upon the *Ground,* my *Sight* with *Gravell* mixt:
> My *Feet* did walke without *Directions* Guide,
> My *Thoughts* did travell farre, and wander wide;
> At last they chanc'd up to a *Hill* to climbe,
> And being there, saw things that were *Divine.*
>   First, what they saw, a glorious *Light* to blaze,
> Whose *Splendor* made it painfull for the *Gaze:*
> No *Separations,* nor *Shadowes* by stops made,
> No *Darknesse* to obstruct this *Light* with *Shade.*
> This *Light* had no *Dimension,* nor *Extent,*
> But fil'd all places full, without *Circumvent;*
> Alwaies in *Motion,* yet fixt did prove,
> Like to the *Twinkling Stars* which never move.
> This *Motion* working, running severall waies,
> Did seeme a *Contradiction* for to raise;
> As to it *selfe,* with it *selfe* disagree,
> Is like a *Skeine* of *Thread,* if't knotted bee.
> For some did go strait in an even *Line,*
> But some againe did crosse, and some did *twine.*[38]

Lewis Thomas describes the mechanism of thought as follows: "Predictable, small-scale, orderly, cause-and-effect sequences are hard to come by and don't last long when they do turn up. Something else almost always turns up at the same time, and then another sequential thought intervenes alongside, and there come turbulence and chaos again. When we are lucky, and the system operates at its random best, something astonishing may suddenly turn up, beyond predicting or imagining."[39]

> Yet at the last, all severall *Motions* run
> Into the first *Prime Motion* which begun.
> In various *Formes* and *Shapes* did *Life* run through,
> *Life* from *Eternity,* but *Shapes* still new;
> No sooner made, but quickly pass'd away,
> Yet while they *were,* desirous were to stay.
> But *Motion* to one *Forme* can nere constant be,
> For *Life,* which *Motion* is, joyes in varietie.
> For the first *Motion* every thing can make,
> But cannot add unto it selfe, nor take.
> Indeed no other *Matter* could it frame,
> It *selfe* was all, and in it *selfe* the fame.
> Perceiving now this fixed *point* of *Light,*
> To be a *Union, Knowledge, Power,* and *Might;*
> *Wisdome, Justice, Truth, Providence,* all one,
> No *Attribute* is with it selfe alone.
> Not like to severall *Lines* drawne to one *Point,*
> For what doth meet, may separate, disjoynt.
> But *this* a *Point,* from whence all *Lines* do flow,
> Nought can diminish it, or make it grow.
> Tis *its* owne *Center,* and *Circumference* round,
> Yet neither has a *Limit,* or a *Bound.*
> A *fixt Eternity,* and so will last,
> All *present* is, nothing to come, or past.
> A fixt *Perfection* nothing can add more,
> All things is *It,* and *It* selfe doth adore.
> My *Thoughts* then wondring at what they did see,
> Found at the last* themselves the same to bee;
> Yet was so small a *Branch,* perceive could not,
> From whence they *Sprung,* or which waies were begot.

Cavendish supplies a marginal gloss for what is "Found at the last*": "*All things come from God Almighty.*" The glorious light of the mind, which turns out to be God's light, is self-involved as any animal: "A fixt *Perfection* nothing can add more / All things is *It,* and *It* selfe doth adore." The paradox of the one/many problem is charmingly enacted by the disagreement between the plural subject, *things,* and singular verb, *is.* The speaker then recognizes her thoughts as diminutive instances of the great force she had perceived as external. Shifting its measures from thought to emotion, the poem next suggests that the passions of paradise may exceed those of earth. The closure dismisses the calculations of astronomy, math, navigation, geometry, and natural philosophy as unequal to the breadth of the heaven. The immeasurable will always outnumber the measurable.

Some say, all that we know of *Heaven* above,
Is that we joye, and that we love.
Who can tell that? for all we know,
Those *Passions* we call *Joy,* and *Love* below,
May, by *Excesse,* such other *Passions* grow,
None in the World is capable to know.
Just like our *Bodies,* though that they shall rise,
And as St. *Paul* saies, see *God* with our *Eyes;*
Yet may we in the *Change* such difference find,
Both in our *Bodies,* and also in our *Mind,*
As if that we were never of *Mankind,*
And that these *Eyes* we see with now, were blind.
Say we can measure all the *Planets* high,
And number all the *Stars* be in the *Skie;*
And *Circle* could we all the *World* about,
And all th' *Effects* of *Nature* could finde out:
Yet cannot all the *Wise,* and *Learned* tell,
What's done in *Heaven,* or how we there shall dwell.

"Those *Passions* . . . / May, by *Excesse,* such other *Passions* grow." When a poet is praised for her wide emotional range, that amplitude includes the various shadings of joy, love, and grief. It does not include queasiness, disgust, and horror. The excesses of certain Cavendish poems, however, are likely to stir "such other *Passions.*" Earlier I divided her verse into two kinds: those that shared the simplicity of George Herbert and those that partook of Richard Crashaw's grotesque sensibility. I've concentrated on the first sort because I like them best and because critical opinion has fastened, unfairly, it seems to me, on the Crashaw-like verses.

Richard Crashaw's poetry offers stupendous examples of ecstatic high seriousness that crashes unwittingly into banal low comedy. The disproportion between the work's intention and its effect are absurd. His excesses are models of camp. The textbook example, from his poem on the tears of Mary Magdalen, finds the pilgrim "follow'd by two faithfull fountaines; / Two walking baths; two weeping motions; / Portable, and compendious oceans."[40] Cavendish's discrepancies of intent and effect sometimes result in Crashaw-like campiness. The poem seems to have an emotive life of its own, quite beyond the author's control. Her conceits can be intensely discomfiting, yet she is naif enough to be unaware of the feelings she stirs. Keats said of the poetical character that "It lives in gusto, be it foul or fair."[41] Cavendish's excesses are at times more foul than fair. Some of her poetry had me resorting to a vocabulary of teenaged squeamishness: Gross! Yucky!

Cavendish's temperament was pragmatic whereas Crashaw's was visionary; her exaggerations are fueled by realism rather than religion. Her sensibility, moreover, was tragic rather than ecstatic. As a result she tends toward gory rather than silly extremes. Her macabre poems seize the facts of physicality, excavate their true, but truly unsavory, implications, and push those implications to fantastic lengths that still retain elements of the realism necessary to horror. But even these poems reflect Cavendish's deep worldview, albeit in bizarre form. Their ghoulish tropes of embodiment violently enforce equity between humans and animals. Rather than "flesh and blood," with its suggestions of divine transubstantiation, the human form is reduced to "meat." By dissolving the difference between flesh and meat, such poems enact the brutality of carnivorism. In one gruesome passage human body parts are up for sale on "*shamble-row*," the butcher's market, along with dead animals ("Of a Travelling Thought"). In "A Battle between King Oberon, and the Pygmees," she writes:

> Here *beasts* and *men* both in ther *bloud* lay *masht*,
> As if that a *French Cook* had them minc'd, *so hasht*,
> Or with their *bloud* a *Gelly* boyle,
> To make a *Bouillion* of the *spoyle*.[42]

Whereas Cavendish's Herbert-like poems are anthropomorphic, her Crashaw-like poems are anthropophagous: they violate taboos concerning the eating of human flesh. Just as animals are personified in her "simple" poems, persons are animalized in her "grotesque" verse. The body's animality does not discount the possibility of divinity: it extends that possibility to beasts, an inclusion that refutes human assumptions of superiority.

I would suggest that horrific events in Cavendish's life forced her ideas into these ghoulish expressions. During the Civil War, Parliamentary troops disinterred and dismembered the bodies of Cavendish's mother and sister. Kathleen Jones writes that "the soldiers made game with the dead ladies' hair in their hats."[43] When news of this defilement and of her brother's execution reached Cavendish, she was disconsolate. The ghastliness seems to have made its way, unmediated, into some of her poems.

Both Cavendish and Richard Crashaw were members of Queen Henrietta Maria's Oxford and Paris courts. Although her bashfulness no doubt prevented conversation, Cavendish might have read Crashaw's manuscripts in circulation. "Extravagant" is often used to describe them both. Richard Crashaw, however, is accorded twelve pages in the *Norton Anthology* (6th edition), whereas Cavendish is allowed three.[44] What is "unique" in Crashaw is deviant in her. The best she can hope for is to be deemed eccentric or outside the center. Historically, "eccentric" is what female poets get to be instead of "original." Yet it seems to me that eccentricity is to postmodernism what originality was to romanticism: a foundational principle. Although Crashaw was ridiculed for his absurd conceits, his work eventually found its audience. Perhaps postmodernism will find new ways to revel in the excesses of Cavendish's outlandish passions.

The gusto that makes some poems unwholesome adds conviction to her best efforts. Her satire on pastoral romance is as good in its way as Sir Walter Raleigh's reply to Marlowe's "Passionate Shepherd."

A Description of Shepherds, and Shepherdesses
The *Shepherdesses* which great Flocks doe keep,
Are dabl'd high with dew, following their Sheep,
Milking their Ewes, their hands doe dirty make;
For being wet, dirt from their Dugges do take.
The Sun doth scorch the skin, it yellow growes,
Their eyes are red, lips dry with wind that blowes.
Their Shepherds sit on mountains top, that's high,
Yet on their feeding sheep doe cast an eye;
Which to the mounts steep sides they hanging feed
On short moyst grasse, not suffer'd to beare seed;
Their feet though small, strong are their sinews string,

Which make them fast to rocks & mountains cling:
The while the *Shepherds* leggs hang dangling down,
And sets his breech upon the hills high crown.
Like to a tanned Hide, so was his skin,
No melting heat, or numming cold gets in,
And with a voyce that's harsh against his throat,
He strains to sing, yet knowes not any Note:
And yawning, lazie lyes upon his side,
Or strait upon his back, with armes spred wide;
Or snorting sleeps, and dreames of *Joan* their Maid,
Or of Hobgoblins wakes, as being afraid.
Motion in their dull brains doth plow, and sow,
Not Plant, and set, as skilfull Gardners doe.
Or takes his Knife new ground, that half was broke,
And whittles sticks to pin up his sheep-coat:
Or cuts some holes in straw, to Pipe thereon
Some tunes that pleaseth *Joan* his Love at home.
Thus rustick Clownes are pleas'd to spend their times,
And not as *Poets* faine, in *Sonnets, Rhimes,*
Making great *Kings* and *Princes* Pastures keep,
And beauteous *Ladies* driving flocks of sheep:
Dancing 'bout May-poles in a rustick sort,
When *Ladies* scorne to dance without a Court.
For they their Loves would hate, if they should come
With leather Jerkins, breeches made of Thrum,
And Buskings made of Freeze that's course, and strong,
With clouted Shooes, tyed with a leather thong.
Those that are nicely bred, fine cloaths still love,
A white hand sluttish seems in dirty Glove.[45]

Cavendish's disdain for affectation is evident in this poem, which mocks the faux shepherds and shepherdesses of idealized courtly love. Kathleen Jones notes that Cavendish's fellow courtiers indulged in a fad for Platonic love, but she scorned such dissembling.[46] Of course, her tendency to be out of countenance made her unpopular at court. In fact, "outness" seems to have been her salient trait. On the page she is not only outspoken but, it seems to me, out of her epoch. Writers are shaped by inherent temperaments as much as by the climate of their age. Affinities spring up across centuries, in defiance of time. Margaret Cavendish has more in common with Whitman's hankering, gross, mystical, nudity than with Milton's sonorous depths. Like Whitman she is "one of the roughs, a kosmos."[47]

Like him she could resist anything better than her own diversity, as her poems, letters, plays, fictions, and essays testify. "I love those best which I create myself," she wrote of her work in *Sociable Letters*.[48]

But a "barbaric yawp" that issued from a woman's pen could only seem vulgar. Imagine the reception that would greet a woman who wrote "I dote on myself . . . there is that lot of me, and all / so luscious."[49] Oddly enough, men poets have been praised for the very qualities that are maligned in Cavendish. The absence of rigorous formal education, counted as a debit for her, is no such thing for Burns, Blake, Clare, Keats, and Whitman. Although Christopher Smart, Blake, and Clare were "mad," their disorder has, if anything, stoked their legends. Cavendish, who was sane, has been slandered as mad and "handled with a Chain," in Dickinson's phrase. Even so sympathetic a reader as Kathleen Jones speculates that "paradoxes," along with "the sheer bulk of Margaret's work," have led to her neglect.[50] Surely both factors would be construed as strengths in a man poet. In reference to her own verse Anne Bradstreet wrote, "If what I do prove well, it won't advance, / They'll say it's stolen, or else it was by chance."[51] Cavendish's single poem in the latest *Norton Anthology* is burdened with the following footnote: "The duchess clearly, *though perhaps not deliberately,* contrasts the world of women . . . with that of . . . Apollonian masculinity."[52] It is hard to understand how a foundational belief that appears across an entire body of work can be regarded as a happy accident.

Cavendish hoped for a posterity in which her work would know "a glorious Resurrection . . . since Time brings strange and unusual things to pass!" It seems to me that she should take her place within a tradition of spontaneous composition and vitality: feral poets whose work Robert Lowell characterized as raw rather than cooked and whose writing process Allen Ginsberg summarized as "first word, best word." Passages of her work show something of the shrewd earthiness of Chaucer, the sincerity of Christopher Smart, the forcefulness of Robert Burns, the innocence of Blake's songs, the heartfelt engagement of John Clare, the robust egotism of Whitman. An anthology of her best poetry and prose would give readers a place to begin. There is scholarly interest in her work right now, so perhaps some enterprising publisher will issue such an "olio" or collection.

After I'd confessed my strange and unusual passion to the reading group, someone said, "Isn't it amazing that she can change you despite the distance of so much time?"

"Yes, and I can change her," I said, too quickly. "By changing the reception of her work." Would that it were so. In a letter "To Poets"

Cavendish writes, "*I have no* Eloquent Orator *to plead for me, as to per-swade a* Severe Judge, *nor* Flattery *to bribe a* Corrupt one; *which makes me afraid, I shall lose my* Suit of Praise. . . . *But if the* Judge *be learned in the* Lawes *of* Poetry, *and honesty from* Bribes *of* Envy; *I shall not need to feare.*"[53] She still has no Eloquent Orator; her writing is its own best defense. Although I am thrown out of countenance by her travails, she seems to have maintained her private equipoise. "*The Worlds dispraises* cannot make me a *mourning garment,*" she noted. "My mind's too big."[54] Her mind—that insatiable, unordinary place.

1. Charles Lamb, "Mackery End, in Hertfordshire," *London Magazine,* July 1821, repr. in *Essays of Elia* (London: J. M. Dent and Sons, 1906), 89.

2. Samuel Pepys, *The Diary of Samuel Pepys,* ed. Robert Latham and William Matthews (London: G. Bell and Sons, 1974), 8:243.

3. Margaret Cavendish to the marquis of Newcastle, in *Sociable Letters* (London, 1664), b1 v.

4. Margaret Cavendish, untitled poem, in *Poems and Fancies* (London, 1653), 212. All Cavendish poems quoted herein are taken from this edition.

5. Margaret Cavendish, *Philosophical Letters* (London, 1664), 40–41.

6. T. S. Eliot, "What Is Minor Poetry?" in *On Poetry and Poets* (New York: Farrar, Straus and Giroux, 1973), 49.

7. T. S. Eliot, "The Metaphysical Poets," in *Selected Essays* (New York: Harcourt, 1950), 245.

8. Virginia Woolf, "The Duchess of Newcastle," in *The Common Reader* (New York: Harcourt, 1948), 111.

9. Douglas Grant, *Margaret the First: A Biography of Margaret Cavendish, Duchess of Newcastle, 1623–1673* (London: Rupert Hart-Davis, 1957), 44.

10. Cynthia M. Tuerk, *Notes and Queries,* n.s., 42 (December 1995): 450–51.

11. Margaret Cavendish, *Orations of Divers Sorts* (London, 1662), 226.

12. Margaret Cavendish, prefatory letter, "To the Two Most Famous Universities of England," in *Philosophical and Physical Opinions* (London, 1663), a1 r–v.

13. Cavendish, *Poems and Fancies,* 70–75.

14. M. H. Abrams et al., eds., *The Norton Anthology of English Literature,* 6th ed. (New York: Norton, 1993), 2:877.

15. Merton M. Sealts Jr., ed., *The Journals and Miscellaneous Notebooks of Ralph Waldo Emerson, 1835–1838* (Cambridge: Belknap–Harvard University Press, 1965), 5:195.

16. Lewis Thomas, "Crickets, Bats, Cats, & Chaos," *Audubon* 94 (March/April 1992): 94.

17. Ibid., 99.

18. E. Toppe, quoted in Cavendish, *Poems and Fancies,* A5.

19. Margaret Cavendish, *The Life of William Cavendish, Duke of Newcastle,* ed. C. H. Firth (London: Routledge and Sons, 1903[?]), 169.

20. Quoted in Grant, *Margaret the First,* 17.

21. G. C. Moore Smith, ed., *The Letters of Dorothy Osborne to William Temple* (Oxford: Clarendon Press, 1928), 41.

22. Grant, *Margaret the First,* 21.

23. Quoted in Kathleen Jones, *A Glorious Fame: The Life of Margaret Cavendish, Duchess of Newcastle, 1623–1673* (London: Bloomsbury, 1988), 154.

24. Robert Paul Wolff, "The Conflict between Authority and Autonomy," in *In Defense of Anarchism* (New York: Harper and Row, 1970), 6–7.

25. Jones, *A Glorious Fame,* 122.

26. Quoted in ibid., 149.

27. Virginia Woolf, *A Room of One's Own* (New York: Harcourt, Brace and World, 1929), 64–65.

28. Quoted in Jones, *A Glorious Fame,* 92.

29. Grant, *Margaret the First,* 126.

30. Mary Midgley, *Wickedness: A Philosophical Essay* (London: Routledge and Kegan Paul, 1984), 127.

31. Cavendish, "An Epistle to Soldiers," in *Poems and Fancies,* 167.

32. Joy Williams, "The Killing Game," *Esquire,* October 1990, 116, 118.

33. Cavendish, *Poems and Fancies,* 110–13.

34. Thomas, "Crickets, Bats, Cats, & Chaos," 99.

35. See Cavendish, *Poems and Fancies,* 53–91.

36. Cavendish, *Orations of Divers Sorts,* 223.

37. Cavendish, *Philosophical and Physical Opinions* (London, 1655), 114.

38. Cavendish, *Poems and Fancies,* 40–42.

39. Thomas, "Crickets, Bats, Cats, & Chaos," 98.

40. Richard Crashaw, "The Weeper," in *The Complete Poetry of Richard Crashaw,* ed. George Walton Williams (Garden City, N.Y.: Doubleday, 1970), 121–37.

41. John Keats to Richard Woodhouse, Oct. 27, 1818, *The Complete Poetical Works and Letters of John Keats* (Boston: Houghton Mifflin, 1958), 336.

42. Cavendish, *Poems and Fancies,* 184.

43. Jones, *A Glorious Fame,* 68.

44. Abrams et al., *Norton Anthology,* 1:1388–99, 1718–20.

45. Cavendish, *Poems and Fancies,* 142–43.

46. Jones, *A Glorious Fame,* 27.

47. Walt Whitman, "Song of Myself [24]," in *The Portable Walt Whitman* (New York: Penguin, 1973), 56.

48. Quoted in Jones, *A Glorious Fame,* 95.

49. Whitman, *Portable Walt Whitman*, 58.

50. Jones, *A Glorious Fame*, 176.

51. Anne Bradstreet, "The Prologue," in *The Norton Anthology of Literature by Women*, ed. Sandra M. Gilbert and Susan Gubar (New York: Norton, 1985), 61–63.

52. Abrams et al., *Norton Anthology*, 1:1718n5 (my italics).

53. Cavendish, *Poems and Fancies*, 121–23.

54. Cavendish, "An Epistle to Mistris Toppe," in *Poems and Fancies*, A5.

TEN

"How coy a Figure"

Marvelry

STEPHEN YENSER

BECAUSE I SENSE THAT THIS meditation might now and again veer into rarefaction, I want to stress its roots in the mundane. The quotidian, which is my turf. Although I now live near and sometimes walk across the intersection of Hollywood and Vine, many years ago, like a lot of Angelenos, I grew up in Kansas, enamored of *Lost Horizon* and *The Wizard of Oz* and other flights of fancy, and aspired to writing up different climes myself. But *plus ça change,* and after all these decades and all these miles, I'm still plodding on, midwestern pedestrian as ever, even if this is Shangri-L.A., the City of Angles, El Lay itself. If this is where the Great Plains meet the Great Fancies, to adapt a phrase from James Merrill, I have evidently been cast as one of the former. It's not my role to invent other worlds after all. Still, there is one film script I can imagine imagining, and it would be based on the life of Andrew Marvell. Although his own origins were common, his doings were charmed, his travels and tastes were broad, his lyrics are wizard, and he would have understood the mercurial, cinematographic ethos of the later twentieth century in the United States better than most of his contemporaries, or indeed mine—or so I think, even though our knowledge of him is as thin in substance as it is thick in mundane fact (which combination itself is of course alluring to the faltering fabulist). I'll make my pitch brief.

After his mother's early death and the quick remarriage of his father, an Anglican minister, when Andrew was seventeen years old and perhaps especially vulnerable regarding issues of authority, Marvell fell under the sway of the cult of his day and left his home in Cambridge to join a Catholic guru in London, whence he was enticed back or abducted by deprogrammers working for his father. The senior Andrew Marvell drowned a couple of years later in strange circumstances and in the company of a woman not his second wife. His father's death seems to have precipitated or permitted Marvell's final departure from Cambridge for London, where he lived until he was twenty-one, at which age he decamped for the Continent, where he perhaps initiated an intermittent career as a spy or a double agent. The precise nature of his relationship to the Dutch government in the 1640s, and again in 1662–63, when he returned to that country for several months, and yet again in 1674, when he surreptitiously represented Dutch interests in England ("Mr. Thomas" was his cryptonym), is forever obscured. Much that we can gather about him, however, comports with the romantic hypothesis of espionage—and leaves room for a certain reconstruction in the film script. Mostly abroad from 1643 through 1647, he learned fencing as avidly as he acquired foreign languages, even as he steered clear of commitment to either side during the Civil War back home. Writing about those years some three decades later in the course of urging religious tolerance in England, he offered an apologia whose rhetoric might have been the envy of some recent prominent American draft dodgers, as well as the citizens of Shangri-La. "Whether it be a war of religion or of liberty," he asserted, "is not worth the labour to inquire. Whichsoever was at the top, the other was at the bottom; but upon considering all, I think the cause was too good to have been fought for." Indeed, "men may spare their pains where nature is at work, and the world will not go the faster for our driving," since "all things happen in their best and proper time, without any need of our officiousness."[1] Those are observations worthy of a doubting "Thomas."

In August of 1678, having served two decades as a member of Parliament from Hull, he—whoever else he really was—slipped away at age fifty-seven. In October 1680 his *Miscellaneous Poems* were published with a brief testimonial to their authenticity, authored, ironically, by one Mary Marvell, *née* Mary Palmer, who claimed Andrew as her "late dear Husband" and who was, although demonstrably his landlady and friend, evidently not his wife. The boundaries of their relationship will never be defined, and—in spite of his poems' many declarations—we know nothing about other possible manifestations of the poet's libido. He seems to have conducted his public life with discretion and his private life in secrecy. Such a summary would square with John Aubrey's tantalizing account of him in his *Brief Lives:* "He was in his conversation very modest," Aubrey testifies, "and of very few words: and though he loved wine he would never drinke harde in company." At the same time, Aubrey somehow knows, he "kept bottles of wine at his lodgeing, and many times he would drinke liberally by himself to refresh his spirits, and exalt his muse."[2] This sentence might remind the reader in a Marvellian mood, or the reader whose own cup runneth over, of the "green pastures" and "still waters" that restore the singer who is so delicately echoed at the end of the fifth stanza in "The Garden."

That still waters run deep is to the point. Whether moderate drinker or functioning alcoholic; whether husband or lover or sexual abstinent; whether skeptic, latitudinarian, temporizer, tergiversator, precocious pacifist, or simply ambivalent soul—he could write poems in warm support of royalist friends, then celebrate a regicide's return in an ode that included a paean to the dead king, then pen an elegy to the regicide, and then endear himself to the restored monarchy and serve in Parliament until his death. Born on Easter Eve, named as his father was named, he always resurrected himself in some new form. Indeed, for centuries known chiefly if hardly credibly as a satirist and politician, he is now regarded as a lyric poet par excellence—in Hugh Kenner's uneasy and suitably slippery assessment, "the greatest minor poet in the English language."[3]

His poetic oeuvre is remarkably "small" (especially if we exclude the satirical and most of the political poems), but it is small as those of Mallarmé and Elizabeth Bishop are small: densely elegant in inverse proportion to length. A writer of what the late Robert M. Adams called hard, beautiful poems, although resident nearer the more amenable Bishop than the recalcitrant Mallarmé, he values conciseness equally with complexity, shuns simplification yet strives for accessibility, loves puzzles but never abandons the sensuous world. In my favorite summation of "To His Coy Mistress," Victoria Sackville-West writes that "the whole poem is as tight and hard as a knot; yet as spilling and voluptuous as a horn of plenty."[4] She might as well have been epitomizing Marvell's lyrical mode. He is in both senses of the word a sensible poet—a doubly sensible poet yet not without his mystical tinge. When Robert Frost averred that he loathed obscurity yet loved dark sayings, he could have been thinking of the famous couplet in which Marvell alludes to the twenty-third Psalm in the course of eulogizing the contemplative mind, capable of "Annihilating all that's made, / To a green Thought in a green Shade."[5] In that verdant, fertile retreat, where all is fungible and fugacious, mercurial Marvell is the master of mutability and metamorphosis.

"The Garden," the source of the famous couplet, is like all instances of its species an imperfect poem, to be sure. (Valéry articulated the law: a lyric is never finished, just left behind.) After a strong first stanza, three workmanlike stanzas intervene before we come to the poem's superb second half. Like most good poems, "The Garden" probably didn't know where it was going until it got there—and by then, evidently, there was no way to bring earlier stanzas quite up to the quality of the closing ones. Stanza 2 treads water as it conventionally opposes the natural world with the social world. Its only memorable lines are its last couplet, "Society is all but rude, / To this delicious Solitude," in which *rude* means ironically both "rustic" or "unpolished" and "vulgar" or "discourteous." Stanza 3 spends most of its eight lines somehow contrasting the beauty of women whose lovers have been selfish enough to cut their names into the garden's trees with the garden's loveliness and then concludes, dismayingly, with the speaker's vow to carve the trees' own names into their bark. Stanza 4 not only manhandles the Daphne and Syrinx myths—which myths, the poet scandalously claims, demonstrate how even Apollo and Pan were happier with their suddenly floral love objects than they would have been with the original nymphs—but also seems casually placed. Wouldn't stanza 4 fit better into the retreat sequence—poet from society, self from lovers, mind from body, soul from self—if it came second or third?

In any event stanza 4, with its metamorphoses, heightens the sexual motif and thus foreshadows stanza 5, where the speaker's solitariness intercepts startlingly the poem's most sensuous language. Far from a retreat from "Passions heat," this stanza represents a fierce if autoerotic sublimation of it. Rather than a return to prelapsarian existence, this stanza suggests a repetition of the fall, from apple through sex, with Nature this time the irresistible temptress:

What wond'rous Life is this I lead!
Ripe Apples drop about my head;
The Luscious Clusters of the Vine
Upon my Mouth do crush their Wine;
The Nectaren, and curious Peach,
Into my hands themselves do reach;
Stumbling on Melons, as I pass,
Insnar'd with Flow'rs, I fall on Grass.

Having thus charmingly disposed of the apparently exhausted body, Marvell can follow the mind's subsequent withdrawal into itself, an environs he magically manages to compare at once to an ocean and to the bower:

Mean while the Mind, from pleasure less,
Withdraws into its happiness:
The Mind, that Ocean where each kind
Does streight its own resemblance find;
Yet it creates, transcending these,
Far other Worlds, and other Seas;
Annihilating all that's made
To a green Thought in a green Shade.

Although the idea that everything on earth has a corresponding type in the ocean (horse and seahorse, and so forth) is just entertaining nonsense, that fact does not affect the claim about the mind, in which indeed everything, on land or in the ocean, including the mind itself, can be compared to something else. But Marvell's concept of the mind, he insists, is of not just an incubator of metaphors but also a generator of "Far other Worlds, and other Seas." If analogy were still an option, the comparison implicit would be to God, especially since the mind's power entails a destructive force capable of "Annihilating all that's made / To a green Thought in a green Shade." I take this couplet to mean that the contemplative mind can extinguish all material things and can plunge into thought itself, where instead of light and dark we find shades and instead of entities insubstantial processes. This is the place or rather the very medium of metamorphosis, beside which myths about its power—like those in Ovid—might seem allegorical and reductive. So perhaps that contrast justifies in retrospect the rather wooden fourth stanza.

The metamorphosis then effected in stanza 7 works in counterpoint, as the soul—*anima* as distinct from the preceding *mens*—also departs from the body but, unlike the mind, takes a form "like [that of] a bird" that glides into a garden tree, where it preens "its silver Wings" in preparation for a "longer flight," presumably to heaven (wherever else that might be by now). Perching there, as it were, the soul "Waves" or weaves "in its Plumes the various Light," which is to say, in parallel to the shades of shades in the preceding stanza, the gradated light, the refracted light, the ever-changing light that is still (nay, therefore) of this world:

Here at the Fountains sliding foot,
Or at some Fruit-trees mossy root,
Casting the Bodies Vest aside,
My Soul into the boughs does glide:
There like a Bird it sits, and sings,
Then whets, and combs its silver Wings;

And, till prepar'd for longer flight,
Waves in its Plumes the various Light.

Beyond that liminal point this poet cannot go. Wallace Stevens, Marvell surely in his mind, also stopped there, in a "green [and] fluent" realm at the end of the third section of "Notes toward a Supreme Fiction," although he tried hard to imagine another world:

They will get it straight one day at the Sorbonne.
We shall return at twilight from the lecture
Pleased that the irrational is rational,

Until flicked by feeling, in a gildered street,
I call you by name, my green, my fluent mundo.
You will have stopped revolving except in crystal.[6]

"When I think on that," Yeats's Soul says, when pondering eternity in "Dialogue of Self and Soul" (a poem in the same genre as some of Marvell's own "dialogues" and closely related to "The Garden"), "my tongue's a stone."[7] As it turns out, Yeats's Soul's "stone" gives his Self a thing to build his worldly church on, and Marvell's "Bird" keeps us in his empirical garden, which in the eighth stanza provokes a sly speculation about Eden before Eve was created:

Such was that happy Garden-state,
While Man there walk'd without a Mate:
After a Place so pure, and sweet,
What other Help could yet be meet!
But 'twas beyond a Mortal's share
To wander solitary there:
Two Paradises 'twere in one
To live in Paradise alone.

The slant rhyme of *Mate* with *meet* across the opening couplets, along with the reader's silent restoration of the term *helpmate* or *helpmeet* that Marvell splits in the fourth line, tells the fuller story rhetorically—a story anticipated by the sexual imagery in stanzas 4 and 5 and recapitulated in the clinching couplet here, where *one* and *alone* are ostensibly identified with *Paradise,* even as the doubling of paradise ("Two Paradises") both conjures the unstated inverse (the redoubled attraction of a paradise with a partner) and so flouts logic that the original proposition calls itself into question. In other words, who believes that last couplet? God didn't (see Genesis 2:18), and so it was that God delivered Eve from Adam's side. And because Marvell didn't believe it either, he sends up his own pronouncement, partly by his flagrant illogic and partly by his repetition of "Paradise[s]," so that the game reader may hear the pair in that word and infer the absurdity of a subtext, a *pair o' dice alone*. Indeed, the lines suggest, the real paradise involves a pair and a gamble, as plucky Eve—who, unlike her earnest companion, was pleased by the visual, gustatory, and epistemological delights of the apple—intuited.

The concluding stanza continues immediately—partly by way of an exotic, occluded pun—from the stanza on Eden:

How well the skilful Gardner drew
Of flow'rs and herbes this Dial new;
Where from above the milder Sun
Does through a fragrant Zodiack run;
And, as it works, th' industrious Bee
Computes its time as well as we.
How could such sweet and wholesome Hours
Be reckon'd but with herbs and flow'rs!

The first lines refer us to the world at large, the fallen world, above which "the milder Sun / Does through a fragrant Zodiack run," so that suddenly the temporality of the world is inseparable from its heavenly fragrance. God mixes the smell of mortality with the scent of eternity. The son of an Anglican minister might well say that it is precisely "the milder S[o]n" who combines these two. Not that we need that hypothesis to be persuaded at the poem's end that time is sacred and indeed essential to our glimpses of perfection: "How could such sweet and wholesome Hours / Be reckon'd but with herbs and flow'rs!" By simply reversing in his last line the "flow'rs and herbes" of this stanza's second line, Marvell frames his *hortus conclusus*—which is not, however, Eden but a larger garden, *the* garden into which his friend Milton's Adam and Eve walk at the end of *Paradise Lost*. The garden of the world. This green sundial or earth wherein we *die all* (the prosody dictates two syllables rather than a diphthong in *Dial*)—perhaps in order (although nothing here insists on spiritual rebirth) to be "new."

"The Garden" is an emerald brilliant with facets or with different "shades" of meaning caused by a "various Light." It begins with a renunciation of "Society," "worldly endeavors," and "incessant Labours" in favor of withdrawal, "repose," and meditation; but it ends with a celebration of a world marked everywhere by time and industry—a celebration so unalloyed that we can note only the irony of the "dust" in *industrious.* To put that another way, it begins by treating the particular remote garden it is set in (although we do not know that the poet had a specific place in mind) as an opposite to the temporal, empirical realm; and it ends by treating the world as a whole as a garden that includes or sublates that realm. How did this happen? The poem followed its aggressive thought.

An emblem of the kind of suave, lucid, serpentine ingenuity that I admire in Marvell can be found in "The Coronet," a poem about, well, about the writing of such a poem as it turns out to be. Such a poem, because the poet explicitly hopes to honor his savior, Jesus Christ, with it, should be a "rich . . . Chaplet" or garland or a "curious Frame," where *curious* means "painstakingly fine" or "elaborate"—and "The Coronet," its simplicity of a sort notwithstanding, surely fills that bill. The poem's intricate structure, which does not allow for stanzas, can be represented by the following groupings:

$$a_5b_4b_4a_5 \ / \ c_4d_5d_4c_5 \ / \ e_5f_4f_4e_5 \ / \ g_4h_4g_4h_4 \ / \ i_5i_5 \ / \ j_5k_5l_5j_5k_5l_5 \ / \ m_5m_5.$$

Only one part's scheme (the first part's) repeats itself (in the third part's) in this wonderful prosodic filigree. "The Coronet" is equally daedalian when it comes to figure. Although the metaphor remains latent throughout, it emerges that the flowers gathered by the speaker are his tropes themselves—or his lines—or the poem as a whole. (If not indeed the capacity of language itself. The poem's twenty-six lines recall the English alphabet—which, however, cannot in the end spell the Word any more than the poem can truly grace God.)

In any event, in the course of writing it, the poet discovers that the poem is unworthy praise of Christ; in implicit contrast to Christ's gift to humanity, his own "fruits" are paradoxically "only flowers"—forever immature, always insubstantial, never nourishing. They cannot but be so because they are mortal, rooted in the fallen world—which is to say bound up with "the Serpent old," who makes his entrance at the poem's exact midpoint, where he is discovered trying to conceal himself among the flowers:

Alas I find the Serpent old
That, twining in his speckled breast,
About the flow'rs disguis'd does fold,
With wreaths of Fame and Interest.

But if that last is a figure a poet might take some pride in, Marvell implies, that is precisely the problem, that ineradicable human wish for "wreaths of Fame and Interest." By this point the poet is in the toils of a double bind because the coronet he had envisioned has transformed itself into a painful crown of thorns (the very sort of thing he had found himself constructing previously and had sought to put by at the poem's outset), as eulogy, chaplet, serpent, and sin have become inextricable.

Inextricable, that is, except by the savior himself, who only could "the Serpent tame, / . . . [and] his slipp'ry knots at once untie, / And disentangle all his winding Snare." But then this poem that seeks to denounce itself qua poem (or worldly enterprise) begins to prove anew the necessity for the savior and thus to justify willy-nilly its own existence because the savior alone can purify and redeem the poet's figures—can rid them of the slippery knots and lubricious negatives they otherwise must traffic in. In the alternative allegorical narrative—but the options come to the same thing—Christ can simply destroy the serpent and

> . . . shatter too with him my curious frame:
> And let these wither, so that he may die,
> Though set with Skill and chosen out with Care.
> That they, while Thou on both their Spoils dost tread,
> May crown thy Feet, that could not crown thy Head.

Even as Marvell seems to welcome his poem's destruction, however, he continues to refine its "curious frame"—so that, for instance, that very phrase shades off into both *inquisitive temperament* and *ungainly body* at the same time that it designates the poem's or garland's *fastidious structure,* with its different flowers "set with Skill and chosen out with Care."

And why not? To be worth sacrificing, the offering must be beautiful. Therefore Douglas Bush's observation that " 'The Coronet' . . . is a religious sacrifice of all poetry,"[8] although not wrong, deserves qualification. One doesn't strew a monarch's path with random bunches of skunkweed and thistles. Far better an exquisite wreath like this one that might both recall God's promise that Christ will bruise his heel on the serpent's head and suggest that the ultimate poem, the poem that renders all others valueless, is Christ's feet—or that mere words must give way to the Word. I don't see how in this notably aesthetic context "thy Feet" can fail to carry such intimations—although it might be that we should think of the poet's own metrical feet as ultimately Christ's, given that the poem is written for the latter. In either case "poetry" is perhaps not so much sacrificed or chastened as it is exalted.

Volatile because creation is restless, virtually indefatigable, Marvell's verse discovers structures within structures. If he were writing now, he would take account of fractals and other instances of asymmetrical synecdoche and nonlinear dynamics. Take "On a Drop of Dew," almost as small a subject as anyone in his day imagined (although Marvell himself in this very poem conjures the dewdrop's "own Tear"), which subject he expatiates on and treats in a prosodic scheme intricately irregular enough to make one want to consider this poem (along with "The Coronet") in the development of the English Pindaric, which Marvell's contemporary Abraham Cowley virtually invented in 1656 (about the time that Marvell was writing this poem) and which tradition runs on through Dryden's ode to Anne Killigrew and Wordsworth's "Intimations" ode. The poem's Neoplatonic conceit is well known: looking in the morning at a dewdrop in a rosebush and foreseeing its evaporation by the sun later in the day, the poet discovers a metaphor for the soul that will return to heaven, its origin. (This cycle is a poetic staple into the twentieth century, when we find it, for example, in Sylvia Plath's "Ariel.") Marvell's poem emphasizes everywhere the circularity inherent in the process. From the first letter of the title, through the initial letter of the first salient word, *Orient* (which here implies "eastern," because the rising sun is in view, and means "brilliant" or "lustrous"), the configuration of the dewdrop, as well as that of both the drop's "Tear" and "the World," to the final image of "th'Almighty Sun," where the reader mindful of the Christian context will substitute the last *o* (for the *u* in *Sun*), the poem continually circles itself.

This circularity manifests itself in part in terms of the natural cycle's balanced antitheses and parallelisms. The drop of dew, understood also to represent "the Soul" by the middle of the poem (the pertinent sentence begins with line 19 of 40 total lines), is poised on the flower:

In how coy a Figure wound,
Every way it turns away:
So the World excluding round,
Yet receiving in the Day.
Dark beneath, but bright above:
Here disdaining, there in Love.
How loose and easie hence to go:
How girt and ready to ascend.

Moving but on a point below,
It all about does upward bend.

The dewdrop or soul is dark or melancholy because of its separation from the Godhead and yet bright or hopeful of reunion, disdainful of the worldly and drawn to the heavenly, eager to depart the earth. In this respect this passage recalls earlier phrases indicating the soul's nostalgia for its origin, such as its being "careless of its Mansion new" (the rosebush, "the humane flow'r") and its shining "with a mournful Light / . . . / Because so long divided from the Sphear" (the celestial orb, heaven).

What we have yet to take into account is, first, Marvell's eroticizing of the language and, then, his poem's corresponding insistent materiality, the quality he attributes to the dewdrop when he marvels at "how coy a Figure wound" it makes. To be "in Love" and yet "disdaining" is precisely—isn't it?—to be "coy" in two senses. One of the more captivating instances of what Roland Barthes dubbed an *enantioseme*,[9] a self-opposing verbal sign (in contemporary American English cf. *cleave* [vb.], *ravel* [vb.], *fast* [adj.]), *coy* means on the one hand modest or secluded or even inaccessible and on the other hand affecting reserve or artful or even lascivious. Whether Marvell's "Coy Mistress" is Janus-faced in such a way, as Robert Herrick's antiprecisianist model in "Delight in Disorder" certainly is, is debatable. But one can hardly dispute the presence of the paradox in this case, as the poem proceeds to show. Even as the soul or drop of dew always "turns away" and is "excluding round," retentive of its integrity, or virginal, we find it also "receiving in the Day," or admitting the ordinary. Moreover, *loose* meant to Marvell (as it does to us) both "unattached" and "morally lax" or "promiscuous," as well as "loosely clad; ungirt; naked" (a sense evoked partly by the appearance of *girt* in the following line), whereas *easie* meant not only "free from constraint" but also "unchaste" (as it still does). In the line in which the soul is "girt and ready to ascend," then, the religious allusion to the virtuous, well-prepared soul (cf. Proverbs 31: 17, Ephesians 6:14) contradicts or qualifies the phrase "loose and easie," which has secular and erotic overtones.

My point is that the drop of dew as presented in these lines is hardly that monad of purity, that dram of unalloyed essence suggested earlier in the poem, where we are told with fitting succinctness—if not indeed with brachylogical license—that it "Round in its self incloses," which is to say encloses a bit of that "clear Region where 'twas born" so that it, "in its little Globes Extent, / Frames as it can its native Element." Its spirituality now appears tinged with sensuousness. Do we begin to resolve the paradox

if we suppose that Marvell is drawing on the tradition whereby the res-
urrected soul is the ardent bride of Christ? He certainly invokes it else-
where, as in "Upon Appleton House," where a cloistered nun provides
this glimpse of her convent's continuous preparation for what a campier
spirit might call the ultimate prom:

> . . . our chast *Lamps* we hourly trim,
> Lest the great *Bridegroom* find them dim.
> Our *Orient* Breaths perfumed are
> With insense of incessant Pray'r.

My feeling, however, is that the venerable allegorical figure, with its rigid
tenor and vehicle (the bride is to the soul as the bridegroom is to Christ),
would be a Procrustean imposition on the pertinent lines in "On a Drop
of Dew," which are—in the basic sense—lubricious. Let's look again, for
example, at these lines on the dewdrop:

> How it the purple flow'r does slight,
>   Scarce touching where it lyes,
> But gazing back upon the Skies,
>   Shines with a mournful Light;
>   Like its own Tear . . .

This passage is an erotic knot of regret and longing. On the one hand,
because the rose is "purple," it has ecclesiastical associations with the
sorrowful and the *penitent* so that the dewdrop's shrinking from the flower
amounts to a renunciation of renunciation or a yearning for transport—
although at the same time the virginal dewdrop is itself explicitly "mourn-
ful" as it gazes moistly up at—its lover? On the other hand, if *purple*
means "royal" or "splendid," the dewdrop's aversion to the worldly (an
aversion itself not unalloyed: "scarce touching" has its flirtatious over-
tones) involves an attraction to the otherworldly so strong that it seems
physical. In the last analysis, then, the sexual and the spiritual simply
cannot be teased apart. That "native Element" the soul embodies consti-
tutes a comparable complexity because Marvell rapidly identifies "the
Soul" not only with "that Drop" of dew that instigated the poem but also
with "that Ray / Of the clear Fountain of Eternal Day" that draws the
dew heavenward and implicitly transmutes it. Moreover, the primordial
light itself was or is already fluid, if we attend to the term *Fountain*.
Liquidity and light, precipitation and evaporation, are intervolved.

So, one might argue, or indeed has begun to argue, are sensuousness and spirituality. That relationship is perhaps one reason for Marvell's concluding the poem with his reference to the manna as described in Exodus. Pierre Legouis pointed out some time ago the aesthetic problem presented by the last four lines, which suddenly introduce an image "slightly different from that of the dew"[10] and which might almost seem a superfluous coda:

> Such did the Manna's sacred Dew destil;
> White, and intire, though congeal'd and chill.
> Congeal'd on Earth: but does, dissolving, run
> Into the Glories of th'Almighty Sun.

"Such" connects "the Soul" with "the Manna," which seems to have been distilled from a "sacred Dew." In other words, as the drop of dew provides Marvell with a paradigm for the soul, so the soul now serves as his model for the manna, with the result that he creates a kind of dialectical progression. But the manna, as Legouis complains, is not the dew. The Bible clearly distinguishes the dew that evaporated earlier in the morning from the manna that remained for the Israelites to gather, and in fact Marvell himself sharply contrasts the two in "Upon Appleton House," stanza 51. One difference is that the manna, although not *natural,* is more substantial and nutritional. Although according to Exodus the ungathered manna itself finally dissolves, rather *like* the dew, it is clearly divine, although somehow material—and even insistently so, because it is "congeal'd and chill . . . on Earth" and thus linked by virtue of the overtones of death-in-life with the corporeal self. Again, Marvell, an ineluctably worldly poet tempted to transcendence—mercurial, hermetic—cannot let us think spirituality apart from materiality.

Marvell's is a metaphysics of double agency in an even more basic sense. As messenger of the gods and as psychopomp, Hermes or Mercury—god of roads and commerce as well as of invention and theft—blurs all borders in the crossing of them. Beyond the relationship between the spiritual and the sensuous is the relationship between the naked concepts of division and unicity, or (to be Germanic) boundableness and boundlessness. This relationship is the matter Marvell addresses in "The Definition of Love," beginning with the paradoxical title, given that the Latinate *Definition* signifies a demarcating of ends or boundaries whereas the four-letter Anglo-Saxon word *Love* implies an overcoming or obliterating of such distinctions. A few readers of this poem think of it as an "expression of passionate ardour" for a particular woman (Legouis), and almost everyone emphasizes its "high abstract tone" (Bush), and at least one sees it specifically as an allegory motivated by "the love of the embodied soul for its heavenly life" (Ann Berthoff).[11] I myself think that its subject, romantically motivated or not, turns out to be the relationship (at once erotic, mathematical, and metaphysical) between the plural and the singular or the different and the identical. If not the "female" and the "male," the beloved and the lover.

The prosodic and rhetorical schemes in "The Definition of Love" themselves generate divisions and convergences as alluring and intricate as those in an astrolabe, or one kind of astrolabe, to appropriate an instrument Marvell refers to in his sixth stanza. The poem's opening lines contain some stark instances:

My Love is of a birth as rare
As 'tis for object strange and high:
It was begotten by despair
Upon Impossibility.

The *abab* quatrain itself adumbrates the theme—as couplets, for instance, could not—because it separates the rhymes yet binds them together in one stanza. Again, in the opening lines, the line break intervenes between the speaker's "Love" and its "object," and the closing pair of lines, which function as a unit and bring together the progenitors of this rare love, undermine the postulate of separation. That is, if "despair" and "Impossibility" can come together to produce a "Love," surely that love, no matter how uncommon, and its object are not necessarily forever separate. Indeed, if we hark back to the overtones of words in the opening lines, we will find some preliminary mitigation of the lovers' separation. *Rare* means not just "exceptional" or "infrequent," and not only that plus "set distantly apart" (cf. Milton: "Among the trees in pairs they rose, they walked; / Those rare and solitairie, these in flocks"),[12] but also *less compacted,* or closer to the empyrean, as fire is rarer than air and therefore the highest of the elements. And because that is the case, *rare* and *high,* which seem at first markers of an insuperable difference, are virtual semantic rhymes that serve to draw the speaker's "Love" and its "object" together.

The agonistic relationship between union and division twists the fourth stanza into its tortuous shape:

For Fate with jealous Eye does see
Two perfect Loves; nor lets them close:
Their union would her ruine be,
And her Tyrannick pow'r depose.

The second line above, whose fulcrum is *nor,* sets perfection against completion in an elegant paradox. To be "perfect," the "Loves" would have to "close," it might seem; but precisely because perfection entails integrity, union is obviated. In other words, on the one hand, the loves are "perfect" because they cannot "close" or *merge;* but on the other hand, because they cannot merge, they cannot "close" or *conclude* and hence are immortal. (Or do I mean mortal?) Meanwhile, the third line pairs *union* with the appropriately imperfectly rhyming *ruine,* and the last word, *depose,* disposes with dispatch of any "close" or resolution we might have been imagining. In the last analysis, then, perfection and endlessness impossibly oppose and unite with each other.

In the second stanza, the first distich, if I may call it that—an independent clause that concerns the speaker's "Despair" at separation (or dispairing) from his beloved, that "divine . . . thing"—opposes the second distich, a dependent clause whose subject is the "Hope" that is all too mortal:

Magnanimous Despair alone
Could show me so divine a thing,
Where feeble Hope could ne'r have flown
But vainly flapt its Tinsel Wing.

Because it takes two wings to fly, that Marvell's rhyme scheme seems to oblige him to use the singular and therefore pathetic "Wing" is convenient. In this as in most of his stanzas—with the possible exception of the fifth and the definite exception of the last—the quatrains fall into two parts. Here is the eighth and concluding stanza, the pièce de résistance:

Therefore the Love which us doth bind,
But Fate so enviously debarrs,
Is the Conjunction of the Mind,
And Opposition of the Stars.

This final stanza is the only one in the poem in which a subject and a predicate are split across—or override—the distich division. Elsewhere, the first distich is separated syntactically from the second, even though the rhymes make the lines mesh like gears. To put that another way, this is the single stanza in which the syntax really enforces the interlacing *abab* quatrain and helps it tie a Gordian knot.

Let me approach this concluding stanza from another direction. The poem numbers thirty-two lines, so there are sixteen rhymes—or eight pairs. Most of the rhyme words highlight either the theme of separation (which is to say division) or that of union (convergence). As it happens, the words of the first kind predominate in the opening three stanzas. Italicizing these words, I'll paraphrase this part of the poem in a fashion that is perhaps tedious—but not, I hope, factitious or eristic: "My love is exceptional or *rare*. It is for a remote being, an object *high* beyond my reach, and it is the paradoxical product of the equally sterile *despair* and *impossibility*. My *despair* is the result of dis-pairing or of realizing how *alone* I am and how nonpareil is my beloved, an isolated *thing* apart, who has in effect *flown* where I cannot follow, because I am—without her—but a single *wing*. I might *arrive* there, where she has been *fixt* like a star, and where my soul already is, if it weren't for Fate, which must *drive* itself *betwixt* us."

With the exception of *arrive* these key end words point to separation. In the fifth stanza, the first two end words, *steel* and *plac'd,* echoing the "Iron wedges" of the third stanza, do so as well. (We might notice in passing, however, that in that earlier stanza the speaker also identified his distant beloved with his own "extended Soul.") But the following two end words, *wheel* and *embrac'd,* might suggest union, and so in context do most of the subsequent rhymes: as Heaven might *fall* into Earth, so the lovers might be *all* one, like the celestial poles in a *planisphere,* and all would be *well* because they would *greet* and *meet* each other who had anyway by nature been truly *parallel.* Meanwhile, the printed poem is itself a *"Planisphere,"* an instrument that projects cosmic spheres on a flat surface and conjoins the heavenly antipodes. As Marvell explains in stanzas 5 and 6, the speaker and his beloved are analogous to the celestial North and South Poles, separated always—except in the case of the planisphere. The poem's own "Lines," "truly *Paralel*" in a visual sense on the page and sometimes parallel syntactically, "meet" in the tropes they compose. Among these conceits is precisely the "oblique" comparison of the poetic lines to lovers, who are by virtue of the poem—like the lovers in "Ode on a Grecian Urn," whose author has to have known "The Definition of Love" by heart—forever joined in their disjunction.

In view of this paradox perhaps the most peculiar line in "The

Definition of Love" is the penult, where "Love" is described in part as "the Conjunction of the Mind." Now it might well be that we are simply meant to understand the plural "minds," especially given that "Mind" is the sphere of the psychic powers (including the emotional, the volitional, the intellectual), but the use of the singular here strikes me as even more pointed than that in the second stanza's "Wing," let alone the fourth stanza's "Eye." The grammar stubbornly interrogates itself: how can an entity conjoin? One response would seem to be, it could do so if it were also more than one thing, if its unicity entailed plurality. If this notion is flatly contradictory, that's perhaps a reason for us to think of God. God is after all Bacon's "mind" inherent in the "universal frame" and Locke's "eternal infinite mind who made and governs all things." If this universal "Mind" were relevant, the latent Christian hierarchy might dictate the lovers' ultimate or essential conjunction because nature's mechanisms are in God's hands. ("Our love is the engagement of [1] the Divine Mind with [2] the stars' opposition to us, and the outcome is inevitable.") And indeed we might hear at the poem's end not "the Stars" or unfortunate destiny but the *rhyme,* "debarrs" with "Stars." Even the debarring stars are made to pair up, so to speak. Who is to tell the green thought from the green shade?

So even as other strategies have demonstrated the lovers' division, forces of convergence have been brought to bear. The basic issue here involves the relationship between one and two, or unicity and plurality, or identity and difference. Rather than simply pitting them against each other, Marvell entangles—or rather reveals the entanglement of—Love and Fate, which are other names for the archetypal paramours and nemeses that this poem always concerns. It's not only that human lovers have spiritual affinities and practical obstacles, or even that (as courtly love decrees) true love is possible only in abstinence, but also that Affinity and Obstacle themselves are forever in an embrace or encounter. It is this poem's discovery that duality and unity are hopelessly bound up. In the last quatrain, where *bind* and *Mind* rhyme, as do *debarrs* and *Stars,* the endgame might seem to result in a draw, then—unless we were to insist that the "Stars" and therefore the elements of "Opposition" or plurality get literally the last word. In that case our dialectic might demand that we attend to the parallelism of the last two ostensibly antithetical lines and notice that *Conjunction* and *Opposition* are themselves conjoined; dual predicate nominatives of "Love," they are the doves that draw the mythic carriage, to turn things around and put them in their proper order. Here the courtly principle extends itself implicitly into metaphysics: Conjunction and Opposition themselves—Identity and Difference, Unicity and Plurality—depend on each other. There is a deep sense in which they *are* the lovers: intertwined, slippery, indivisible forever.

But in the beginning I swore allegiance to the quotidian. So I'll conclude with what is one of the least metaphysical (if nonetheless confounding) of Marvell's lyrics, "The Gallery," which is also one of the most captivating portraits of the "cruel lover" in the early seventeenth century, the golden era of that jaundiced genre. Although the poem's effect, chiefly a function of the relationship between structure and tone, presupposes the reader's acceptance of it as a dramatic monologue, the speaker's address to his lover, which comprises eight stanzas, at no point contains a hint of the atrabilious. Indeed, there's almost nothing "personal" about it, thanks in part to the poem's rigorous adherence to its central figure, according to which the beloved's various moods and acts appear as descriptions of different painted portraits of her. From the outset, the speaker's "Soul" (or "Mind"—here *anima* and *mens* are used interchangeably, perhaps because the speaker's "several lodgings" or psychic compartments have been combined "into one") is insistently a "Gallery" devoted to "Pictures" of the beloved. (If he were writing the poem today, I suspect, Marvell's metaphor would have been a filmic montage.)

In the first stanza she—her name is Clora—is courteously invited to tour and judge the speaker's memorial collection of portraits of her:

> *Clora* come view my Soul, and tell
> Whether I have contriv'd it well.
> Now all its several lodgings lye
> Compos'd into one Gallery;
> And the great *Arras*-hangings, made
> Of various Faces, by are laid;
> That, for all furniture you'l find
> Only your Picture in my Mind.

The scaldingly curatorial second stanza comes out of nowhere:

> Here Thou art painted in the Dress
> Of an Inhumane Murtheress;
> Examining upon our Hearts
> Thy fertile Shop of cruel Arts:
> Engines more keen than ever yet
> Adorned Tyrants Cabinet;

Of which the most tormenting are
Black Eyes, red Lips, and curled Hair.

How gently, how conventionally, how utterly contrarily this stanza's first
and last lines frame the other six, with their overtones of Grand Guignol,
and thus permit the transition to the sharply contrasting third stanza.
Hardly has the shocked reader taken in the enormity of Clora's deeds
(among them a promiscuity that just barely warrants mention in that
plural "our Hearts") than he or she is whisked back into *la vie en rose* in
the stanza on Aurora:

But, on the other side, th'art drawn
Like to *Aurora* in the Dawn;
When in the East she slumb'ring lyes,
And stretches out her milky Thighs;
While all the morning Quire does sing,
And *Manna* falls, and Roses spring;
And, at thy Feet, the wooing Doves
Sit perfecting their harmless Loves.

If these lines strike us right off as a touch saccharine, not to say uberous,
they seem the less so for being somewhat reassuring after the preceding
glimpse of horrors.

No sooner have we settled back into plush cliché, however, than Mar-
vell's speaker switches vocabulary again. Resuming the murder plot from
the second stanza, he confronts the beloved with scenes of her handiwork,
including a grisly haruspication (divination by means of entrails, which
of course presumes a disemboweling) and the subsequent disposal of the
offal:

Like an Enchantress here thou show'st,
Vexing thy restless Lover's Ghost;
And, by a Light obscure, dost rave
Over his Entrails, in the Cave;
Divining thence, with horrid Care,
How long thou shalt continue fair;
And (when inform'd) them throw'st away,
To be the greedy Vultur's prey.

It's with a sense of balance satisfied and with some relief that we come to
the fifth stanza, enchanting enough to conjure both Enobarbus's report

of Cleopatra on the Nile and Botticelli's representation of the birth of Venus:

> But, against that, thou sit'st a float
> Like *Venus* in her pearly Boat,
> The *Halcyons,* calming all that's nigh,
> Betwixt the Air and Water fly.
> Or, if some rowling Wave appears,
> A Mass of Ambergris it bears.
> Nor blows more Wind than what may well
> Convoy the Perfume to the Smell.

The poem comes to a seeming conclusion in stanza 6, which summarizes all of the "Pictures" in the psychic gallery and recommends them above even those in the collections of Charles I and the dukes of Mantua in Italy:

> These Pictures and a thousand more,
> Of Thee, my Gallery do store;
> In all the Forms thou can'st invent
> Either to please me, or torment:
> For thou alone to people me,
> Art grown a num'rous Colony;
> And a Collection choicer far
> Then or White-hall's, or Mantua's were.

And thus "The Gallery" might neatly enough have ended.

"But," as the actual final stanza begins (like stanzas 3 and 5—Marvell is the poet of "but"), it does not. Instead of a bland summary, we end on what seems a sweet and pastoral note, apparently meant to confirm the third and fifth stanzas' amatory views of the seductive lover:

> But, of these Pictures and the rest,
> That at the Entrance likes me best:
> Where the same Posture, and the Look
> Remains, with which I first was took.
> A tender Shepherdess, whose Hair
> Hangs loosely playing in the Air,
> Transplanting Flow'rs from the green Hill,
> To crown her Head, and Bosome fill.

This "extra" stanza, then (rather like the "extra" lines at the end of "A Dialogue between the Self and Body"), unbalances the poem. But in which direction, in the last analysis? By cagily deferring until now the portrait that was at "the Entrance" of both the little exhibit and the relationship (the poet's presentation of the portraits thus differs significantly from the speaker's physical arrangement of them), Marvell introduces us only at the end of the tour to the fairest, most innocent version of his mistress. This concluding yet original figure is not "Like to Aurora" or "Like Venus," with the overtones of calculation and artificiality that those similes imply, but simply "A tender Shepherdess." Are we to gather that the original beloved was an innocent who was later somehow to fall into sadistic perfidy? Or is to think along such lines to be taken in anew?

Like the term *loose* in "On a Drop of Dew," *loosely* is surely loaded, and "Transplanting" gleams with irony, given that Clora has plucked or cut the flowers in order to adorn herself and to seduce admirers. It's not transplantation but violation that we witness here (as in stanza 3 of "The Garden"). Moreover, seeing fit to "crown" herself, Clora might come across as a usurping "Tyrant" (my term harks back to stanza 2), as well as a "Murtheress" and an "Enchantress," and the flowers might substitute for trophies. If so, among the trophies would be the speaker's heart. In this light the "Posture" of "tender Shepherdess" would appear to be the invidious mistress's masterwork of disguise.

At the same time, there's no denying the appeal to the speaker of that "tender Shepherdess." Unless we take him to be a kind of dotard, then, the poet leaves us with a predicament: in spite of his damning knowledge of her, if not indeed because of it, the speaker worships this woman. For the poet, if not for the speaker, her name, Clora, would have strong overtones of verdancy and fecundity, green thoughts and green shades. Is she—in her endless variety and various illumination—Marvell's volatile Muse? Is she about to stride even now at the green light—or against the red: it makes no difference—across the intersection of Hollywood and Vine? I have to think so.

NOTES

1. Quoted in Pierre Legouis, *Andrew Marvell* (Oxford: Oxford University Press, 1968), 10.

2. John Aubrey, *Aubrey's Brief Lives,* ed. Oliver Lawson Dick (London: Secker and Warburg, 1950), 196.

3. Hugh Kenner, *Seventeenth Century Poetry: The Schools of Donne and Jonson* (New York: Holt, Rinehart, and Winston, 1964), 444.

4. Victoria Sackville-West, *Andrew Marvell* (London: Faber and Faber, 1929), 52.

5. Quotations from Marvell's verse are taken from *The Poems and Letters of Andrew Marvell,* ed. H. M. Margoliouth, 3d ed., vol. 1 (Oxford: Clarendon Press, 1971).

6. Wallace Stevens, "Notes toward a Supreme Fiction," in *The Collected Poems of Wallace Stevens* (New York: Knopf, 1971), 406–7.

7. W. B. Yeats, "A Dialogue of Self and Soul," in *The Collected Poems of W. B. Yeats* (New York: Macmillan, 1951), 231.

8. Douglas Bush, *English Literature in the Earlier Seventeenth Century, 1600–1660* (Oxford: Oxford University Press, 1962), 168.

9. Roland Barthes, *Roland Barthes,* trans. Richard Howard (New York: Farrar, Straus and Giroux, 1977), 45.

10. Legouis, *Andrew Marvell,* 70.

11. Legouis, *Andrew Marvell,* 76; Bush, *English Literature,* 173; Ann Berthoff, *The Resolved Soul: A Study of Marvell's Major Poems* (Princeton: Princeton University Press, 1970), 88.

12. John Milton, *Paradise Lost,* 7:460–61, in *John Milton,* ed. Stephen Orgel and Jonathan Goldberg (Oxford: Oxford University Press, 1990), 502.

ELEVEN

Saint John the Rake

Rochester's Poetry

THOM GUNN

I DISCOVERED ROCHESTER WITH WONDER and delight when I was in my teens, with the 1948 British publication of Ronald Duncan's selection, hardly a scholarly edition but a good starting point, with a stringently Poundian introduction. It contained some poems no longer attributed to Rochester, but they were in a vigorous style equal to his median work. It also contained "The Imperfect Enjoyment," which only five years later V. de Sola Pinto was constrained to omit by the publishers of his Muses' Library edition "owing to the risk of prosecution in this country [Britain] under the existing laws" (xlix). Things were to get worse before they improved; but fuller editions have succeeded these, and now that censorship has been pretty well overturned in Britain and the United States, there is a wealth of texts available to the horny teenager and the blameless scholar alike.

I suddenly realized a few years ago, looking at some Titians in the Prado (and particularly at similar paintings on the subject of "Venus and the Organist," a pairing I do not profess to understand), that a lot of what we like to think of as high art may have been commissioned in the first place as pornography for the upper class; and I agree with Thomas Waugh's statement in his *Hard to Imagine* (Waugh 8) that it is both impossible and undesirable to distinguish between the pornographic and the erotic, the difference being in the mind of the describer, who is likely to be concerned rather with excellence of execution than with the intention or effect of the subject matter. What sexually excites us and is expensive or classy or "classic" is thus called erotic, whereas what sexually excites us and is crudely done or mass produced and easily available is called pornographic. Paintings with good brushwork are erotic; graffiti are pornographic. But really, you get aroused by what you can find—and if all I found available in those pubertal years were certain classic texts like Chaucer, Petronius, and Rochester, it was not proof of my educated taste but of what I could lay my hands on. (To be exact, I was first aroused by the sleeping bag episode in *For Whom the Bell Tolls,* which at the time might have been considered evidence of tasteful masturbation. I admit it with shame. Nothing is more unfashionable than yesterday's bestseller.)

I make this emphasis to note by way of a start the naughty-boy aspect of Rochester's poetry in the deliberate excess and the elaborate and extreme ingenuity of its sexuality. That is a given—there is comparatively little in his poetry that is not sexual. Might it not be, however, that to focus on sexuality only is no more limiting than to focus on spirituality only? It is, after all, one intense part of a life rather than another, although perhaps in the event a less complex one.

THE COMEDY OF SEX

I always took the maxim "A hard cock has no conscience" to be a modern Cockney expression, because I first heard it in a London pub, until I found it was also a Latin commonplace of two thousand years ago. The member without conscience may be the cause of tragedy, but in literature it is more likely to attract comedy. Sex lands us in funny and often ungraceful bodily positions, the male organs normally kept covered popping out with their own unexpected force, for example. And our inordinate hungers tempt us into laughable intrigues and project us into ridiculous social situations. These are the constituents of farce, but if we take comedy in a larger sense, we must remember that its most obvious definition in drama insists on a happy ending, and what could be a more obviously successful outcome to a story than the orgasm achieved? Sexual subject matter is hospitable to comedy on several counts, then. Thus "The Miller's Tale," many of Shakespeare's comedies, Donne's elegies, and the wealth of popular songs at any time of history. To disregard the comedy of sex is to oversolemnize our humanity.

D. H. Lawrence and the good newspaper columnists who follow him teach us that sex should not be casual and that it is the sacrament accompanying love, but we know well that it often isn't—that there is so much of the animal remaining in us that we might as well accept it; we "carry on like alley cats," we say, or "we fuck like dogs," and rejoice that we have been granted such an unlimited scope for mindless happiness. Rochester's poetry is not always happy, some of it being misanthropic and misogynistic, and the toll of keeping up his reputation with what must have been frequent and frightful hangovers is certainly paid in the cynicism of some of his poetry, but he is on the whole wonderfully high-spirited, and it is difficult not to like a poet who can conclude a drinking song with these words: "With wine I wash away my cares, / And then to cunt again" (Vieth 53).

THE DESIRE TO SHOCK

For all his Hobbesian self-buttressing, Rochester based his reputation less on instinctual behavior than on exploits originating in bravado. Reputation was of supreme importance to him, being tied in to his self-image with the tightness of the stage performer. The dedicated libertine had to adhere to a demanding physical régime that in fact led to his early death. "To the Postboy" (Vieth 130–31) is a curious although trivial example of his self-awareness. On being asked "the readiest way to Hell," the boy, an expert in planning roadmaps, answers by punning on the poet's title and the name of the town in Kent: "The readiest way, my Lord, 's by Rochester."

David M. Vieth, Rochester's resourceful editor, calls this poem "half-boastful, half-penitential" (130). Rochester was on occasion both a bully and a brute, and we might not think the penitence nearly great enough given the specific offenses, for it is mitigated by the boastfulness, the bravado, the thoroughgoingness, and ultimately the dedication of Rochester's drudgery in the service of libertinage. The poem is a dull one, but for the sheer obstinacy behind it the poet deserves an existential sainthood like the one Genet was awarded by Sartre. I spoke of a hard physical régime; the word *régime* was perhaps his word too, occurring in the title of the poem "Régime de Vivre" (Lyons 42), which, although of doubtful provenance, characteristically implies just a touch of self-criticism in spite of uncharacteristically loose versification and diction. "Look how disgusting I am," he says. "What a good boy am I!" And we sense his boredom at the same time.

> I rise at eleven, I dine about two,
> I get drunk before seven, and the next thing I do,

I send for my whore, when for fear of a clap,
I spend in her hand, and I spew in her lap;
Then we quarrel and scold, till I fall fast asleep,
When the bitch growing bold, to my pocket does creep.
Then slyly she leaves me, and to revenge the affront,
At once she bereaves me of money and cunt.
If by chance then I wake, hot-headed and drunk,
What a coil do I make for the loss of my punk!
I storm, and I roar, and I fall in a rage.
And missing my whore, I bugger my page.
Then crop-sick all morning I rail at my men,
And in bed I lie yawning till eleven again.

The libertine Rochester is of course defiant, and the defiance is connected
with one of the most frequent effects of all pornography, which is not
only to excite but also to *shock*—that is, to shock some into disgust and
others into still greater excitement. The great shock here is in the casu-
alness of line 12. There are other approving references to homosexuality
in Rochester's work, two of them to be taken up below, but I see little
more profit in speculating about whether Rochester was bisexual than in
postulating that Apollinaire really enjoyed copulating with wounds. The
poet is caught between the desire to excite and the desire to shock, taking
the risk that the latest item might just turn off the reader who is repelled
by homosexuality. The whole thing reads like an improvisation, one thing
following another as it occurs in the poet's mind, but the introduction of
buggery is completely gratuitous and stands to the rest perhaps in the
same way as the presence of bisexuality to the heterosexuality of certain
stag films noted by Thomas Waugh in *Hard to Imagine,* where he aptly
alludes to what he calls "an erotics of pansexuality" (Waugh 319).

Such an erotics is evoked far more subtly, although to much the same
general effect, at the end of Rochester's "Love a woman" (Vieth 51), which
has been justifiably enough included in *Gay Love Poetry,* a recent anthol-
ogy edited by Neil Powell. Three-fourths of the poem seem like familiar
ground: in general tone it resembles Suckling's "Out upon it," in which
the gentleman-sensualist's nod to compliment is subsumed by a slick cyn-
icism. In Suckling's poem the compliment to the lady is pure sentimen-
tality, but then sentimentality has never been in conflict with cynicism.
(There is a tradition of the gangster's affection for little children.) Roch-
ester's misogyny might seem even more distasteful, but he is a cleverer
man than Suckling, and nothing overrides distaste so well as the wit of
an intelligent speaker.

Love a woman? You're an ass!
　'Tis a most insipid passion
To choose out for your happiness
　The silliest part of God's creation.

Let the porter and the groom,
　Things designed for dirty slaves,
Drudge in fair Aurelia's womb
　To get supplies for age and graves.

Farewell, woman! I intend
　Henceforth every night to sit
With my lewd, well-natured friend,
　Drinking to engender wit.

I said that the sentiments are familiar, and of course they are handled with the utmost skill: in the first stanza misogyny; in the second a combination of misogyny and snobbery, justified by its imagery of grime, mining, and grave digging, and in its consequential lighthearted disgust at sex for procreation. The exaggeration is comic. The third stanza subsides into a Horatian acceptance of comfortable limitation: drink and dirty stories with a good-natured crony. *We* drink to engender wit rather than copulate to engender babies; *our* dirt is in the head rather than in the body. But the fourth stanza turns the whole poem around:

Then give me health, wealth, mirth, and wine,
　And, if busy love entrenches,
There's a sweet, soft page of mine
　Does the trick worth forty wenches.

It is all the more surprising in that we had assumed we were in familiar territory. Our assumption was incorrect. We are either delighted or shocked in our surprise; but Rochester's delicacy here (as opposed to the brute indelicacy of "Régime de Vivre") is the more likely to charm us, while the poet's fatigue emerges as wit. We are forced surely to appreciate the sheer cleverness of the diction: the page is "sweet [and] soft" and clean by comparison with Aurelia, and he "does the trick," sex with him being a simple skill or knack, a trick quickly performed, as opposed to the hard and filthy labor of mining new "supplies for age and graves." The imagery and ideas knit together with the consistency of a John Donne.

We speak far too readily of the Renaissance lyric as a courtly form and only a courtly form. It is less limited, deriving as it does from popular song in the first place, and in the best hands often refreshing itself from the same source. Ralegh's poetry supplies obvious examples, but you don't have to read widely to find other cases in which the court calls on anonymous ballad, street cry, or riddle as models. Much of Rochester's poetry, too, derives from the subject matter—the joyous anarchy of pansexuality—in the obscene song. I don't know how many such anonymous songs survive from Rochester's time, but there are plenty of modern equivalents. There is for example the lengthy narrative, like "The Good Ship Venus" or "Eskimo Nell," structured so loosely that it can accrete innumerable instances of hyperbolic sexual activity, a new audacity to each stanza. In "The Good Ship Venus":

> One day the captain's daughter
> Fell headlong in the water—
> Delighted squeals
> Showed little eels
> Had found her sexual quarter.

Such a song is Rochester's "Signior Dildo" (Vieth 54–59), of which the hero is "a noble Italian . . . in a plain leather coat" (they had to make do with what they could before the invention of latex). He works his way through the ladies of London, with a new joke to each stanza, being finally challenged by Count Cazzo (or Penis) and "a rabble of pricks." At last he escapes down Pall Mall, pursued by his foes:

> The good Lady Sandys burst into a laughter
> To see how the ballocks came wobbling after,
> And had not their weight retarded the foe,
> Indeed 't had gone hard with Signior Dildo.

The same note is struck, of surrealistic sexuality, the language is plain, even improvisatory, and the forced rhyming characteristic of many a ballad is both parodied and exploited by the transference of stress to the second syllables of such words as *windów* and *dildó*.

The plain colloquial diction is common in Rochester's poetry and carries over into his numerous epigrams, and the jolly, rather comfortable tone appears in a lot of other poems, notably the facetious dialogue that starts "Quoth the Duchess of Cleveland to Counselor Knight" (Vieth 48), which ends: "For I'd rather be fucked by porters and carmen / Than thus be abused by Churchill and Jermyn." The courtier poet recommends the superior potency of laborers to those of his fellow-courtiers—and the class scorn and fatigued tone of "Love a woman" are reversed.

MISCELLANY

For the rest: "A Song of a Young Lady, to her Ancient Lover" (Vieth 89) is static but confusing, given that we are bound to ask how far Rochester wants the speaker to be heard as serious or joking. I like it less than I did when I was myself young, in my advancing years tending to frown on attempts to poke fun at gerontophiles.

There are also certain "serious" or nonsexual poems, the two most commonly anthologized being "Upon Nothing" (Vieth 118–20), an extended conceit more clever than convincing, and "A Satire against Reason and Mankind" (Vieth 94–101), which hardly affords much competition to the satires that Dryden, Pope, and Johnson will write. It turns out that the "reason" he attacks is only "false reasoning" and that "right reason" or "true reason" meet with his approval after all. "True reason"

> . . . distinguishes by sense
> And gives us rules of good and ill from thence,
> That bounds desires with a reforming will
> To keep 'em more in vigor, not to kill.

This has the familiar winning impudence, it is true. The tone of the poem is that of the expostulating essayist, one that we shall also find in the work of the three later satirists: but their most brilliant writing will be in the illustrative character sketch or incident or analogy rather than in the argument itself. (I am thinking of the accounts of Zimri, Atticus, or Charles XII.) Nevertheless, he is capable of some superb lines. I might point to "Huddled in dirt the reasoning engine lies, / Who was so proud, so witty, and so wise." If I understand the entry in the *OED* rightly, the word *engine* still had its earlier sense of ingenuity (or natural ability) at the same time as its later, which is alone ours, of mechanical contrivance. Thus it makes a splendid pun. And in the lines Empson admired, Rochester says of "wretched man": "For fear he arms, and is of arms afraid, / By fear to fear, successively betrayed." Rochester was a poet who *thought;* but he always thought most profoundly about sex. There is not much else here so impressive as the lines from the attributed poem "Pindaric" (Lyons 80) where of a modern Messalina he says:

When she has jaded quite
Her almost boundless appetite,
Cloyed with the choicest banquets of delight,
She'll still drudge on in tasteless vice,
(As if she sinned for exercise)
Disabling stoutest stallions every hour.

The fifth of these lines is surely great poetry, where Rochester enjoys his subject matter and at the same time manages to imply a certain perverse set of standards in describing it, in the application of which he is exquisitely witty.

"The Imperfect Enjoyment" (Vieth 37–40), which V. de Sola Pinto was not allowed to reprint, has a lot more substance, to my mind, than any other of the longest poems in couplets. I doubt I can imagine a better description of orgasm, which occurs early (too early!) in the poem.

In liquid raptures I dissolve all o'er,
Melt into sperm, and spend at every pore.
A touch from any part of her had done't:
Her hand, her foot, her very look's a cunt.

I do not remember ever having read a similar attempt to convey the sudden breakdown of tactile distinction that occurs in the moments before climax. The poem is not mock-heroic in most of its diction, but in tone rather, since most of the language is plain and direct, that of an educated man using occasional poetic circumlocution just enough to make fun of it, in phrases like "her balmy brinks of bliss." To parody the heroic is only a subsidiary intention. The poem is written with a consistent inventiveness and an energy of language that is ironic in light of its subject, which for the remaining fifty lines is that of impotence, for his penis, having been "stiffly resolved" before, "Now languid lies in this unhappy hour, / Shrunk up and sapless like a withered flower." He predicts its future:

Worst part of me, and henceforth hated most,
Through all the town a common fucking post,

On whom each whore relieves her tingling cunt
As hogs on gates do rub themselves and grunt.

His elaborate curse follows, concluding one of the great works of sexual comedy.

It is, however, comparatively simple in its feeling, as much of Rochester's poetry is. Sexual activity is a good in itself, and impotence is a comic inadequacy. And this is the point at which I have to answer my earlier question, whether to focus exclusively on sexuality is no more limiting than to focus similarly on the spiritual. It is, because the subject matter is capable of less complexity and less variety. The perfect sexual union was attainable in the first part of this poem, but the perfect union with God can never be attained, although there are degrees of closeness that may be distinguished, and thus religious poetry may have a more complex matter to present. The poet woos God, yearns, and is unable to attain. (It is of course interesting that when St. John of the Cross did claim to such a union, he used a sexual analogy. Rochester, characteristically, reversed the procedure in his version of "Why dost thou shield thy lovely face.") Most of Rochester's poetry is comparatively simple in feeling, and in being deliberately amoral it lacks all subtlety other than the aesthetic subtleties of style. But he is a supremely talented stylist; thus when we do come to Rochester the moralist, we find him standing high on the shoulders of Rochester the amoralist, and we are reading superior poetry indeed, poetry of weight and perpetual interest, in which he ventures on judgments inescapably intertwined with a full attempt to understand experience. That is, the experience and the judgment are so closely connected that the one is inconceivable without the other. The two best poems I would attribute to Rochester the moralist are "The Disabled Debauchee" (Vieth 116–17) and "Absent from Thee" (Vieth 88–89).

ROCHESTER THE MORALIST

"The Disabled Debauchee" is a highly sophisticated satire, as devastating as Johnson's "A Short Song of Congratulation" of a century later and more subtle in that it puts even its own point of view in doubt. It starts with an epic simile, apparently serious, although there is already something potentially comic about the word *crawls,* as though the retired admiral were an infant or a tortoise, but we are invited to take it in earnest for the moment until adjectives like *wise* and *bold* can be better assessed on our learning their true context. Such learning starts with the fourth stanza, where the other part of the simile—now revealed to be mock heroic—is worked out in detail. "Impotence" is a sexual pun, as "deprived of force" also turns out to be, and we are presented with a series of discrepancies—"the unlucky chance of war" with that of wine, the dangerous billows of the real sea with those of debauchery, the broadsides from the ship with those across the table, the scars of battle with those of syphilis, and so on. The poem, then, is about discrepancies between behavior and the language describing it, moving from the apparent seriousness of the first three stanzas, through the spunky and amusing defiance of the middle part of the poem (the defiance with which we are already familiar), to the contempt of the last third, in which the satire is turned back on the apparently unwitting speaker, the debauchee of the title, who is clearly in a sense Rochester himself, even though equally clearly Rochester is director of that satire. The retired hero recounts his advice to the newly enlisted rake:

> I'll tell of whores attacked, their lords at home;
>   Bawds' quarters beaten up, and fortress won;
> Windows demolished, watches overcome;
>   And handsome ills by my contrivance done.

The very vigor and thoroughness of the language ridicules the conduct of the debauchee, whose valor is to attack defenseless women, to break windows like a rebellious child, to wreck the houses of pimps and overpower old men: it leads us at once to see the handsome feats as tawdry, trivial, and cowardly.

There follows a remarkable stanza that was sometimes omitted in the reprinting of the poem as late as the Muses' Library edition but is undoubtedly Rochester's, both for its skill and its subject-matter:

> Nor shall our love-fits, Chloris, be forgot,
>   When each the well-looked link-boy strove t'enjoy,
> And the best kiss was the deciding lot
>   Whether the boy fucked you, or I the boy.

Possible reasons for omission are obvious: an early editor's uneasiness with the sudden appearance of bisexuality or even with the sexual unscrupulousness of the linkboy's employers. There may have been an additional, less conscious reason for bowdlerization, however. A genuine authorial enthusiasm seems to be present in the brief anecdote, which also lacks the implied self-condemnatory qualifiers directed earlier at the debauchee's conduct in such obviously ironic evaluations as "wise and daring," "honorable," and "handsome." I recognize in it the pansexuality of other poems, and see how in context this is all part of the bully's lack of discrimination and feeling, but have to admit to finding the ingenuity of the situation exciting. Sexual manipulation is usually fun to read about (think of Laclos), so long as you are not being victimized by it yourself.

The sexual frisson this stanza may give me complicates but does not destroy the force of the satire. Returning to the poem I am merely warned that I too approach the status of the contemptible speaker:

> With tales like these I will such thoughts inspire
>   As to important mischief shall incline:
> I'll make him long some ancient church to fire,
>   And fear no lewdness he's called to by wine.
>
> Thus, statesmanlike, I'll saucily impose,
>   And safe from action, valiantly advise;
> Sheltered in impotence, urge you to blows,
>   And being good for nothing else, be wise.

The earlier and simpler ironic technique is taken up again: "important mischief" sounds more like the work of a fallen angel than the pathetic naughtiness of the action described. There is probably room for a pacifist interpretation of the poem (one that Rochester himself would have been unlikely to share), by which the rake is not only contrasted to a warrior but the warrior is compared to the rake. Such an anachronistic reading would do no harm to the poem. In fact, in the last stanza Rochester does widen the scope of attack to include the retired but still vocal politician, a cowardly busybody, his supposed wisdom being exactly comparable to that of the speaker. Rochester bruises both rake and statesman with one stone.

It is an astonishing poem, especially when compared with the defiant and often joyful celebrations of the rake's life that we have read in Rochester's other poems. "The Disabled Debauchee" astonishes because it criticizes the rake's conduct as the ultimate not in boldness but in timidity—precisely the habit he has heretofore held in contempt. And as for the linkboy stanza, where the rake appears as a wit, a Dorimant, that should not raise the speaker of the rest of the poem in our estimation so much as lower the Dorimant to the level of the other: the boy has not exactly been consulted in the disposal of his destiny, and he is as helpless before two adults, his employers, as the whores and watchmen of the previous stanza. (Whether he will enjoy the experience is not brought into question.)

We do know something, sifting through the anecdotes, about the kind of rake Rochester was. I am not concerned with the last-minute repentance, which is reported only by interested parties. If it took place, it must have done so as the effect of illness. For the rest I have suggested that he was a kind of existential saint in his life, and what I mean is this. It is easy and common to be lightly cynical. I have already described a mild cynicism as the natural companion of sentimentality, each being an easy and comfortable attitude unaccompanied by vigor of thought or feeling. They derive from a trivializing of experience: if all life is trifling, then of course the affections are trifling too. But for Rochester, as later for Blake, the devils were angels and the angels were devils. He did not trifle; he went to extremes, becoming a *dedicated* libertine and a saint of debauchery. His defiance was full-time, and he was not one of those poets who jot down the exceptional piece of smut during a life's work of nonsexual poetry. His corpus was pornographic, his nonsexual poetry exceptional. However, when he wrote about his life, he was eventually forced to think more deeply about it, too, his judgment emerging most demonstrably in his choice of words. So, although he was always serious in his slightest poetry, and serious in the midst of the wildest humor while he pursued his sexual obsession, he had to make choices in language—and choosing one word rather than another is likely to be a moral choice. From, let us say, believing that his defiance was "handsome," he was forced to consider what handsome behavior actually consisted of—firing an old church, breaking a window? His career is thus superlatively interesting, both artistically and morally, because he took his language as seriously as his debauchery. The result is that in "The Disabled Debauchee" the humor is a sort of sanity. The poetry is no longer merely defiant. The act of writing has become itself a form of behavior that is corrective to the physical behavior of daily conduct and a judgment on it. It does not remedy it, being a different order of behavior, but I find nobility in the very inconsistency.

There remains one other poem in my list:

Absent from thee, I languish still;
    Then ask me not, when I return?
The straying fool 'twill plainly kill
    To wish all day, all night to mourn.

Dear! from thine arms then let me fly,
    That my fantastic mind may prove
The torments it deserves to try
    That tears my fixed heart from my love.

When, wearied with a world of woe,
    To thy safe bosom I retire
Where love and peace and truth does flow,
    May I contented there expire,

Lest, once more wandering from that heaven,
    I fall on some base heart unblest,
Faithless to thee, false, unforgiven,
    And lose my everlasting rest.

The language and syntax are more formal than those of the other poem—
less direct, more courtly, although far from the circumlocutions of courtly
preciosity. He strikes once more the note of the Cavalier poets: we hear
the decorous tone, as he languishes and strays and expires, the gracefulness
of the whole performance, the slight irony of *plainly,* and the balance of
the antithesis in the fourth line. But here no more than in the previous
poem is Rochester to have his cake and eat it too—he is too honest, it
seems, to *enjoy* the paradox suggested in the second stanza, that he is
unfaithful to the lady in order that the return to her may seem all the
sweeter. In the expression of this stanza, however, he makes us aware of
the full complexity of his emotion; even within the limits of his under-
stated vocabulary it is felt as a paradox painful to live through. (*Deserves*
is an extraordinary word, when you come to think of it.) The alliteration
of the ninth line may be heard as an indication of simpler feeling, and it
is a simpler feeling that he most wants—a freedom from the fate of being
Rochester. She ("Dear!") is a constancy, like a baby's mother or God, from
whom love and peace and truth flow. I have always thought that Rochester
sees himself here as Milton's Satan, damned by having absented himself
from heaven, "wandering" as he does in search of sexual adventure, and
in doing so "straying" from God—and losing all possibility of return. The

unbroken movement of the poem's second half is an appropriately continuous presentation of his situation, hoping to die in the "safe bosom" of the Absolute in "everlasting rest," so as to avoid the temptations of the real and imperfect world in what I can only call the descending meanings of the alliterating words *fall, faithless, false,* and *unforgiven*—for to be unforgiven by the source itself of love is the worst of all. The whole of the last stanza is in fact a fabric of alliteration, the *l* and the *st* sounds knitting together to give force and finality to the last line and the *w* sounds (*once* and *wandering*) suggesting acts of unfaithfulness easy and almost inevitable. It could be an unpleasant poem, or else a silly one, if it were to simply embody the bad faith that is his subject. Instead, Rochester is not the victim of his theme. His poem looks forward to the psychological complexity of, say, Baudelaire or Proust. Or it may be compared to Hardy's magnificent "I'll say I'll seek her" as a first-person examination of helplessness.[1]

I do not attempt to disentangle the implicit Christianity of this poem from the assertions of atheism elsewhere. The Christian terms are Rochester's; they are not inserted by me. They are, however, analogies, not professions of faith. In any case he is helpless as the straying Christian might be helpless. He has free will, but he has to operate among the specifics of this world and cannot live an inactive life of passive contemplation (or maybe of sleep) in the bosom of the absolute. He is in an impossible fix. The neatness and apparent lightness are part of the whole paradox, essential to it: Rochester is in control of a statement about lack of control. The vigor of the verse movement shows up in minute metrical variations (initial trochees) but is also apparent in the complex syntax of the final sentence, which must be shared by two stanzas, containing as it does two statements that either support or deny one another ("may I expire lest I lose my everlasting rest"). In the smooth context of the courtly "song" such small exercises of energy are equivalent to more effortful displays in a showier context. The slightly elevated diction, too, is justified by the contrast with the raw and unelevated things it really refers to, the moments of sensual ecstasy, for example, so great that all distinction between body parts is elided, as in "The Imperfect Enjoyment."

In discussing both poems I have taken pains to emphasize Rochester's interest in the incongruities between conduct and the description of it. To condemn conduct and to persist in it creates writing of great *complexity,* and I have unashamedly used this word as a term of appreciation, fully aware that many readers may find it old-fashioned, reminding them of midcentury critics. So I should state, with my own defiance, that two of the most interesting pursuits I can find in literature are the expression of energy and the exploration of complexity within that energy. Of course, when speaking of complexity, I distinguish mere complications, mystifications, and blunders from our subtly self-contradictory emotional processes, seldom completely conscious, never completely understood. The full Rochester, as we are finally allowed to read him, emerges as a more and more admirable poet. He visits a large number of sexual sites and deals with his findings in a variety of ways, sometimes casually, sometimes carefully, to report on the consistencies and discrepancies between language and experience. It's a big subject he takes on, and he takes it on completely and seriously—first attempting to express all its energy and finally facing up to its full complexity.

NOTE

1. The two poems resemble one another in the sadness of the situation, over which the speaker has resigned control. But for once Rochester rejects the comedy implicit in it, although Hardy typically does not (but Hardy's, as always, is a strange kind of comedy).

BIBLIOGRAPHY

Lyons, Paddy, ed. *Rochester: Complete Poems and Plays.* London: Everyman, 1993.

Pinto, Vivian de Sola, ed. *Poems by John Wilmot, Earl of Rochester.* Muses' Library ed. London: Routledge and Kegan Paul, 1953.

Powell, Neil, ed. *Gay Love Poetry.* New York: Carroll and Graf, 1997.

Vieth, David M., ed. *The Complete Poems of John Wilmot, Earl of Rochester.* New Haven: Yale University Press, 1968.

Waugh, Thomas. *Hard to Imagine.* New York: Columbia University Press, 1996.

TWELVE

Edward Taylor

What Was He Up To?

ROBERT HASS

EDWARD TAYLOR'S POEMS—I think the story is by now well known—
were discovered in a bound manuscript book in Yale University Library
in the middle of the 1930s by a scholar named Thomas Johnson. Taylor
had died in the village of Westfield, Massachusetts, in the summer of
1729. His tombstone said he was eighty-seven years old. He had arrived
in the Massachusetts colony sixty-one years before, in 1668, when the
entire English settlement in the New England forests consisted of some-
thing between twenty and thirty thousand souls and the village of West-
field not much more than a hundred. Johnson published a few of Taylor's
poems in an antiquarian journal in 1937. A first book of the poems, *The
Poetical Works of Edward Taylor*, followed in 1939, after which poets and
scholars began to read him and write about him. In 1960—just between
the publications of Robert Lowell's *Life Studies* and John Ashbery's *The
Tennis Court Oath*—Donald Stanford's *The Poems of Edward Taylor* put
all of Taylor's major poems before American readers. It was a somewhat
belated literary debut.

It was also an imposing, rather startling body of work. At the center of
it was a sequence of 219 poems, written from 1682 to 1724, from the time
Taylor was forty years old until he was eighty-two, entitled "Preparatory
Meditations before my Approach to the Lords Supper. Chiefly upon the
Doctrin preached upon the Day of administration." There was also an
ambitious long poem on Calvinist doctrine, made out of thirty-six indi-

vidual poems and several thousand lines, called *Gods Determination;* eight miscellaneous lyrics written, the scholarly guess is, sometime before 1689; a formal elegy on the death of his first wife from 1689; another on the death of one of Taylor's colleagues, the Hartford minister Thomas Hooker, in 1697; an undated poem in couplets, called "A Fig for Thee Oh! Death"; two other undated poems in couplets, "The Martyrdom of Deacon Lawrence" and "The Persian Persecution"; and a piece in what was his characteristic form, the rhymed six-line stanza of the "Preparatory Meditation," called "The Sparkling Shine of Gods Justice." There was more work, none of it adding much to our sense of Taylor's accomplishment, and it has been printed in the intervening years.

Almost everything about Edward Taylor and his poetry was unexpected. The unexpectedness of the poetry itself lay in the intersection of its quality, its quantity, its history, and its style, the peculiarities of its style. That a large body of poetry had turned up, written by a Puritan parson in the latter years of the seventeenth century in a village on the remotest western frontier of colonial New England, was not so surprising given the culture of literacy among the Puritan English colonists and the level of education required of Puritan ministers. The first surprise was that it was so good. Scholars in the 1940s were quite prepared to recognize its provenance, if not its value. Serious study of the intellectual and theological foundations of New England were flourishing; and, more crucially, it was the high tide, in English departments, of the study of the seventeenth-century poets, the metaphysicals from Donne through Traherne, to whom modernist practice and the essays of T. S. Eliot had given so much authority. Students of the poems saw immediately what tradition Taylor belonged to and how deeply he was rooted in it. Another surprise was that a poet so good—although the assessments of how good he was were quite mixed—had lain unnoticed for so long.

The next surprise had to do with the ways in which he puzzled notions of Puritan austerity. He was very often a playful poet, on occasion an ecstatic poet, and his imagery was, well, more than metaphysical. By 1941 Austin Warren had published an essay titled "Edward Taylor's Poetry: Colonial Baroque."[1] Warren was trying to account for lines like these:

Shall Heaven, and Earth's bright Glory all up lie
    Like Sun Beams bundled in the sun, in thee?
Dost thou sit Rose at Table Head, where I
    Do sit, and Carv'st no morsell sweet for mee?[2]

Even if you grant the pun on *rose* and the risen Christ, there is still a rose sitting at the head of a table carving meat, a rose that is also the sun, and a pun on *son*. This was not the aesthetic of George Herbert; it much more resembled the writing of Richard Crashaw, whose *Steps to the Temple* was published in 1646, and Crashaw was a Roman Catholic. So this was a Puritan minister in the 1680s on the remotest American frontier writing an often ecstatic poetry in a style strongly reminiscent of George Herbert but verging on a continental, Roman Catholic baroque, a minister who also, it should be added, was the author of a number of virulently anti-Papist works. The Puritans of Boston recognized the baroque style when they saw it. Michael Wigglesworth, the author of New England's most popular poem, *Day of Doom,* sternly rebuked a poetry made of "strained metaphors, far-fetch't allusions, audacious & lofty expressions . . . meer ostentation of learning & empty flashes of a flourishing wit," declaring that such writers "daub over their speech with rhetorical paintments" and "winding, crocked, periphrasticall circumlocutions & dark Allegoric mysteries."[3] This tells us that there was something un-Protestant about this adamantly Calvinist cleric.

The next set of surprises had to do with what must be called the quaintness and homeliness of his style. In his introduction to Donald Stanford's 1960 edition of Taylor's poems, Louis Martz enumerates what were seen to be the deficiencies of Taylor's verse: the clumsiness of his meters and his rhymes; his "strangely assorted diction," mixing low and learned terms with what seem to be coinages and dialect words; and the effects of "his use of the homeliest images to convey the most sacred and reverend themes."[4] To these charges might be added at least two others. Alongside the baroque in Taylor is a curious literalness and methodicalness of imagination: if the Lord is like wine, you are apt to get a solid stanza on every phase of the fermentation process. And finally for a Puritan, he is, rather surprisingly, inclined to load down the Lord with a profusion of descriptive terms that have the feel of a plain man's idea of high life: precious stones, the finest linen, the best wine, rare sugars, ointments, and perfumes. Perfumes, above all. One of the distinct characteristics of the divine in Taylor's world is that it smells wonderful. (This from a poet who, in 1696, twenty-five years after he arrived there, could still speak of Westfield's "foggy damps assaulting my lodgen in these remotest swamps." It's not so difficult to guess why the terms of his praise give the impression that God existed in a sort of eternal duty-free shop.) Martz is at pains to defend Taylor against the charge that he was a bumpkin, "a burlap

Herbert," and he does so by appealing to the deeply learned, passionately earnest man discernable beneath what he nevertheless regards as "the surface crudities" of his verse.

This issue, what to make of Taylor's style, is one of the subjects I want to take up, but there remains the last wonder in this inventory of Taylor's surprises to be dealt with. It is that all the evidence suggests that he created this body of work in private and in more or less total isolation. Over the course of his life he sent a few verses to friends and family members in letters, and he courted his first wife with a popular New England form, the anacrostic poem; but beyond this there is no evidence that he shared his poetry with anyone. There is no correspondence to suggest that he wrote to Cambridge or Hartford friends about it. Although the "Preparatory Meditations" seem to have been written on the same subjects as his sermons, there's no suggestion that he ever read his poems to his congregation. He made no effort to publish them, and although he copied out this large body of work very carefully and bound it in rough leather manuscript books, he explicitly forbade its publication upon his death. This doesn't mean that he didn't share his work. He may have had a literary correspondence that has been lost. He may have had a circle of friends among the Westfield farmers who took an interest in verse. He may have read his poems to one or both of his wives or to his children in his later years. We don't know. We know very little about his life. But there's nothing to indicate that he had a community of readers.

It is a set of facts—and gaps—one looks at with a mixture of disbelief and recognition. Emily Dickinson, after all, lived just north and east of him in Amherst, but she at least sent her poems to Thomas Higginson and Helen Hunt Jackson, and a few to magazines, and got to enjoy the reputation of a poet, recluse, and snob. Edward Taylor's privacy, like his culture, is a harder thing to read. He was an Englishman. He was born in Leicestershire, in the southern midlands, which made him an atypical colonist. The great majority of them came from East Anglia, the Home Counties, and the southwest of England.[5] Leicestershire was the birthplace of George Fox. It seems to have been more Quaker than Puritan in its leanings. It's hard to know how much this means. Michael Wigglesworth, with his dour view of verbal excess, came from Yorkshire. However eccentric Taylor was to the home culture of the other New England colonists, he had an English education and a profoundly Puritan theology.

So one ought to be a little skeptical of any impulse to claim him as an American, or proto-American, poet. In his early years in Westfield he went through King Philip's War, the last concerted attempt of the New England Indians to drive out the European invaders, and his poems make no mention of it. The imagery of the natural world in his poems is English, and his poems are full of English folk technologies and games and turns of speech, recently and wondrously transplanted, it is true, but that new rooting seems not to enter his imagination. He was among the founders of New England culture, certainly of the culture—somewhat different from Boston's—of the Connecticut River valley. Still, the only thing that seems American about him—presciently so—is this strange absence of a social context for his work. He seems—as Anne Bradstreet does in her private and unpublished poems—an early instance of the solitariness, self-sufficiency, and peculiarity of the American imagination.

THE ISSUE OF HIS STYLE

Which is why I want to return to the issue of his style. Here is one of his lines that has stuck in my head, a "volunteer," as they say of garden weeds: "Let Conscience bibble in it with her Bill." It's almost nonsense verse: the alliteration of *bibble* and *bill;* the string of assonances in the short *i* sound, *bibble in it with* and *bill;* and the odd word *bibble.* Here we come to the issue of Taylor's diction. He is a poet who sends you to dictionaries. His word of choice is not *dabble,* which, according to the *OED,* came into the language in the late sixteenth century, probably from the Dutch, and which Shakespeare used, in *Richard III,* to describe "A Shadow like an Angell, with bright hayre Dabblel'd in blood," and Tennyson used, in *The Princess,* to describe someone "Dabbling a shameless hand" in the "holy secrets of this microcosm," and which seems to have been ascribed to the feeding behavior of ducks around 1661, so that Wordsworth could use it in 1789 in "The Evening Walk"—"Where the duck dabbles 'mid the rustling sedge"—and John Clare, gorgeously, in 1821—"The long wet pasture grass she dabbles through." It is not this word.

Nor *dibble,* which I first came across in Cowper's "Yardley Oak," where there is "a skipping deer, with pointed hoof dibbling the glebe." A dibble was an instrument for poking holes in the ground for planting. The noun shows up in manuscripts as early as 1450, the verb in 1583. Keats found a use for it in *Endymion* ("In sowing-time ne'er would I dibble take"), and it seems to have disappeared from all but horticultural uses by the end of the nineteenth century. It had an even briefer life as a variant on *dabble.* Michael Drayton's *Polyolbion* in 1622: "And near to them you see the lesser dibbling teale," and it is applied to the activities of fishermen by a Mr. Chetham in *The Angler's Vade-mecum:* "When you angle at ground in a clear Water, or dibble with natural Flies," in the 1680s.

So both *dibble* and *dabble* were, theoretically, available to Edward Taylor, but what came to his mind was *bibble,* which arrived in English from French or Norman French in both transitive and intransitive forms. In Stanyhurst's 1583 translation of the *Aeneid* there are "fierce steeds" that "Xanth stream gredilye bibled," and its intransitive form—which the *OED* describes as obsolete—gets used by John Skelton in 1529: "Let me wyth you bybyll." The word is applied to ducks as early as 1552, and the last use of it cited in that dictionary occurs in 1861, in a work by M. B. Edwards called *Tale of the Woods,* in a section devoted to "The Eider Duck": "How pleasant it is to glide through the grass, / And bibble the dew-drops as I pass!" Whether Taylor's choice was dictated by the assonance or the alliteration, or by regional dialect, or by the sheer silliness of the word—it calls to mind a child blowing bubbles in milk—we have no way of knowing. What we do know is that it is not a duck exactly but a conscience behaving like a duck that is doing the bibbling. Which is enough to tell us that we are—the provenience of the word aside—in the seventeenth century.

Moreover, there is the matter of what this duck-like conscience is bibbling in. It's bibbling in rose water. Here is the stanza, from the fourth of Taylor's "Preparatory Meditations," in which the line appears:

> God Chymist is, doth Sharons Rose distill.
>   Oh! Choice Rose Water! Swim my Soul herein.
> Let Conscience bibble in it with her Bill.
>   Its Cordiall, ease doth Heart burns Caus'd by Sin.
>   Oyle, Syrup, Sugar, and Rose Water such.
>   Lord, give, give, give; I cannot have too much.

Taylor himself was, probably as a matter of necessity, something of a chemist. As a person of education he served as doctor as well as minister to the village of Westfield. His library included a five-hundred-page manuscript in his own hand, *Dispensatory,* extracted from sources like *The English Physician Enlarged* (1666) and *Pharmacopoeia Londensis* (1685), which described the medicinal properties of herbs, drugs, oils, and gums and the manner of their preparation.

This stanza condenses various ways of turning rose petals into medicine. But its proposition is to meditate on a verse from the Song of Solomon: "I am the Rose of Sharon." The rose of Sharon is a species of hibiscus, not a rose, but let that be. The metaphor is part of a song sung by a bride for herself in an ancient erotic Hebrew folk song; Christian typology—to get the full strangeness of it—had converted the bride into a figure for Christ. So the rose water and the rose oil, and the rose sugar and the rose syrup here are imagined applications of seventeenth-century technologies to the blood of Christ. God is the chemist who distilled a healing rose water from the blood of his son's crucifixion—an event of such joy that the seventeenth-century Calvinist conscience can bibble in it.

It is not surprising that the first twentieth-century commentators on Taylor found him exceedingly quaint and strange. They were also inclined to see him as a rather clumsy amateur, and a line like "Oyl, Syrup, Sugar, and Rose Water such" might have served as an example. One supposes that he means to say that these items also have medicinal properties, and the commentators might have guessed that Taylor has forced the syntax in his effort to secure the rhyme. But what the word *bibble* should tell us is that we can't be sure about this. Given a mind so embedded in its own time, it seems quite possible that "Oyl, Syrup, Sugar, and Rose Water such" was perfectly idiomatic Leicestershire English. We simply cannot know.

And we might have the same trouble with a line that seems a perfect example of what scholars took to be Taylor's naivete: "Its Cordiall, ease doth Heart burns Caus'd by Sin." It looks as if the poet, having wandered into his pharmaceutical metaphor, has—if not inadvertently, certainly ludicrously—turned sin into a form of indigestion. But there is no doubt that he's making a joke about sin and indigestion—it's, in fact, an instance of the metaphysical "wit" that attracted the attention of midcentury scholars to him in the first place. This does seem to be an aspect of his sense of humor and also of his theology: given the saving blood of Christ, sin is a mere indisposition. It is also possible that other meanings of *heartburn* had more force in Taylor's English. The word is first cited by the *OED* with reference to digestion in 1597. It shows up around the same time as a joke in *Much Ado about Nothing:* "How tartly that Gentleman lookes, I never can see him, but I am heartburn'd an howre after." It also, however, was used to describe feelings of passionate enmity—"heart-burning Hate," Spenser writes in *The Faery Queen.* How much sting of this second meaning there is inside the joke I think it's impossible to gauge. In either case, although Donne might have assayed such a metaphor, George Herbert, to whom Taylor is so often compared, would probably not. It is a little too low and a little too risible. And it is for me one of the things that's wonderful about him. He is a poet full of verbal wonders.

And this is one of the pleasures and strangenesses of reading him. His contemporaries, like Marvell, and his great antecedents, like Donne and Herbert and Milton and Vaughan and Crashaw, have become the seedbed of educated English. Their diction defined its possibilities, and their lines are the echo chamber in which English verse came to have resonance. Taylor, who was not absorbed in this way, both because he was not naturalized by generations of poets and schoolmasters and because he was always in some sense an outsider—not university educated, not a Londoner, not even an East Anglian like most Puritan ministers—presents us with a fresher and more radical version of one of the main experiences that poetry has to offer: the intimate confrontation with another mind, embodied in the verbal habits of another time.[6] Perhaps this effect will change over the years as poets and schoolchildren come to know his lines, but now, some sixty years after the recovery of his verse, it still seems newly decanted, as if—I don't know whether this metaphor should refer to rose water or to wine—it had been salvaged from the sea and the bottles opened and the odor were as sharp and unfamiliar as the day it was bottled.

THE ORGANIZATION OF HIS POEMS

The poem in which these lines occur, "Meditation 4. Cant. 2.1. I Am the Rose of Sharon," was written in April of 1683. It is, as the title indicates, a meditation on an image from the bride's song in Song of Solomon. It is a place to continue an interrogation of Taylor's style and to look at the related issue of the organization of his poems. The poem is organized, like all of the "Preparatory Meditations," as a sort of prayer. Its purpose is not so much union with God, at which the practice of meditation aimed, but preparation for the union that occurred, for Taylor, in the Lord's Supper. Each of the meditations begins by laying out a theme suggested by a scriptural text; the middle part of the poem develops the theme, and the poem ends with a supplication, which is both a way of praising God and an expression of the desire for union with Him. "Lord blow the Coal: Thy Love Enflame in mee," the first meditation ends. "Yet may I Purse, and thou my Mony bee," ends the second. And the third, more ecstatically, "Lord, breake thy Box of Ointment on my Head." A bed of coals, cash and a purse, a box of ointment: the range and heterogeneity of his imagery is a bit dizzying, as if the entire world existed to be a compendium of likenesses to this relationship.

It is striking, and moving to me, that the very last of the meditations, written more than forty years after these early poems, takes as its theme another line from the Song of Solomon, "I am sick of Love." It also ends with a supplication—it is his final supplication—that the gift of his poetry might be accepted. This is a theme throughout the second series of meditations, and it is accompanied often by a sense of the inadequacy of his art. The tone is profoundly subdued:

> Had I but better thou shouldst better have.
>   I nought withold from thee through nigerdliness,
> But better than my best I cannot save
>   From any one, but bring my best to thee.
>   If thou accepst my sick Loves gift I bring
>   Thy it accepting makes my sick Love sing.

One of the interesting things that this anguish in the later poems tells us about the intention of Taylor's art, and therefore about the formal organization of the meditations, is that they were intended as an offering, and although Taylor believed that no human action could bring a person to God, he seems to have hoped that his gift would be accepted. This tells us in turn something about the middle part of his poems, in which he is concerned to develop, or at least elaborate, his theme: it is his way of making a gift of his imagination to his God. This explains something to me about the joy, the giddiness and strangeness of the early meditations, as well as the feeling of gravity and exhaustion in many of the late ones. This is a subject I will return to shortly, but for now it is enough that we understand what is at stake for Taylor—beside doctrine—in the development of the poems.

Let's look now at Meditation 4. The first two stanzas deploy the theme by making a little allegory:

> My Silver Chest a Sparke of Love up locks:
>   And out will let it when I can't well Use.
> The gawdy World me Courts t'unlock the Box,
>   A motion makes, where Love may pick and choose.
>   Her Downy Bosom opes, that pedlars Stall,
>   Of Wealth, Sports, Honours, Beauty, slickt up all.
>
> Love pausing on't, these Clayey Faces she
>   Disdains to Court; but Pilgrims life designs,
> And Walkes in Gilliads Land, and there doth see
>   The Rose of Sharon which with Beauty shines.

Her Chest Unlocks; the Sparke of Love out breaths
To Court this Rose: and lodgeth in its leaves.

This is quaint enough. So far as vehicle and tenor are concerned, it's a bit hard to know exactly what the silver chest represents, but one does not pause long at this literal level in Taylor. The image itself is probably entirely conventional, but there is something quite pleasing and memorable about that peddler's stall of a downy bosom, and there is a Tayloresque pleasure in the last phrase of the stanza, "slickt up all." The passage has the slight crazing of metaphorical slippage, like a pane of crazed glass, that seems to me so distinctive in Taylor. The speaker in the poem has a silver box, and in the box is a spark of love, which is feminine in gender. Then Love, the spark inside the box carried, presumably, by the speaker, goes walking in Gilead and encounters a rose, wherewith she—Love—unlocks the box she is in, and out of it breathes the Spark, now converted by a pun into a beau or suitor—this sense of "spark" appears in Shakespeare's *Timon* in about 1600 and was stage slang by the time of Etherege—who is prepared to court the rose. The last line of the stanza, which is perhaps the only one that is graceful in a traditional way, gives a luxuriant rhythm to its slightly erotic sense of arrival.

The slippage at the literal level has been treated by the critics I have read as either an instance of his crudeness, although most of them have found it a charming crudeness in the way of folk art, or have tried to make a case for it as an effect of the baroque. I think it is an effect of the baroque, but saying so doesn't take us very far. I also think that it is charming, although not crude, if by crude one means inadvertent. There are, after all, only a certain number of guesses one can make about this writing. One is that Taylor did not notice the inconsistency or the unsettling malleability of his metaphors. Another is that he noticed and it was in fact an aesthetic effect that he aimed at. A third, somewhere between the two, is that he noticed and didn't mind because it was theological or doctrinal or—perhaps—emotional exactness he was aiming at. A fourth, slightly different, is that he noticed and, although it was not at the center of his intention, he liked the effect of the slippage, liked the freedom and the oddness of it, had what might be thought of as a cheerfully Platonist disregard for mere consistencies that resembles and anticipates in a curious way (as the baroque sometimes does) the attitude of surrealism. To say it another way, it seems likely that he saw and liked the aesthetic and cognitive effects of his imagery. He may have believed they mirrored his mind. In any case they became one of the habits of his mind.

Here are the next two stanzas, in which he contemplates the rose:

No flower in Garzia Horti shines like this:
  No Beauty sweet in all the World so Choice:
It is the Rose of Sharon sweet, that is
  The Fairest Rose that Grows in Paradise.
  Blushes of Beauty bright, Pure White, and Red
  In Sweats of Glory on Each Leafe doth bed.

Lord lead me into this sweet Rosy Bower:
  Oh! Lodge my Soul in this Sweet Rosy bed:
Array my Soul with this sweet Sharon flower:
  Perfume me with the Odours it doth shed.
  Wealth, Pleasure, Beauty Spirituall will line
  My pretious Soul, if Sharons Rose be mine.

This is the spark's courting song. He has rejected the downy bosom of the sluttish world and fallen in love with the blushing rose. The writing, like much of Taylor's writing in the meditations, would be conventional if it were not so odd. There is, first of all, something appealing in its exhilaration. The music—"the Fairest Rose that Grows in Paradise"—is in places like this reminiscent of Broadway lyrics. And then there are Taylor's particularities of imagination: the dew on the rose becomes "Sweats of Glory on Each Leafe," and this leads to what can only be described as sexual euphoria in the next two lines (they are hard to read without thinking of Blake's "The Sick Rose" as their underside). And finally there is this sort of showering dispersal of the image. The bower of the rose becomes a bed, and then apparel, and then perfume, and then some luxurious spiritual lining—he does not say what kind, a rose-petal lining, presumably, in place of sable or lamb's wool. And there is also the suggestion in "pretious" that the soul has become a jewel in a rose-petal setting.

These two pairs of stanzas are instances of two ways that Taylor's effects occur. In the first two stanzas, being literal about the allegory—one notices, for example, that the world courts the soul, but the soul is not courted by the rose (that would be contrary to Calvinist doctrine); the rose does the courting—releases the imagination to dream silver boxes and downy bosoms and pedlars' stalls and clayey faces and walks in Gilead and courting sparks in a whirligig of images. In the second pair of stanzas, not being literal in the elaboration of the metaphor of the rose as a blushing lover cascades insensibly into beds and flowery raiments and the soft linings of garments and a jewel.

The next stanzas are characteristic in a different way. George Herbert, in his poem on this trope, had mentioned the restorative properties of roses and hence of Christ, but Taylor the physician-poet is downright methodical in his development of this conceit, and once it has seized his attention, the courtship metaphor is abandoned altogether, having served its purpose. The next passage—in a manner almost Joycean—sits right at the edge of parodying a pharmaceutical manual:

> The Blood Red Pretious Syrup of this Rose
> > Doth all Catholicons excell what ere.
> Ill Humors all that do the Soule inclose
> > When rightly usd, it purgeth out most clear.
> > Lord purge my Soul with this Choice Syrup, and
> > Chase all thine Enemies out of my land.
>
> The Rosy Oyle, from Sharons Rose extract
> > Better than Palma Christi far is found.
> Its Gilliads Balm for Conscience when she's wrack't
> > Unguent Apostolorum for each Wound.
> > Let me thy Patient, thou my Surgeon bee.
> > Lord, with thy Oyle of Roses Supple mee.

[The *OED* records uses of *supple* as a transitive verb, meaning "to soften or mollify a wound," from 1526 to 1688. The last use is by Bunyan: "Lord, supple my wounds, pour Thy wine and oil into my sore."]

> No Flower there is in Paradise that grows
> > Whose Virtues Can Consumptive Souls restore
> But Shugar of Roses made of Sharons Rose
> > When Dayly usd, doth never fail to Cure.
> > Lord let my Dwindling Soul be dayly fed
> > With Sugar of Sharons Rose, its dayly Bread.

[The verb *dwindle* first appeared in print in Shakespeare's plays; it was used to mean a shrinking in size or value; usages with the shading "degenerate" show up in several seventeenth-century texts. "Shugar" was made by crystallizing the juices of many different plants, often for medicinal purposes. The word *succor* derives from one pronunciation.]

God Chymist is, doth Sharons Rose distill.
    Oh! Choice Rose Water! Swim my Soul herein.
Let Conscience bibble in it with her Bill.
    Its Cordiall, ease doth Heart burns Caus'd by Sin.
    Oyle, Syrup, Sugar, and Rose Water such.
    Lord, give, give, give; I cannot have too much.

The final stanza in this passage brings us back—with what seems like artistic self-assurance—to the metaphor on which it has been floated:

But, oh! alas! that such should be my need
    That this Brave Flower must Pluckt, stampt, squeezed bee,
And boyld up in its Blood, its Spirits sheed,
    To make a Physick sweet, sure, safe for mee.
    But yet this mangled Rose rose up again
    And in its pristine glory, doth remain.

And the poem concludes with two more stanzas, which gather up its praise and frame its supplication:

All Sweets, and Beauties of all Flowers appeare
    In Sharons Rose, whose Glorious Leaves out vie
In Vertue, Beauty, Sweetness, Glory Cleare,
    The Spangled Leaves of Heavens cleare Chrystall Sky.
    Thou Rose of Heaven, Glory's Blossom Cleare
    Open thy Rosie Leaves, and lodge me there.

My Dear-Sweet Lord, shall I thy Glory meet
    Lodg'd in a Rose, that out a sweet Breath breaths.
What is my way to Glory made thus sweet,
    Strewd all along with Sharons Rosy Leaves.
    I'le walk this Rosy Path: World fawn, or frown
    And Sharons Rose shall be my Rose, and Crown.

The middles are usually the best of Taylor's poems. The endings, like this one, sometimes have an air of haphazard recapitulation. But it is not always easy to tell. It's hard to know, for example, whether the triple repetition "Glory Cleare," "Heavens cleare Chrystall Sky," and "Glory's Blossom Cleare" is a horn flourish of insistence—it picks up on a superior medicine's ability to produce clear purges—or a failure of invention. The one definite invention in it is the final transformation of the dew on the roses into stars in the sky. And that vernacular phrase in the penultimate line—"World fawn, or frown"—seems to try to make some gesture back to the little Bunyanesque allegory with which the poem began. One does not mind the ending, but one notices that when Taylor strings together abstract nouns, he is at his least compelling. One grants the breathless ardor that "In Vertue, Beauty, Sweetness, Glory Cleare" is intended to convey and prefers the strange mix of homeliness and sublimity in the metaphors.

George Herbert addresses this problem of adequate praise in "The Windows":

Lord, how can man preach thy eternall word?
    He is a brittle crazie glasse:
Yet in thy temple thou dost him afford
    This glorious and transcendent place,
    To be a window, through thy grace.

But when thou dost anneal in glasse thy storie,
    Making thy life to shine within
Thy holy Preachers; then the light and glorie
    More rev'rend grows, & more doth win:
    Which else shows watrish, bleak, & thin.

Doctrine and life, colours and light, in one
    When they combine and mingle, bring
A strong regard and aw: but speech alone
    Doth vanish like a flaring thing,
    And in the eare, not conscience ring.

Herbert, as he worked his way out from under the influence of Donne, developed a style of impressive clarity and simplicity, but even he does not do much with a line like "this glorious and transcendent place." He does not, however, risk rapture, so he does not, when he uses this diction, invite the distaste that some of the commentators have expressed toward Taylor's batteries of abstract nouns and adjectives. The style allows Herbert to achieve quietly brilliant effects—"Which else shows watrish, bleak, & thin," "but speech alone / Doth vanish like a flaring thing." Taylor's surfaces are too animated for such accuracies of perception and description. His famous lines, like the ones about the creation in "The Preface" to *Gods Determination*—

Who Spread its Canopy? Or Curtains Spun?
Who in this Bowling Alley bowld the Sun?

—or the ones in Meditation 8, where his subject is a line from John, "I am the Living Bread"—

> Doth he bespeake thee thus, This Soule Bread take.
>> Come Eate thy fill of this thy Gods White Loafe?
>> Its Food too fine for Angells, yet come, take
>> And Eate thy fill. Its Heavens Sugar Cake.

—come not from precision and purity of diction but from the sense of an unpredictable imagination taking delight in its own inventions. Although Meditation 4 ends with the triple insistence of God's clearness, the poem itself elects to be a "crazie glasse." As a writer one might have to choose between the styles of Herbert and Taylor, but as a reader, happily, one does not. Herbert's "The Windows" is a clearly marshaled argument without a word to spare. Taylor's organization, such as it is, is a kind of rough framework on which to spin out the rush of constantly self-transforming metaphors that are his gift: flaring things, one after another.

The third Meditation, "Thy Good Ointment," is one of the strangest of Taylor's poems and one of the most vivid examples of his practice. And more than enough, I think, to give a sense of what "the baroque" means in him. It's a sort of homemade verbal equivalent to a Bernini fountain, sweetly eschatological, and Calvinist to the core. It begins by taking up the odor of ointments:

> How sweet a Lord is mine? If any should
>> Guarded, Engarden'd, nay, Imbosomd bee
> In reechs of Odours, Gales of Spices, Folds
>> Of Aromaticks, Oh! how sweet was hee?
>> He would be sweet, and yet his sweetest Wave
>> Compar'de to thee my Lord, no Sweet would have.

Reek in the seventeenth century was applied—the *OED* says—to any "dense or unctuous smoke." The modern sense of a disagreeable odor didn't come in until the late nineteenth century. *Fold* was a pen or enclosure; it was also a wrapping or covering and, interestingly, an embrace. Shakespeare, in *Troilus and Cressida:* "Weake wanton Cupid Shall from your necke unloose his amorous fould." *Wave* in the seventeenth century meant both the displaying on an ensign—important for, possibly the source of, the military metaphor to come, as well as any motion of swaying to and fro. Herrick: "A winning wave (deserving note) / In the tempes-

tuous petticoat." The run of "Guarded, Engarden'd, nay, Imbosomed" is
particularly wonderful, I think. He does manage to imbosom us in reeks
of odors, gales of spice.

His elaboration in the next stanza is perhaps unnecessary, but the ba-
roque principle seems to be that if you can keep inventing metaphors,
you do:

> A Box of Ointments, broke; sweetness most sweet.
>   A surge of spices: Odours Common Wealth,
> A Pillar of Perfume: a steaming Reech
>   Of Aromatick Clouds: All Saving Health.
>   Sweetnesse itself thou art: And I presume
>   In Calling of thee Sweet, who art Perfume.

And then, having glossed the scriptural image, he proceeds to the devel-
opment. Watch what happens. As the poem proceeds, nostrils get mixed
up with nipples, and the military metaphor wanders in, with the bore of
a gun, called to mind presumably by the shape of nostrils:

> But Woe is mee! who have so quick a Sent
>   To Catch perfumes pufft out from Pincks, and Roses
> And other Muscadalls, as they get Vent,
>   Out of their Mothers Wombs to bob our noses.
>   And yet thy sweet perfume doth seldom latch
>   My Lord, within my Mammulary Catch.

"Muscadalls" are probably muscatel grapes, from which a strong sweet
wine came. The Puritans took the grape from England to New England.
"These Muscadell grapes," a grower wrote in 1601, "like wel and love cold
countries."[7] But there was also a muscadel pear brought from Norfolk to
Massachusetts. And best of all, "muscadines" were a kind of sweetmeat
perfumed with musk; a cookery book from 1665 says that they went by
the name of Kissing Comfits. As for "bob," here is a description of a fight
from 1605: "The fellowe . . . got the foole's head under his arme, and bobd
his nose."[8] The "Mothers Womb" is presumably the earth, but that line
is wonderfully strange.

The curious, in fact startling, "Mammulary Catch" gets taken up in
the next stanza:

> Am I denos'de? or doth the Worlds ill sents
>   Engarison my nosthrills narrow bore?

Or is my smell lost in these Damps it Vents?
  And shall I never finde it any more?
  Or is it like the Hawks, or Hownds whose breed
  Take stincking Carrion for Perfume indeed?

This is my Case. All things smell sweet to mee:
  Except thy sweetness, Lord. Expell these damps.
Breake up this Garison: and let me see
  Thy Aromaticks pitching in these Camps.
  Oh! let the Clouds of thy sweet Vapours rise,
  And both my Mammularies Circumcise.

Shall Spirits thus my Mammularies suck?
  (As Witches Elves their teats,) and draw from thee
My Dear, Dear Spirit after fumes of muck?
  Be Dunghill Damps more sweet than Graces bee?
  Lord, clear these Caves. These Passes take, and keep.
  And in these Quarters lodge thy Odours sweet.

Explicating this is probably as hopeless as explaining a joke, but bear with me. The general idea is pretty clear: have I lost my sense of smell, he asks, that I can't distinguish the scent of the Lord from the foul vapors of the world? *Muck* in the seventeenth century meant, unequivocally, animal dung. This conflict is made elaborate at first by the military metaphor. The nostril becomes the bore of a gun, which suggests the idea of warfare between the Lord and the World, whose army has pitched camp in the speaker's nostrils. And Taylor prays for the Lord's army to expel them— with more puns on the nostril in the ideas of clearing caves and taking passes.

Complicated enough. But "Mammulary Catch" sets off another set of metaphors that could perhaps have only occurred to a seventeenth-century physician. *Mamilla* refers to the nipple of the female breast. *Mamillary* was a technical term for any nipple-like projection and came to be applied to the papilla of the tongue and nostrils. The *OED* cites Crook, *The Body of Man*, 1615: "The mamillary processes which are the Organes of smelling." By 1648 John Beaumont had made a joke of this bit of technical jargon in *Psyche:* "By the Mammillar Processions, I Embrace those pleasures which my Sweets impart." That clears up "Mammulary Catch" and perhaps even "Mammularies Circumcise," that is, scour my nostrils, which are dulled to the sweetness of the Lord. But it does not clarify "both my Mammularies," even if the phrase means "both my nasal passages," because Taylor's mind has already been nudged from papillae to breasts:

> Shall Spirits thus my Mammularies suck?
>   (As Witches Elves their teats,) and draw from thee
> My Dear, Dear Spirit after fumes of muck?

So, "And both my Mammularies Circumcise" is as surreal as it seems. It refers to no known surgical procedure. He wants the foreskin off the nipples of his spiritual sense of smell. That elves sucking at the teats of witches should wander into this is quite delicious. And there is a final set of puns on *spirit,* which means here not just "soul" or "sprite" but also "wind," conceivably "strong spirits," and most probably "professional kid-nappers." The *OED* cites two instances from the seventeenth century: Whitelock, 1645: "An Ordinance against such who are called Spirits, and use to steal away, and take up children"; and the *London Gazette,* 1686: "The frequent Abuses of a lewd sort of People, called spirits, in Seducing many of his Majesties Subjects to go on Shipboard." It is a wild run.

The poem ends with the supplication, which is smooth and conventional enough, save for the exuberance of the first line, the somewhat less strange second line in which the hair is powdered with the talcum of grace, and the need to tie things up, which introduces food for the nose into the fifth:

> Lord, breake thy Box of Ointment on my Head;
>   Let thy sweet Powder powder all my hair:
> My Spirits let with thy perfumes be fed
>   And make thy Odours, Lord, my nosthrills fare.
>   My Soule shall in thy sweets then soar to thee:
>   I'le be thy Love, thou my sweet Lord shalt bee.

Meditations 3 and 4 are typical of the early meditations. They do, in a general way, follow the prescriptions in Richard Baxter's 1650 account of meditative practice, which Professor Martz has demonstrated to inform the organization of meditative poems throughout the period. The organization is tripartite, corresponding, as Martz points out, to the division of the faculties of the mind into memory, understanding, and will. The first part recalls a scriptural text, the second submits it to understanding, and the third disposes the will, although in Taylor's case will doesn't count for much. He simply asks his God to close the gap between them. It is the idea of understanding, the development of the theme, in Taylor that makes this organization seem the roughest of structures. Inside the development it is certainly not rational understanding to which doctrine is submitted but a wild, playful efflorescence of imagination. He makes poems as vigorous, strange, dreamy, and sometimes comic as any Joseph Cornell box, and like Cornell he makes them out of the smallest oddments and particulars of his culture.

Meditations 3 and 4 were not among the poems Thomas Johnson printed in the journal article that announced the discovery of Taylor's manuscript, and they were not among the poems published in the *Poetical Works* of 1937. They were perhaps too peculiar altogether to excite Johnson's admiration, or possibly he decided to introduce Taylor to the world in less eccentric modes. Nor are they included in any of the anthologies of American poetry that I am aware of. What usually represents the early meditations is "Meditation 8. I am the Living Bread," and it is through the lines I quoted earlier—

Come Eate thy fill of this thy Gods White Loafe?
Its Food too fine for Angells, yet come, take
And Eate thy fill. Its Heavens Sugar Cake.

—that most readers, if they read him, come to know the mix of homeliness and literalness and imaginative play that characterizes Taylor's images. They also get another Tayloresque line in the last stanza, delicious in its rhythms: "Yee Angells, help: This fill would to the brim / Heav'ns whelm'd-down Chrystall meele Bowle, yea and higher." That run of six strong stresses does its work triumphantly. A "whelm" was a wooden drainpipe. Originally, whelms were made from tree trunks, split in half vertically, hollowed out, and "whelmed down" or, as the *OED* says, "turned with the concavity downwards to form an arched watercourse." The word is said to survive to the present in Midlands dialect. It's one of the lines that gives me the impression that Taylor's rhythms are at their surest when he is nearest the language of the particulars of his world.

And the opening of the poem is also like Taylor in that it does not— as if he cannot, or like a playwright would not, do without a double plot—simply develop the imagery of bread:

I kening through Astronomy Divine
    The Worlds bright Battlement, wherein I spy
A Golden Path my Pensill cannot line,

From that bright Throne unto my Threshold ly.
And while my puzzled thoughts about it pore
I finde the Bread of Life in't at my doore.

When that this Bird of Paradise put in
    This Wicker Cage (my Corps) to tweedle praise
Had peckt the Fruite forbad: and so did fling
    Away its Food; and lost its golden dayes;
    It fell into Celestiall Famine sore:
    And never could attain a morsell more.

Alas! alas! Poore Bird, what wilt thou doe?
    The Creatures field no food for Souls e're gave.
And if thou knock at Angells dores they show
    An Empty Barrell: they no soul bread have.
    Alas! Poore Bird, the Worlds White Loafe is done.
    And cannot yield thee here the smallest Crumb.

This movement from the stars to the lie of a threshold, and the intro-
duction of the bird of the soul tweedling in its cage, and the move from
that to the pecked fruit of Eden and celestial famine are very different
from the conceits of Donne and Herbert, which are brought under the
control of the intellectual force of their arguments. The cascade of meta-
phor and analogy in Taylor is restless and vertiginous, and it was probably
the formulaic structure of meditative verse that allowed him both to
loosen his imagination and give it a form. This perhaps explains why,
having come on the form of the meditations in 1682, he persisted in it
for forty years. It gave him access, as John Milton described it in *The
Reason of Church Government,* to "what the mind at home in the spacious
circuits of her musing hath liberty to propose to herself."

The term *baroque* was introduced into critical discourse about art by
the German scholar Heinrich Wölfflin. He used it to describe the differ-
ence between what he saw as the harmonies of the high Renaissance and
what came after. "The Baroque," he observed, "never offers us perfection
and fulfillment, or the static calm of 'being,' only the unrest of change
and the tension of transience."[9] It was this, perhaps, that the form of the
meditative lyric allowed Taylor both to explore and to fend off, just as
the worldly specifics in his poems, the processes of brewing and baking
and metallurgy, the unguents and powders and medicines, the children's
games and gambling games, allowed him to celebrate a world he was
bound in conscience to deplore.

It's hard to read Taylor without wondering where these poems came from or to wonder that they came at all, let alone that they came from what was, literally, the remotest edge of European civilization. When Ezra Pound invented the belatedness of Hugh Selwyn Mauberly—

> For three years, out of key with his time,
> He strove to resuscitate the dead art
> Of poetry; to maintain "the sublime"
> In the old sense . . .

—he did not have before him the example of Taylor's belatedness. John Donne died in 1631, George Herbert two years later. Richard Crashaw was dead in 1649, when Taylor was five years old. Henry Vaughan, twenty years older than Taylor, died in 1695, but he had written and published almost all his poetry by 1655, when Taylor was thirteen years old. Long before Taylor arrived in New England, the style of English poetry had changed, as styles do. This was already reflected in the first book of poetry to come from New England, Anne Bradstreet's *The Tenth Muse Lately Sprung Up in America,* which was published in 1650. Bradstreet's poems, written twenty or so years before any Taylor poems that can be dated, were nevertheless much closer to the English style in midcentury. Her large, ambitious poems were skillful, learned, and written in the new smooth couplets that were becoming fashionable. They were also pretty conventional. Here are some lines about summer, from the set of poems on the four seasons:

> Now go those frolic swains, the shepherd lads,
> To wash the thick clothed flocks with pipes full glad
> In the cool streams they labour with delight
> Rubbing their dirty coats till they look white;
> Whose fleece when finely spun and deeply dy'd
> With robes thereof kings have been dignifi'd.[10]

It was the sound in poetry that people then admired. Now it glazes the eyes, both the rhythm and the diction. Nothing in it is really seen. And although the knowledge that the New England economy, like the economy of Bradstreet's native Lincolnshire, was based on sheep raising gives the subject some force, the conventional images—compare them to the smell of the barnyard in Taylor—drain it away.

The poems of Bradstreet that we read today are, for the most part, the personal ones that she did not publish in her lifetime. These lines, for example, are from a poem addressed to her husband. She was about to give birth to a child, which was, as she knew, a risky business. She uses the couplet again, but listen to the difference:

How soon, my Dear, death may my steps attend,
How soon't may be thy lot to lose thy friend,
We both are ignorant, yet love bids me
These farewell lines to recommend to thee,
That when the knot's untied that made us one,
I may seem thine, who in effect am none.

It's *soon't* that tells us how closely she is listening to her own voice; it's a bit of speech one can still hear among country people in Norfolk and Suffolk. And there is this, from another poem to her husband, which carries the same plainness and earnestness: "If ever two were one, then surely we. / If ever man were loved by wife, then thee." The rest of the poem is conventional, but these lines in Bradstreet with their adamant and Protestant plainness, their attention to speech and the inner movement of feeling, seem almost to leap forward 140 years; they anticipate both the strictures of Wordsworth in the preface to the *Lyrical Ballads* and the sound of his poems.

Taylor, when he arrived in Boston in 1668, at the age of twenty-six, seems to have brought with him the poetic practices of 1633, when both Donne's poems and Herbert's *The Temple* were first published. It's not possible to date his early work with any exactness, but there is evidence that the miscellaneous poems were written before 1691, the year that Taylor made a fair copy of the first forty meditations and the eight Occasional Poems. And the miscellaneous poems are numbered. The sixth of them, "Upon Wedlock and the Death of Children," can be dated to the events that occasioned the poem, the deaths of two of his children in infancy, the youngest of whom died in 1682. The poem after that, "Upon the Sweeping Flood," is dated by Taylor to August 1683. If this is an indication that the poems are arranged in chronological order by date of composition, it allows us to assume that the first five of these poems were written before 1682 and may have been written in the order in which they occur in the manuscript.[11]

How much before 1682, the year he began the meditations, they were written, it's not, as far as I know, possible to say. I have seen attributions that suggest they were written after 1673 (when Taylor was about thirty) on the grounds that the earliest of his poems that can be dated, the acrostic verses contained in letters to his first wife when he was courting her, are crude and that the miscellaneous poems, because they represent an advance over this apprentice work, must have been written afterward. The argument doesn't seem very persuasive given that it's perfectly possible to write quite bad poetry after having written some that isn't. So what we are left to guess is that the first five of the miscellaneous poems were written before Taylor began the meditations and that they represent, possibly in the order that he wrote them, the apprentice work he wished to preserve for himself.

In any case the first of these poems is a pure imitation of Donne. It's entitled "When Let by Rain." It has a Donne-like stanza, with lines of irregular length and an invented rhyme scheme, Donne's colloquial diction, his abruptness of entry, and his subject, ambivalence about departure. The first stanza looks like this:

> Ye Flippering Soule,
> > Why dost between the Nippers dwell?
> Not stay, nor goe. Not yea, nor yet Controle.
> > Doth this doe well?
> > > Rise journy'ng when the skies fall weeping Showers.
> > > Not o're nor under th'Clouds and Cloudy Powers.

The development is Taylor. He cannot settle on a metaphor:

> Is this th'Effect,
> > To leaven thus my Spirits all?
> To make my heart a Crabtree Cask direct?
> > A Verjuicte Hall?
> > > As Bottle Ale, whose Spirits prisond nurst
> > > When jog'd, the bung with Violence doth burst?
>
> Shall I be made
> > A sparkling Wildfire Shop
> When my dull Spirits at the Fireball trade
> > Do frisk and hop?
> > > And while the Hammer doth the Anvill pay,
> > > The fireball matter sparkles ery way.

I will resist the temptation to gloss this, but it's evident that we are already in the territory of his love of the details of the home crafts. He does not do what Donne so often does, marshal the metaphors into a surprising argument. He takes the smithy metaphor through one more stanza and then, in a sudden and terse ending, drops it:

> One sorry fret,
>   An anvill Sparke, rose higher
> And in thy Temple falling almost set
>   The house on fire.
>   Such fireballs droping in the Temple Flame
>   Burns up the building: Lord forbid the same.

What this suggests is that he took from Donne a racy freedom of diction and the use of the conceit, but he was not tempted by, or up to, or persuaded by the ingenuity of Donne's intellectual force.

The next poem, "Upon a Spider Catching a Fly," will remind some readers, in its subject, of Donne's "The Flea," but its style, the short-lined, knotty stanza, is much closer to Herbert. The language is brilliant, playful, and offers a more intensely observed description of the natural world than anything in either Donne or Herbert. It begins by addressing the spider:

> Thou sorrow, venom Elfe.
>   Is this thy play,
> To spin a web out of thyselfe
>   To Catch a Fly
>   For Why?
>
> I saw a pettish wasp
>   Fall foul therein.
> Whom yet the Whorle pins did not clasp
>   Lest he should fling
>   His sting.
>
> But as affraid, remote
>   Didst stand hereat
> And with thy little fingers stroke
>   And gently tap
>   His back.

Then he contrasts the spider's treatment of the wasp with its treatment of a fly:

Whereas the silly Fly,
    Caught by its leg
Thou by the throate tookst hastily
    And 'hinde the head
        Bite Dead.

This is very good writing, and the stanza form has a comic daintiness, or wariness. After it he draws out the theological implications and the moral in an argument that I, and others, have found rather confusing. So far as his development is concerned, what's interesting about the poem is the language ("Thou sorrow, venom Elfe" could hardly be bettered), the humor, and the closeness of observation. It is certainly more disciplined about sticking with the metaphor, but it does not have what goes with this in Herbert, the deftness and clarity of thought. And, in fact, Taylor doesn't quite stick with the metaphor. At the end of the poem he abandons the insects, assuring the Lord that if He frees humankind from the spider's net of the world,

We'l Nightingaile sing like
    When pearcht on high
In Glories Cage, thy glory, bright,
    And thankfully,
        For joy.

And ends, one also notices, with an English, not a North American, bird.

The next poem, "Upon a Wasp Child with Cold," returns to the subject of insects. It's written in tetrameter couplets, a form much more congenial to midcentury writers. He must have been working in this form at about the same time Andrew Marvell was, and there are passages in which he deploys it so brilliantly and playfully that one wishes he had explored it a little more. Here, for example, is the description of the wasp dealing with an icy northern wind:

Doth turn, and stretch her body small,
Doth Comb her velvet Capitall.
As if her little brain pan were
A Volume of Choice precepts cleare.
As if her sattin jacket hot
Contained Apothecaries Shop
Of Natures recepts, that prevails
To remedy all her sad ailes,

As if her velvet helmet high
Did turret rationality.

The poem ends, in less distinguished fashion, with a wish to learn from
the wasp a nimble spirit in the world's cold winds.

The fourth miscellaneous poem, "Huswifery," is the one by which Tay-
lor is most widely known. It's written in the Herbert stanza he was to use
in the meditations. It has Taylor's technological thoroughness, and, like
Bradstreet's lines, it describes a principal feature of the colonial English
domestic economy; he looks at what happens to the wool once Bradstreet's
swains have sheared the sheep, and he turns it into an ingenious lesson
in Calvinist theology. Reading it, one feels that it must have been the very
poem that a scholar looking for a Puritan metaphysical poet, composing
homely verses on the colonial frontier, might have written. But it is not
at all typical of Taylor, mainly because it is—although one might not
notice if one doesn't know his other work—humorless and static:

Make me, O Lord, thy Spining Wheele compleate.
    Thy Holy Worde my Distaff make for mee.
Make mine Affections thy Swift Flyers neate
    And make my Soule thy holy Spoole to bee.
    My Conversation make to be thy Reele
    And reele the yarn theron spun of thy Wheele.

Make me thy Loome then, knit therein this Twine:
    And make thy Holy Spirit, Lord, winde quills:
Then weave the Web thyselfe. The yarn is fine.
    Thine Ordinances make my Fulling Mills.
    Then dy the same in Heavenly Colours Choice,
    All pinkt with Varnisht Flowers of Paradise.

Then cloath therewith mine Understanding, Will,
    Affections, Judgment, Conscience, Memory
My Words, and Actions, that their shine may fill
    My wayes with glory and thee glorify.
    Then mine apparell shall display before yee
    That I am Cloathd in Holy robes for glory.

It is his most perfect poem in Herbert's mode, but it is certainly not his
liveliest. And it is not where the drama of his writing lay, in that cross
between the literalness that's in this poem, the attention to the stuff of
the world, and his teeming, endlessly transforming imagination. Nor does

the poem contain the great peaks and abysses of emotion that the meditations suggest were the core of his spiritual experience. It seems a pity, for that reason, that this is the poem by which he is so often represented. It is well enough made, and the working out of the metaphor has its virtue, but it does not get at what is most his own in Taylor's verse. Hopkins's description of a "Pied Beauty" seems near the mark—"All things counter, original, spare, strange; / Whatever is fickle, freckled (who knows how?)"—although Taylor at his best is hardly spare.

HIS RESONANCE

It was probably sometime after "Huswifery" (but not long after, given that he had found his way to Herbert's six-line stanza) that Taylor undertook the meditations. I think the best of them are in the fifty poems or so of the first series, written between 1682, when he was forty years old, and 1692, when he was fifty. Something got released in him in those poems. It was partly no doubt the form that freed him to make his fountaining inventions, but it must also have been that it gave him a way to probe the relation on which he had staked his life. To examine this argument requires a brief look at Taylor's theological convictions. I have never understood how practicing Calvinists dealt with the conviction of their absolute helplessness before their God or how, having once experienced election, they sustained the experience of it. I think it is no accident that very early in the meditations—it is the fourth poem in the series—Taylor placed one of three poems that are not based on scriptural citations and do not seem to have been texts chosen for his sermons on the occasion of the Lord's Supper. Each of them has a separate title. This poem is called "The Experience." It seems to be an account of his own conversion experience, which seems to have occurred when he received the sacrament.

Over the course of his life Taylor's theology—he lived into his middle eighties—grew to be antique. His conservatism apparently tried the patience of his church, and the issue on which he resisted change was just this one of who was eligible to receive the sacrament. The doctrine of his youth was clear. No one was permitted to the Lord's Supper who had not had a conversion experience and who was not therefore absolutely certain of salvation. Taylor's lifelong nemesis and rival was a popular minister in nearby Northampton named Solomon Stoddard, who insisted, as Norman Grabo puts it, "that no man could know he was saved with absolute certainty" and concluded that "the only safe course, therefore, was to admit all well-behaved Christians to the sacrament in hopes that they might thereby secure saving grace."[12] Taylor resisted this view vehemently, and over the course of his life the tide of opinion turned against him. His tenacity, this poem suggests, was rooted in the deepest experience of his life.

And it's interesting that this issue, which preoccupied him as a minister, bears so directly on the subject and occasion of the meditations. It makes a reading of "The Experience" illuminating because the poem must have been written in Westfield, in the early years of his ministry, about the moment in his earlier life that confirmed his election and his faith and drove him out of England. It gives us a glimpse into the experience on which his convictions and his sacramental poems were based:

> Oh! that I always breath'd in such an aire,
>   As I suckt in, feeding on sweet Content!
> Disht up unto my Soul ev'n in that pray're
>   Pour'de out to God over last Sacrament.
>   What Beam of Light wrapt up my sight to finde
>   Me neerer God than ere Came in my minde?
>
> Most strange it was! But yet more strange that shine
>   Which filld my Soul then to the brim to spy
> My Nature with thy Nature all Divine
>   Together joyn'd in Him thats Thou, and I.
>   Flesh of my Flesh, Bone of my Bone. There's run
>   Thy Godhead, and my Manhood in thy Son.
>
> Oh! that that Flame which thou didst on me Cast
>   Might me enflame, and Lighten ery where.
> Then Heaven to me would be less at last
>   So much of heaven I should have while here.
>   Oh! Sweet though Short! Ile not forget the same.
>   My neerness, Lord, to thee did me Enflame.
>
> I'le Claim my Right: Give place, ye Angells Bright.
>   Ye further from the Godhead stande than I.
> My Nature is your Lord; and doth Unite
>   Better than Yours unto the Deity.
>   Gods Throne is first and mine is next: to you
>   Onely the place of Waiting-men is due.
>
> Oh! that my Heart, thy Golden Harp might bee
>   Well tun'd by Glorious Grace, that e'ry string
> Screw'd to the highest pitch, might unto thee
>   All Praises wrapt in sweetest Musick bring.

I praise thee, Lord, and better praise thee would
If what I had, my heart might ever hold.

Not a very strong poem, I think. Taylor does better with some of these
themes elsewhere, for example in Meditation 44, in the second series:

You Holy Angells, Morning-Stars, bright Sparks,
    Give place: and lower your top gallants. Shew
Your top-saile Conjues to our slender barkes:
    The highest honour to our nature's due.
    Its neerer Godhead by the Godhead made
    Than yours in you that never from God stray'd.

What's interesting about it though is that the poem is not about having
had the experience once and for all but about having had it and longing
for it, for the reassurance of the sensation of being at one with divinity.
And also that this longing takes the form of desire for adequate praise:

Oh! that my Heart, thy Golden Harp might bee
    Well tun'd by Glorious Grace, that ev'ry string
Screw'd to the highest pitch, might unto thee
    All Praises wrapt in sweetest Musick bring.

It tells us something about the forty-year labor of the meditations and
connects Taylor's poetic and spiritual practices to a permanent state of
distance and supplication, which he hoped his imagination might—but
must also have believed could not—overcome, at least in this world.

It's this sense of longing, I think, that makes him a poet who still
resonates with readers altogether remote from his theology. His euphoria
and anguish, rooted in his faltering belief in the power of his own imag-
ination, seems in many ways to echo down to the present. It makes me
think, first of all, of the Coleridge of "Dejection: An Ode," suffering from
"A grief without a pang, void, dark, and drear, / A stifled drowsy unim-
passion'd grief" and hoping that the sounds of a coming storm "Might
now perhaps their wonted impulse give, / Might startle this dull pain, and
make it move and live!"

The terms are different. Although Coleridge addresses his semiallegor-
ical "Lady" in much the same terms that Taylor addresses his God, Cole-
ridge seems to think, as Taylor, at least officially, could not, that the
solution could come from himself:

> Ah! from the soul itself must issue forth
> A light, a glory, a fair luminous cloud
>   Enveloping the Earth—

Still one feels, listening to him, that Taylor and Coleridge are engaged in the same conversation. This is clearly not a matter of influence. The connection, I think, is this: at least since Taylor's time, the dilemmas of English Protestant spirituality have visited English poetry with the problem of sustaining an imaginative and inward relationship to whatever the sources of meaning are.

It's not quite the case that if you substitute Nature for God and imagination for grace, Taylor and Coleridge are writing the same poem—you have to squint a little to blur the philosophical niceties—but it is nearly the case. That's one of the reasons why it has come to seem that, when the English metaphysical tradition died with Edward Taylor in the remote fastnesses of New England in 1729, American poetry had already begun. A hundred and forty years after his death, a little further up the Connecticut River watershed, Emily Dickinson would be writing lines that seem to take up the same issues:

> There's a certain Slant of light,
> Winter Afternoons—
> That oppresses, like the Heft
> Of Cathedral Tunes—
>
> Heavenly Hurt, it gives us—
> We can find no scar,
> But internal difference
> Where the Meanings, are—

And eighty years after that, downriver in Hartford, Wallace Stevens, with neither a living God nor the wounding absence of God to refer meaning to, would still be revolving the problem in a poem called, appropriately enough, "The Poems of Our Climate." In it he is meditating on newly fallen snow and wrestling with the longing for a perfection elsewhere:

> Say even that this complete simplicity
> Stripped one of all one's torments, concealed
> The evilly compounded, vital I
> And made it fresh in a world of white,
> A world of clear water, brilliant-edged.

Still one would want more, one would need more,
More than a world of white and snowy scents.

There would still remain the never-resting mind,
So that one would want to escape, come back
To what had been so long composed.
The imperfect is our paradise.
Note that, in this bitterness, delight,
Since the imperfect is so hot in us,
Lies in flawed words and stubborn sounds.

I think it's in this way, his theology aside, that I find myself reading Taylor. Some critics have taken Taylor's complaints about the crudeness of his art as confirmation of their judgment of it. I think that's both to misjudge his poems and to miss his point. There is art enough in his poems, and there could never be, for him, art enough in the flawed words. It's that that makes the final poem in the meditations, written when he was eighty-one, so moving. The scripture he is meditating on at the end also comes from the Song of Solomon: "I am sick of Love." By some last irony, the first stanza is not entirely legible. In Stanford's edition it reads like this:

Heart sick my Lord heart sick of Love to thee!
     * * * * * * * * * * * * * * pain'd in Love oh see
Its parchments ready to crack, it was so free.
     It so affects true love * * * * * * * * * * * * * *
     As taken * * * * sends my Lords pledge
     But seeing its so small and hence not fledge.

But it is fledged enough, although it looks like the metaphors, after Taylor's fashion, have mixed up a book and a bird.

NOTES

1. Austin Warren, "Edward Taylor's Poetry: Colonial Baroque," *Kenyon Review* 3 (summer 1941): 355–71.

2. From "The Reflexion." Quotations from Taylor's poems come from *The Poems of Edward Taylor,* ed. Donald Stanford (New Haven: Yale University Press, 1960).

3. Wigglesworth's remarks occur in "The Prayse of Eloquence" (notebook located in the New England Historical and Genealogical Society), cited by Karl Keller, *The Example of Edward Taylor* (Amherst: University of Massachusetts Press, 1975), 304.

4. Louis Martz, foreword to Stanford, *The Poems of Edward Taylor,* xiii–xvii.

5. For an account of the origins of the Puritan migration, see David Hackett Fischer, *Albion's Seed: Four British Folkways in America* (Oxford: Oxford University Press, 1989). There is also a study of Leicestershire pronunciation in Taylor's rhymes. See Bernie Eugene Russell, "Dialectical and Phonetic Features of Edward Taylor's Rhymes: A Brief Study Based upon a Computer Concordance of His Poems," 6 vols., Ph.D. diss., University of Wisconsin, 1973.

6. In *Albion's Seed* Fischer offers several examples of the sharp differences between East Anglian and Midlands speech. Horses in East Anglia *neighed;* in the Midlands they *whinnied.* East Anglians were *scared,* when folk from the Midlands were *frightened. Rotten* wood was *dozie* in the Midlands, a word Taylor uses in the phrase "Dozie Beam." He also uses *millipuff* for *fuzzball.* The *OED* gloss of this word is particularly happy. It cites Josselyn, *Voyage to New England,* in 1674: "Fuss-balls, mullipuffes, called by the Fishermen Wolves-farts, are to be found plentifully." See also Craig Carver, *American Regional Dialects: A Word Geography* (Ann Arbor: University of Michigan Press, 1987).

7. *OED,* s.v. "muscatel."

8. *OED,* s.v. "bob."

9. Heinrich Wölfflin, *Renaissance and Baroque,* trans. Kathrin Simon (Ithaca: Cornell University Press, 1966). The book appeared in German in 1888. Wölfflin's remark is quoted from Harold B. Segal, *The Baroque Poem: A Comparative Survey* (New York: Dutton, 1974), 16.

10. Quotations from Bradstreet's poems are from *The Works of Anne Bradstreet,* ed. Jeannine Hensley (Cambridge, Mass.: Harvard University Press, 1967). For the three quotations I use here, see, respectively, pp. 68 ("The Four Seasons of the Year"), 224 ("Before the Birth of One of Her Children"), and 225 ("To My Dear and Loving Husband").

11. See the discussion of chronology in Thomas Davis, *A Reading of Edward Taylor* (Newark: University of Delaware Press, 1992), 15–17, 48–49.

12. Norman Grabo, *Edward Taylor* (Boston: Twayne, 1961), 32.

CONTRIBUTORS

CALVIN BEDIENT is professor of English at the University of California, Los Angeles. His books include *Eight Contemporary Poets* (Oxford University Press, 1974), nominated for a National Book Award; *In the Heart's Last Kingdom: Robert Penn Warren's Major Poetry* (Harvard University Press, 1984); and *He Do the Police in Different Voices: "The Waste Land" and Its Protagonist* (University of Chicago Press, 1986). The recipient of a Guggenheim Fellowship and a frequent reviewer, Bedient is also the author of a book of poems, *Candy Necklace* (Wesleyan University Press, 1997), and an editor of the New California Poetry Series, published by the University of California Press.

EAVAN BOLAND is professor of English at Stanford University. The author of twelve books of poetry, including *The Lost Land* (Norton, 1998) and *An Origin like Water: Collected Poems 1967–1987*, she is also the author of *Object Lessons: The Life of the Woman and the Poet in Our Time* (Norton, 1995), a volume of prose, and coeditor (with Mark Strand) of *The Making of a Poem: A Norton Anthology of Poetic Forms* (Norton, 2000). Her awards include a Lannan Foundation Award in Poetry and an American Ireland Fund Literary Award.

ALICE FULTON is professor of English at the University of Michigan, Ann Arbor. She is the author of five books of poetry, most recently *Felt* (2001) and *Sensual Math* (1995), both published by Norton. A collection of her essays, *Feeling as a Foreign Language: The Good Strangeness of Poetry*, appeared from Graywolf Press in 1999. Among her many honors, she has received fellowships from the John D. and Catherine T. MacArthur Foundation and the Guggenheim Foundation.

LINDA GREGERSON is professor of English at the University of Michigan, Ann Arbor. She is the author of two books of poetry, *Fire in the Conservatory* (Dragon Gate, 1982) and *The Woman Who Died in Her Sleep* (Houghton Mifflin, 1996). A third book of poems will appear from Houghton Mifflin in 2002. The recipient of many awards, including a Guggenheim Fellowship, she is also the author of two books of literary criticism, *The Reformation of the Subject: Spenser, Milton, and the English Protestant Epic* (Cambridge University Press, 1995) and *Negative Capability: Contemporary American Poetry* (University of Michigan Press, 2001).

THOM GUNN is retired senior lecturer of English at the University of California, Berkeley. *Boss Cupid*, published in 2000 by Farrar, Straus and Giroux, is his twelfth volume of poetry. His *Collected Poems* appeared from the same publisher in 1994. He is also the author of several volumes of critical essays, most recently *Shelf Life: Essays, Memoirs, and an Interview* (University of Michigan Press, 1993), and has edited, among other works, *The Selected Poems of Fulke Greville* (University of Chicago Press, 1968). A recipient of many awards, including a MacArthur Fellowship, he lives in San Francisco.

ROBERT HASS is professor of English at the University of California, Berkeley. His books of poetry include *Sun under Wood: New Poems* (Ecco Press, 1996), *Human Wishes* (Ecco Press, 1989), *Praise* (Ecco Press, 1979), and *Field Guide* (Yale University Press, 1973). He has also cotranslated several volumes of poetry with Czeslaw Milosz, most recently *A Treatise on Poetry* (Ecco Press, 2001), and is the author or editor of several other collections of essays and translations, including *The Essential Haiku: Versions of Basho, Buson, and Issa* (Ecco Press, 1994) and *Twentieth Century Pleasures: Prose on Poetry* (Ecco Press, 1984), which received the National Book Critics Circle Award. He served as poet laureate of the United States from 1995 to 1997.

ANTHONY HECHT is retired university professor in the Graduate School of Georgetown University. His seventh book of poems, *The Darkness and the Light*, was published by Knopf in 2001. He is the author of several books of critical essays, including *Obbligati* (Atheneum, 1986) and *On the Laws of the Poetic Art* (Princeton University Press, 1995), based on the Andrew Mellon Lectures in the fine arts, and of a critical study of the poetry of W. H. Auden, *The Hidden Law* (Harvard University Press, 1993). A collection of essays on poetry and religion, *Melodies Unheard,* is forthcoming from Johns Hopkins University Press. Among his many honors, Hecht received the Robert Frost Medal for 2000 from the Poetry Society of America.

WILLIAM LOGAN is alumni/ae professor of English at the University of Florida. He is the author of five volumes of poetry, most recently *Vain Empires* (Penguin, 1998) and *Night Battle* (Penguin, 1999). He has also published two books of essays and reviews, *All the Rage* (University of Michigan Press, 1998) and *Reputations of the Tongue* (University Press of Florida, 1999), the latter a finalist for the National Book Critics Circle Award in Criticism. Among his honors are the Peter I. B. Lavan Younger Poets Award from the Academy of American Poets and the Citation for Excellence in Reviewing from the National Book Critics Circle.

HEATHER MCHUGH is Milliman Distinguished Writer-in-Residence each spring at the University of Washington in Seattle. At other times she works with poets at the low-residency MFA Program for Writers at Warren Wilson College. Her most recent books, published by Wesleyan University Press, include *GLOTTAL STOP: 101 Poems by Paul Celan,* a translation with her husband Nikolai Popov (University Press of New England, 2000); *The Father of the Predicaments,* a volume of poems (Wesleyan University Press, 1999), and a collection of critical essays, *Broken English: Poetry and Partiality* (Wesleyan University Press, 1993). *Hinge & Sign: Poems 1968–1993* (Wesleyan University Press, 1994) was a finalist for the National Book Award. In 1999 she was elected a chancellor of the Academy of American Poets.

CARL PHILLIPS is professor of English at Washington University, St. Louis. He is the author of five books of poems, most recently *The Tether,* published by Farrar, Straus, and Giroux in 2001, and *Pastoral,* published by Graywolf Press in 2000. *From the Devotions* (Graywolf Press, 1998) was a finalist for the National Book Award. He is the recipient of a number of awards and fellowships, including ones from the Guggenheim Foundation, the Library of Congress, and the Academy of American Poets.

JONATHAN F. S. POST is professor of English at the University of California, Los Angeles, and former chair of the Department. He is the author of *Henry Vaughan: The Unfolding Vision* (Princeton University Press, 1982) and *Sir Thomas Browne* (G. K. Hall, 1987). Most recently, he has published *George Herbert in the Nineties: Reflections and Reassessments* (George Herbert Journal: Special Studies and Monographs, 1995, with Sid Gottlieb) and *English Lyric Poetry: The Early Seventeenth Century* (Routledge, 1999). He has been a Fellow of the National Endowment for the Humanities and the Guggenheim Foundation.

PETER SACKS is professor of English at Harvard University. He is the author of five collections of poems, most recently *Natal Command* (University of Chicago Press, 1997), *O Wheel* (University of Georgia Press, 2000), and *Necessity* (forthcoming from Norton, 2002). An author of essays and reviews on poetry and on art, he received the Christian Gauss Award for *The English Elegy: Studies in the Genre from Spenser to Yeats* (Johns Hopkins University Press, 1985).

STEPHEN YENSER is professor of English at the University of California, Los Angeles. His book of poems, *The Fire in All Things* (Louisiana State University Press, 1993) won the Walt Whitman Award from the Academy of American Poets. He is the author of three books of criticism, *A Boundless Field: American Poetry at Large* (University of Michigan Press, 2001), *The Consuming Myth: The Work of James Merrill* (Harvard University Press, 1987), and *Circle to Circle: The Poetry of Robert Lowell* (University of California Press, 1975). He is also coeditor (with J. D. McClatchy) of the *Collected Poems of James Merrill* (Knopf, 2001).

INDEX

Herbert, George *(continued)*
lery," 153–55; "Avarice," 150; "The Ban-
quet," 158; "Business," 150; "The
Church-Floor," 149; "Church-Lock and
Key," 140, 149; "The Church Militant,"
138, 158; "Church-Monuments," 149;
"The Church-Porch," 138; "Clasping of
Hands," 147; "The Collar," 155, 157;
"Coloss. 3.3 Our Life is hid with
Christ in God," 148, 149; "Confession,"
146; "Constancy," 149, 150; "Content,"
149; *The Country Parson,* 136–37, 143,
146, 150–51; "The Cross," 136; "Dia-
logue," 155; "Divinity," 149; "Dullness,"
136; "Easter-wings," 139; "Frailty," 149;
"Good Friday," 138–39; "Humility," 149;
"Jordan (I)," 145; "Jordan (II)," 145, 155;
"Justice (I)," 141–42, 149, 152; "Love
(III)," 159; "Mattens," 139–40, 149;
"Misery," 152; "Paradise," 147–48; "The
Pearl. Matth. 13.45," 151; "Prayer (I),"
143, 150; "Providence," 146; "The Pul-
ley," 156–57; "The Quiddity," 145; "Re-
pentance," 141; "The Reprisal," 138;
"The Sacrifice," 138; "Sin (II)," 140,
149; "Sunday," 150; "The Temper (I),"
144–45; "The Thanksgiving," 138;
"Trinity Sunday," 149; "A True
Hymn," 158; "Vanity (I)," 150; "The
Windows," 141, 146, 149, 270–71; "A
Wreath," 147
Herrick, Robert, 71, 80–81, 101; "Delight
in Disorder," 230, 271–72
Higginson, Thomas, 260
Hobson, Thomas, 165
Holbein, Hans, 20, 21, 36n13
Hollander, John, *Vision and Resonance,*
169
Homer, 26
Hooker, Thomas, 258
Hopkins, Gerard Manley, 19, 58n12, 137,
144; "As Kingfishers Catch Fire, Drag-
onflies Draw Flame," 19; "Pied
Beauty," 283; "The Wreck of the
Deutschland," 57
Horace, 96, 169
Howard, Richard, 241n9
Huizinga, Johan, 57, 58n13, 112, 134n3
Hunt, Clay, 114

Ines, Sor Juana, 22, 25, 34n8

Jackson, Helen Hunt, 260
James I, 90, 95
John of the Cross, Saint, 250
Johnson, Samuel, 248; "A Short Song of
Congratulation," 250
Johnson, Thomas, 257, 275
Jones, Kathleen, 204, 214, 215, 216,
218nn23,25,26,28,43,46, 219nn48,50
Jonson, Ben, 4, 5, 7–8, 9, 71, 86–108, 161,
170; *The Alchemist,* 94; "A Celebration
of CHARIS in ten Lyrick Peeces," 8,
99, 100; *Conversations with Drummond,*
93, 96, 102, 161; *Cynthia's Revels,* 101;
Eastward Ho, 92; "An Elegie," 101; *The
English Grammar,* 86; *Epigrams,* 87;
"Epistle to Elizabeth Countesse of Rut-
land," 93; "Epistle to Katherine, Lady
Aubigny," 89, 94–95; "An Epistle to Sir
Edward Sacvile, now Earle of *Dorset,*"
91; "His Excuse for loving," 100; "A
Hymne On the Nativitie of my Sav-
iour," 105, 107; "A Hymne to God the
Father," 103; *Isle of Dogs,* 92; "My Pic-
ture Left in Scotland," 100; "Of
Death," 102; "On Lucy Countesse of
Bedford," 88, 91; "On My First
Daughter," 101; "On My First Sonne,"
98, 106–7; "On Poet-Ape," 94; "On
Sir John Roe," 102; "A Sonnet, To the
noble Lady, the Lady Mary Worth," 94;
"To Alphonso Ferrabosco, on his
Booke," 95; "To Clement Edmonds, on
His Caesars Commentaries observed,
and translated," 97; "To Heaven," 104;
"To Mary Lady Wroth," 89; "To Mr.
Josuah Sylvester," 96; "To my chosen
Friend, The learned Translator of Lu-
can, Thomas May, *Esquire,*" 96; "To
My Meere English Censurer," 87; "To
My Muse," 93; "To Person Guiltie," 92;
"To Sir William Jephson," 90; "To the
. . . Earle of Pembroke," 92; "To the
Immortal Memory and Friendship of
That Noble Pair, Sir Lucius Cary and
Sir H. Morison," 14, 169; "To the
Same; On the Same," 97; "To Thomas
Earle of Suffolke," 89; "To William

18, 104; *Henry IV,* 167; *A Midsummer Night's Dream,* 163; *Much Ado about Nothing,* 263; *Poems: Written by Wil. Shake-speare, Gent.,* 163; *Richard III,* 261; *Romeo and Juliet,* 163; "So shall I live, supposing thou art true" ("Sonnet 93"), 21; *The Taming of the Shrew,* 195; "That time of year thou mayst in me behold" ("Sonnet 73"), 18; *Timon of Athens,* 171, 266; *Troilus and Cressida,* 271; *Venus and Adonis,* 161; *The Winter's Tale,* 171

Shelley, Percy Bysshe, *Adonais,* 177

Sidney, Sir Philip, 40n28, 41–58, 64, 183; *An Apology for Poetry,* 5; *Astrophil and Stella,* 18; *The Countess of Pembroke's Arcadia,* 41, 42, 58; "Farewell Ô Sunn," 42; "Since Wailing Is a Bud," 41; "Yee Gote-heard Gods," 6, 43–50

Sidney family, 9

Signorelli, Luca, 20

Simic, Charles, 10; "Elegy in a Spider's Web," 15n2

Skelton, John, 262

Smart, Christopher, 216

Smart, J. S., 162, 174n2

Sola Pinto, V. de. *See* Pinto, Vivian de Sola

Spenser, Edmund, 34n8, 38n19; *Amoretti,* 33n5; *The Faery Queen,* 263; *The Shepherd's Calendar,* 42–43

Stanford, Donald, 257, 259, 287, 287n2;

Stanyhurst, Richard, 262

Stein, Arnold, 124, 134n10

Stein, Gertrude, 79, 110, 111

Stevens, Wallace, 34n8, 79, 110, 241n6; "Notes toward a Supreme Fiction," 225; "The Poems of Our Climate," 13, 286–87

Stoddard, Solomon, 283

Suckling, Sir John, "Out upon it," 245

Surrey, Henry Howard, Earl of, 17, 21, 23, 24, 26, 31, 57, 170, 188

Swift, Jonathan, 170

Swinburne, Algernon Charles, 101

Sylvester, Josuah, 96

Tasso, Torquato, 161

Taylor, Edward, 11, 12, 13, 257–88; *Dispensatory,* 262; "The Experience," 283–85; "A Fig for Thee Oh! Death," 258; *Gods Determination,* 258, 270; "Huswifery," 282–83; "The Martyrdom of Deacon Lawrence," 258; "Meditation 3," 271; "Meditation 4. Cant. 21. I Am the Rose of Sharon," 264–69; "Meditation 8," 271, 275; "Meditation 44," 285; "The Persian Persecution," 258; *The Poems of Edward Taylor,* 257; *The Poetical Works of Edward Taylor,* 257, 275; "Preparatory Meditations before my Approach to the Lords Supper," 257, 258, 260, 262, 264; "The Reflexion," 258; "The Sparkling Shine of Gods Justice," 258; "Upon a Spider Catching a Fly," 280–81; "Upon a Wasp Child with Cold," 281–82; "Upon the Sweeping Flood," 278; "Upon Wedlock and the Death of Children," 278; "When Let by Rain," 279–80

Tennyson, Alfred, *The Princess,* 261

Theocritus, 43

Thomas, Edward, 79, 84n19

Thomas, Lewis, 200, 208, 211, 217n16, 218n17, 218n34, 218n39

Titian, 16n13, 21, 242

Toppe, Elizabeth, 202, 218n18

Tottel, Richard, 26

Traherne, Thomas, 258

Tudor, Henry, 30

Tuerk, Cynthia, 195, 217n10

Tuve, Rosemond, 114

Valency, Maurice, 57, 58n14

Valéry, Paul, 223

Van Eyck, Jan, 20

Vaughan, Henry, 264, 277; "The Book," 60

Vega, Garcilaso de la. *See* Garcilaso de la Vega

Vermeer, Jan, 110

Vesalius, Andreas, 60

Vieth, David M., 82n3, 83n6, 244, 256

Virgil, 58n3; *Aeneid,* 262; *Eclogues,* 43

Wallace, David, 30, 39n27

Walpole, Horace, 204

Warren, Austin, 13; "Edward Taylor's Poetry: Colonial Baroque," 258, 287n1

Warwick, Countess of, 178

Designer: Nola Burger
Compositor: Binghamton Valley Composition
Text: 11.25/13.5 Adobe Garamond
Display: Perpetua
Printer and binder: Friesens